Teach Yourself
VISUALLY™
MacBook

Visual

by Brad Miser

WILEY

Wiley Publishing, Inc.

Teach Yourself VISUALLY MacBook

Published by
Wiley Publishing, Inc.
10475 Crosspoint Blvd
Indianapolis, IN 46256

Published simultaneously in Canada

Library of Congress Control Number: 2008921208

ISBN: 978-0-470-22459-5
Manufactured in the United States of America

10 9 8 7 6 5 4 3 2

Trademark Acknowledgments

Contact Us

For general information on our other products and services please contact our Customer Care Department within the U.S. at 800-762-2974, outside the U.S. at 317-572-3993 or fax 317-572-4002.

For technical support please visit www.wiley.com/techsupport.

WILEY
Wiley Publishing, Inc.

US Sales

Contact Wiley
at (800) 762-2974 or
fax (317) 572-4002.

Praise for Visual Books

"Like a lot of other people, I understand things best when I see them visually. Your books really make learning easy and life more fun."

John T. Frey (Cadillac, MI)

"I have quite a few of your Visual books and have been very pleased with all of them. I love the way the lessons are presented!"

Mary Jane Newman (Yorba Linda, CA)

"I just purchased my third Visual book (my first two are dog-eared now!), and, once again, your product has surpassed my expectations.

Tracey Moore (Memphis, TN)

"I am an avid fan of your Visual books. If I need to learn anything, I just buy one of your books and learn the topic in no time. Wonders! I have even trained my friends to give me Visual books as gifts."

Illona Bergstrom (Aventura, FL)

"Thank you for making it so clear. I appreciate it. I will buy many more Visual books."

J.P. Sangdong (North York, Ontario, Canada)

"I have several books from the Visual series and have always found them to be valuable resources."

Stephen P. Miller (Ballston Spa, NY)

"Thank you for the wonderful books you produce. It wasn't until I was an adult that I discovered how I learn — visually. Nothing compares to Visual books. I love the simple layout. I can just grab a book and use it at my computer, lesson by lesson. And I understand the material! You really know the way I think and learn. Thanks so much!"

Stacey Han (Avondale, AZ)

"I absolutely admire your company's work. Your books are terrific. The format is perfect, especially for visual learners like me. Keep them coming!"

Frederick A. Taylor, Jr. (New Port Richey, FL)

"I have several of your Visual books and they are the best I have ever used."

Stanley Clark (Crawfordville, FL)

"I bought my first Teach Yourself VISUALLY book last month. Wow. Now I want to learn everything in this easy format!"

Tom Vial (New York, NY)

"Thank you, thank you, thank you...for making it so easy for me to break into this high-tech world. I now own four of your books. I recommend them to anyone who is a beginner like myself."

Gay O'Donnell (Calgary, Alberta, Canada)

"I write to extend my thanks and appreciation for your books. They are clear, easy to follow, and straight to the point. Keep up the good work! I bought several of your books and they are just right! No regrets! I will always buy your books because they are the best."

Seward Kollie (Dakar, Senegal)

"Compliments to the chef!! Your books are extraordinary! Or, simply put, extra-ordinary, meaning way above the rest! THANK YOU THANK YOU THANK YOU! I buy them for friends, family, and colleagues."

Christine J. Manfrin (Castle Rock, CO)

"What fantastic teaching books you have produced! Congratulations to you and your staff. You deserve the Nobel Prize in Education in the Software category. Thanks for helping me understand computers."

Bruno Tonon (Melbourne, Australia)

"Over time, I have bought a number of your 'Read Less - Learn More' books. For me, they are THE way to learn anything easily. I learn easiest using your method of teaching."

José A. Mazón (Cuba, NY)

"I am an avid purchaser and reader of the Visual series, and they are the greatest computer books I've seen. The Visual books are perfect for people like myself who enjoy the computer, but want to know how to use it more efficiently. Your books have definitely given me a greater understanding of my computer, and have taught me to use it more effectively. Thank you very much for the hard work, effort, and dedication that you put into this series."

Alex Diaz (Las Vegas, NV)

Credits

Project Editor
Chris Wolfgang

Acquisitions Editor
Stephanie McComb

Copy Editor
Scott Tullis

Technical Editor
Griff Partington

Editorial Manager
Robyn Siesky
Business Manager
Amy Knies

Sr. Marketing Manager
Sandy Smith

Manufacturing
Allan Conley
Linda Cook
Paul Gilchrist
Jennifer Guynn

Book Design
Kathie Rickard

Production Coordinator
Kristie Rees

Layout
Carrie A. Cesavice
Andrea Hornberger
Jennifer Mayberry

Screen Artist
Jill Proll

Illustrators
Ronda David-Burroughs
Cheryl Grubbs

Proofreader
Betty Kish

Quality Control
Jessica Kramer

Indexer
Johnna VanHoose

Vice President and Executive Group Publisher
Richard Swadley

Vice President and Publisher
Barry Pruett

Composition Director
Debbie Stailey

About the Author

Brad Miser has written more than 25 books, his favorite topics being anything related to Mac computers or products starting with "i," such as iTunes, iPhones, and iPods. In addition to *Teach Yourself Visually MacBook*, Brad has written *My iPhone*, *Absolute Beginner's Guide to iPod and iTunes*, *Sleeping with the Enemy: Running Windows on a Mac*, and *Special Edition Using Mac OS X, v10.5 Leopard*. He has also been a co-author, development editor, or technical editor on more than 50 other titles.

In addition to his passion for silicon-based technology, Brad enjoys steel-based technology and rides his motorcycle whenever and wherever possible. A native of California, Brad now lives in Indiana with his wife Amy; their three daughters, Jill, Emily, and Grace; and a rabbit named Bun-Bun.

Brad would love to hear about your experiences with this book (the good, the bad, and the ugly). You can write to him at bradmacosx@mac.com.

Author's Acknowledgments

While my name is on the cover, it takes many people to build a book like this one. Thanks to Stephanie McComb who made this project possible and allowed me to be involved. Chris Wolfgang deserves extra credit for leading me through the details; I'm sure working with me was a challenge at times. Griff Partington did a great job of keeping me on my toes to make sure this book contains fewer technical gaffs than it would have without his help. Scott Tullis transformed my stumbling text into something people can read and understand. Thanks also to my agent, Marta Justak, for managing the business of the project and being a support for me during the writing process.

On my personal team, I'd like to thank my wife Amy for her tolerance of the author lifestyle, which can be both odd and challenging. My delightful daughters Jill, Emily, and Grace are always a source of joy and inspiration for all that I do, for which I'm ever grateful.

Table of Contents

chapter 1   Explore the MacBook

chapter 2   Look Through Mac OS X Finder Windows

chapter 3 Manage the Desktop with the Dock, Exposé, Spaces, and the Dashboard

chapter 4 Work on the Mac Desktop

Table of Contents

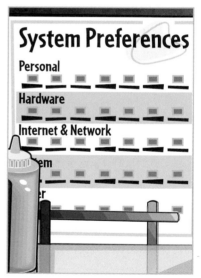

chapter 7 Connect to a Network and the Internet

chapter 8 Surf the Web

Table of Contents

chapter 9   E-mail

chapter 10   Use .Mac

chapter 11

Listen to Music and Watch Video with iTunes

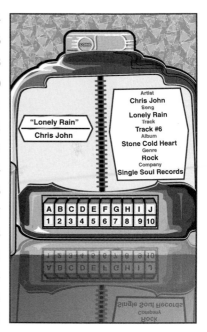

Table of Contents

Create Photo Books and Other Projects with iPhoto

 Chat

chapter **14** Manage Contacts

chapter **15** Manage Calendars

Table of Contents

chapter 18 Connect a MacBook to Other Devices

chapter 19 Maintain and Troubleshoot MacBook

How to use this book

How to Use this Teach Yourself VISUALLY Book

Do you look at the pictures in a book or newspaper before anything else on a page? Would you rather see an image instead of read about how to do something? Search no further. This book is for you. Opening *Teach Yourself VISUALLY MacBook* allows you to read less and learn more about the MacBook computer.

Who Needs This Book

This book is for a reader who has never used a MacBook or the software it runs. It is also for more computer literate individuals who want to expand their knowledge of the different features that MacBook has to offer. You don't need much experience with MacBook to be able to learn from this book because it begins at the beginning, such as powering up MacBook and using its trackpad. If you already know how to do these tasks, don't worry because that's only the start. You'll learn how to get the most out of MacBook, even if you have used it for sometime, such as learning about networking and managing the desktop.

Book Organization

Teach Yourself VISUALLY MacBook has 19 chapters. Chapter 1 gets you started with powering up MacBook, using the trackpad, and other essential tasks.

Chapter 2 helps you learn to look at the world through Mac OS X Finder windows, including changing views, using the Sidebar, and making the toolbar work for you.

In Chapter 3, you take command of the desktop using Expose, Spaces, and the Dashboard.

Chapter 4 teaches you how to move around on MacBook's desktop, create and use files and folders, and work with disks and discs.

You explore how to use applications on MacBook in Chapter 5. Topics include installing applications, opening documents, and saving documents.

In Chapter 6, you learn how to make MacBook your own by personalizing it in many ways. These include setting desktop pictures, configuring the trackpad and keyboard, and creating and managing user accounts.

No MacBook is an island. In Chapter 7, you learn how to connect MacBook to different kinds of networks, the most important of which is the Internet.

Now that you're on the 'net, Chapter 8 shows you how to surf the Web. From moving to Web sites quickly and easily, to saving and emailing Web pages, you'll find out how to perform some really useful Web tasks.

Chapter 9 helps you e-mail like a pro (is there really a professional e-mailer?). You learn how to set up e-mail accounts and how to use Mac OS X's excellent Mail application to read, send, and organize e-mail.

A .Mac account empowers you to do a lot of great things, including accessing an online disk, creating and publishing your own Web pages, and keeping information in sync. Chapter 10 shows you how.

Chapter 11 fills you in on the basics of iTunes music and video. You learn how to stock the shelves of your iTunes Library and how to listen and watch the great content you store there. Of course, no discussion of iTunes is complete without iPods and iPhones, so these devices make an appearance too.

Digital photos are great, and iPhoto is just the application you need to store, organize, and use your own photos. In Chapter 12, you can see how easy these tasks are.

If you like to communicate with other people in real time, chatting is a great way to do it. With iChat, you can chat with text, audio, and video. Chapter 13 shows you how.

When you communicate with people, you need to manage and use contact information. Chapter 14 explains how using Mac OS X's Address Book.

Chapter 15 enters the picture with iCal. If you're memory challenged like I am (and even if you're not), having a way to manage the times and dates that are important is helpful. You can use iCal to create and manage your own calendars, share those calendars with others, and access calendars people share with you.

Computers certainly did not eliminate the need for paper; in Chapter 16, you'll learn how to print your documents in a number of ways. If you want to save a few trees and distribute documents electronically, you'll learn that too.

One of the nice things about MacBook is that you can take it with you. Chapter 17 provides information about moving around with yours.

While MacBook contains all the hardware devices you must have; there are lots more you need, such as external hard drives and mice. In Chapter 18, you learn how to connect MacBook to these devices.

Last, but not least, in Chapter 19 you focus on tasks that are important to keep MacBook running in top form. You learn what to do if MacBook's condition becomes something less than that too.

Chapter Organization

This book consists of sections, all listed in the book's table of contents. A *section* is a set of steps that show you how to complete a specific computer task.

Each section, usually contained on two facing pages, has an introduction to the task at hand, a set of full-color screen shots and steps that walk you through the task, and a set of tips. This format allows you to quickly look at a topic of interest and learn it instantly.

Chapters group together three or more sections with a common theme. A chapter may also contain pages that give you the background information needed to understand the sections in a chapter.

What You Need to Use This Book

To use this book, you need a MacBook running Mac OS X (of course, you can read the book even if you don't have a MacBook, but it won't be nearly as much fun). The Leopard version (10.5) of Mac OS X is used for the steps and screenshots so you'll get the most from the book if your MacBook runs Leopard too.

Using the Trackpad

This book uses the following conventions to describe the actions you perform when using the trackpad:

Point

Slide your finger on the trackpad. The pointer on the screen follows your finger motion on the trackpad. Pointing to something is how you indicate that you want to do something with whatever you point to.

Click

Press the trackpad button once. You generally click the trackpad button on something to select it. This is equivalent to a single mouse click and to a left-button click on a two-button mouse.

Double-click

Press the trackpad button twice. Double-clicking something on the computer screen generally opens whatever item you have double-clicked.

Ctrl+click (AKA Right-click)

Hold the Ctrl key down and press the trackpad button; this is the equivalent of pressing the right button on a two-button mouse. When you right-click anything on the computer screen, a shortcut menu containing commands specific to the selected item is shown (this is called a contextual menu).

Click and Drag, and Release the Trackpad Button

Drag your finger on the trackpad to point to an item on the screen. Press and hold down the trackpad button to select that item. While holding the button down, move your finger so the pointer (to which the item will be attached) moves to where you want to place the item and then release the button. You use this method to move an item from one area of the computer to another.

The Conventions in This Book

A number of typographic and layout styles have been used throughout *Teach Yourself VISUALLY MacBook* to distinguish different types of information.

Bold

Bold type represents the names of commands and options that you interact with. Bold type also indicates text and numbers that you must type into a dialog box or window.

Italics

Italic words introduce a new term and are followed by a definition.

Numbered Steps

You must perform the instructions in numbered steps in order to successfully complete a section and achieve the final results.

Bulleted Steps

These steps point out various optional features. You do not have to perform these steps; they simply give additional information about a feature.

Indented Text

Indented text tells you what the program does in response to you following a numbered step. For example, if you click a certain menu command, a dialog box may appear, or a window may open. Indented text may also tell you what the final result is when you follow a set of numbered steps.

Notes

Notes give additional information. They may describe special conditions that may occur during an operation. They may warn you of a situation that you want to avoid, for example the loss of data. A note may also cross-reference a related area of the book. A cross-reference may guide you to another chapter, or another section with the current chapter.

Icons and buttons

Icons and buttons are graphical representations within the text. They show you exactly what you need to click to perform a step.

 You can easily identify the tips in any section by looking for the TIPS icon. Tips offer additional information, including tips, hints, and tricks. You can use the TIPS information to go beyond what you have learned in the steps.

Explore the MacBook

With MacBook, you can virtually explore the world, communicate with just about everyone you know, create the next great American novel, make that novel into a movie, listen to music, watch TV, and manage an iPod or iPhone. Before you dive into all that amazing functionality, take a quick tour of MacBook to get familiar with its layout and how you interact with it.

Here you can learn about the MacBook's major features from the outside, including its controls, ports, and other areas that you use to control your MacBook and to connect it to other devices.

Tour MacBook

● **Display**

The MacBook's display provides a sharp, bright, and colorful view into all that you do

● **iSight camera**

Use the built-in iSight camera to video conference, take photos, and more

● **Microphone**

Input audio-to-audio conference and record your voice or other sound

● **Keyboard**

Along with the standard letter and number keys, you have function keys to control your MacBook

● **Trackpad**

Enables you to move the cursor on the screen just by sliding your finger

● **Trackpad button**

Click the button to perform actions

● **Ports**

Connect MacBook to other devices, such as drives, iPods, and so on

● **Sleep indicator light**

Pulses when MacBook is asleep, glows solid when MacBook is on but its display is dimmed

● **Disc drive**

Use or burn CDs and DVDs

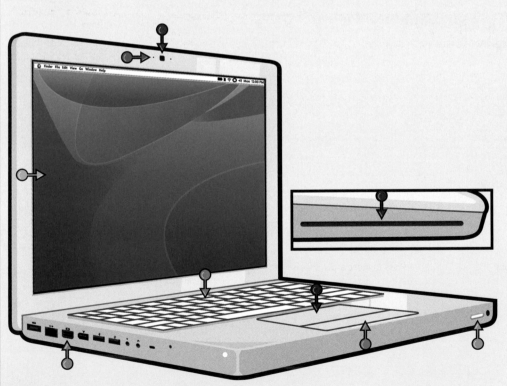

MACBOOK KEYBOARD

● **Brightness keys**

Press F1 to decrease your screen's brightness or F2 to increase it

● **Volume keys**

F3 mutes MacBook, F4 turns the volume down, and F5 turns it up

● **Num Lock key**

Press F6 to transform m, j, k, l, u, i, and o keys into number keys for easier number entry

● **Video mode key**

When MacBook is connected to an external display or projector, press this to use mirroring or dual displays

● **Standard function keys**

Press to perform specific functions, such as opening the Dashboard

● **Eject key**

Press to eject a CD or DVD

● **Command keys**

Press to invoke keyboard shortcuts

● **Scroll keys**

Press to move around the screen

● **Power button**

Press to turn MacBook on; press and hold to force MacBook to turn off

continued

MacBooks are elegantly designed and are simple and easy to use. But do not let that fool you; they are very powerful and extremely capable computers that can do just about anything you want them to.

MACBOOK PORTS

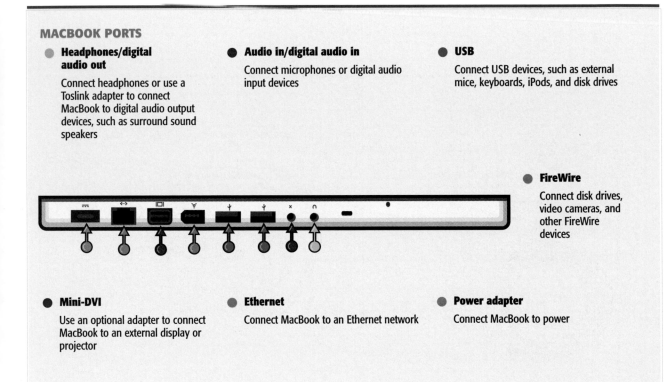

Headphones/digital audio out

Connect headphones or use a Toslink adapter to connect MacBook to digital audio output devices, such as surround sound speakers

Audio in/digital audio in

Connect microphones or digital audio input devices

USB

Connect USB devices, such as external mice, keyboards, iPods, and disk drives

FireWire

Connect disk drives, video cameras, and other FireWire devices

Mini-DVI

Use an optional adapter to connect MacBook to an external display or projector

Ethernet

Connect MacBook to an Ethernet network

Power adapter

Connect MacBook to power

MACBOOK COMPANIONS

● **Power adapter**

Transforms standard outlet power to what MacBook needs to run and charges its battery

● **Power cord**

Connects to the power adapter to enable you to connect MacBook to a power outlet

● **Remote**

Control MacBook from afar, such as when you are listening to music or watching movies

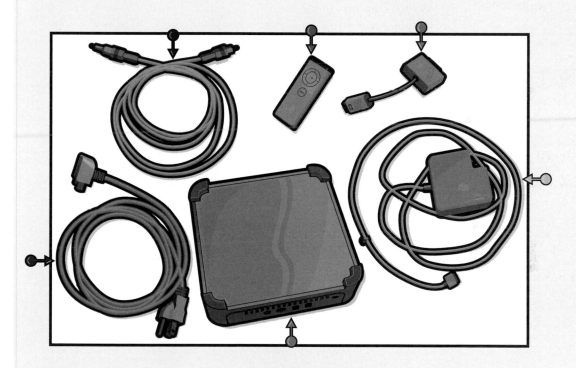

● **Mini-DVI adapter**

An optional Mini-DVI adapter enables you to connect MacBook to external displays for more screen room

● **Toslink adapter and audio cable**

An optional Toslink adapter and digital audio cable enable you to connect MacBook to digital audio devices, such as surround sound speakers

● **External hard drive**

Every MacBook user should have an external hard drive to back up important files and for extra working room

Start Up and Log In

Starting a MacBook is not much of a challenge. After you turn MacBook on, you might also need to log in to start using it (which is not a challenge either). That is because Mac OS X supports multiple user accounts so that each person who uses MacBook can have his own resources. You created at least one user account when you first turned MacBook on.

Mac OS X includes an automatic login feature, which bypasses the login process. If this feature is turned on, you do not have to log in to start using MacBook. If it is not turned on, you need to know a user name and password to be able to log into a user account.

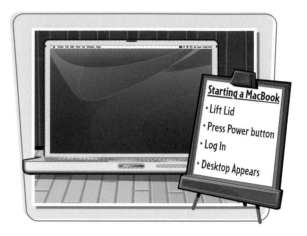

Starting a MacBook
- Lift Lid
- Press Power button
- Log In
- Desktop Appears

Start Up and Log In

START UP

 Open MacBook by lifting up its lid.

② Press the Power button.

MacBook turns on and starts the boot process.

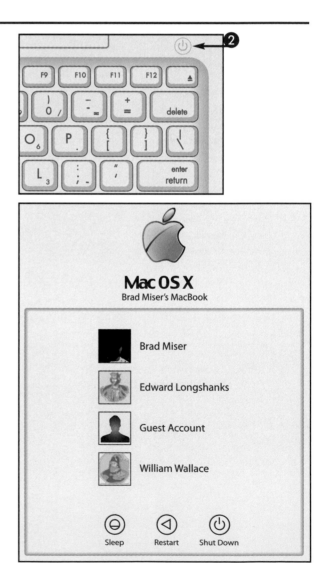

LOG IN WITH THE USER LIST

① Start up MacBook.

The Login window appears, showing a list of user accounts on MacBook.

② Slide your finger over the trackpad until the pointer is over the appropriate user account.

③ Press the trackpad button to select the account.

The Password field appears.

④ Enter the password for the user account.

⑤ Point to the **Log In** button and click the trackpad button or press Return.

You log into the user account and the Mac OS X desktop appears.

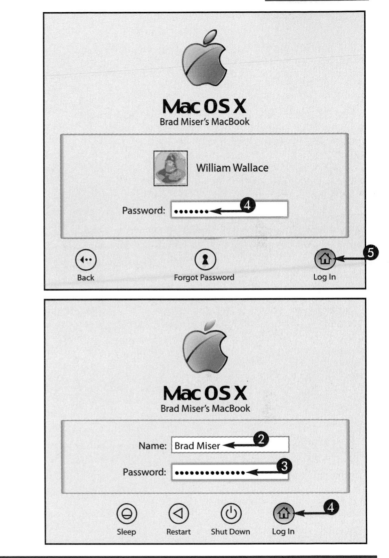

LOG IN WITH A USER NAME

① Start up MacBook.

The Login window appears, showing the Name and Password fields.

② Enter the name of the user account in the Name field.

③ Enter the password for the account in the Password field.

④ Point to the **Log In** button and click the trackpad button or press Return.

You log into the user account and the Mac OS X desktop appears.

 TIPS

What if I forget my password?

If you enter an incorrect password or do not enter a password correctly, the Login screen shudders when you try to log in. This lets you know that the password you provided does not work. Try entering it again. If that does not help, click the Forgot Password button and a password hint appears on the screen. If you still cannot login, try a different user account.

WRONG!

What kind of user accounts are there?

An administrator account enables you to configure various aspects of the system; the first user account you created during the first time you started your MacBook is an administrator account. Standard accounts cannot access very many of the configuration tools and can be limited even further. Guest accounts also have limited access to the system. The root account is the most powerful, but you use that one only in specific situations.

Accounts
· Administrator
· Standard
· Guest
· Root

Explore the Mac OS X Desktop

MacBooks operate through the Mac operating system, which is currently in version 10.5, more commonly called OS X Leopard.

The Mac OS X desktop is the overall window through which you view all that happens on MacBook, such as looking at the contents of folders, working on documents, and surfing the Web.

Explore the Mac OS X Desktop

● **Menu bar**

A menu bar always appears at the top of the screen so you can access the commands it contains

● **Hard drives**

MacBook stores its data, including the software it needs to work, on hard drives. It includes one internal hard drive, but you can connect external drives too

● **CD or DVD**

CDs and DVDs are also incredibly useful for storing your own data

● **Folders**

Containers that you use to organize files and other folders stored on MacBook

● **Files**

Documents (text, graphics, movies, and songs, for example), applications, or other sources of data

● **Finder windows**

You view the contents of folders in Finder windows

● **Application/document windows**

When you use applications, you use the windows those applications present, which can be for documents, Web pages, and games

FINDER MENU BAR AND MENUS

● **Apple menu**

This menu is always visible so you can access special commands, such as Shut Down and Log Out

● **Finder menu**

Where you control the Finder application itself, such as to empty the trash or set preferences

● **File menu**

Use commands on this menu to work with files and Finder windows

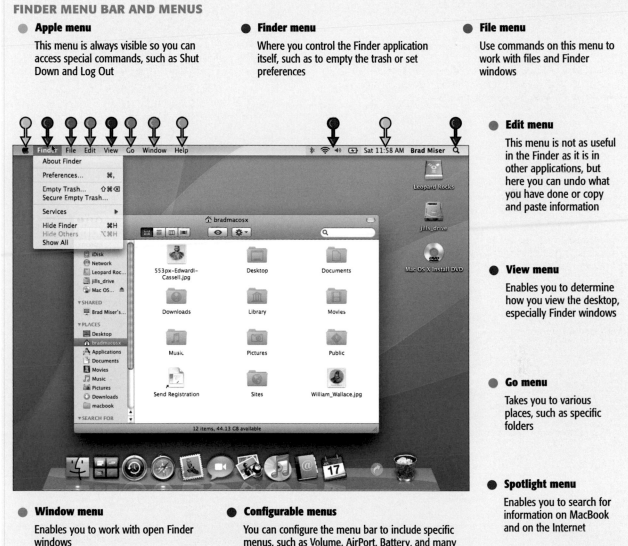

● **Edit menu**

This menu is not as useful in the Finder as it is in other applications, but here you can undo what you have done or copy and paste information

● **View menu**

Enables you to determine how you view the desktop, especially Finder windows

● **Go menu**

Takes you to various places, such as specific folders

● **Spotlight menu**

Enables you to search for information on MacBook and on the Internet

● **Window menu**

Enables you to work with open Finder windows

● **Help menu**

Use when you need help with Mac OS X or the other applications

● **Configurable menus**

You can configure the menu bar to include specific menus, such as Volume, AirPort, Battery, and many more

● **Clock**

Here you see the current time and day

continued

The Finder application controls the Mac OS X desktop, so you see its menu bar whenever you work with this application. The Dock and Sidebar enable you to access items quickly.

FINDER WINDOWS

● **Close button**

Click to close a window

● **Minimize button**

Click to shrink a window and move it onto the Dock

● **Maximize button**

When clicked, a Finder window expands to show you as much as possible; click it again to return to the previous size

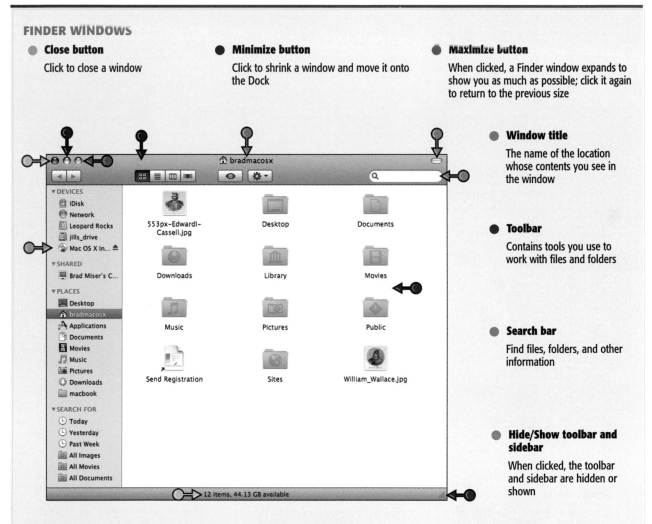

● **Window title**

The name of the location whose contents you see in the window

● **Toolbar**

Contains tools you use to work with files and folders

● **Search bar**

Find files, folders, and other information

● **Hide/Show toolbar and sidebar**

When clicked, the toolbar and sidebar are hidden or shown

● **Sidebar**

Enables you to quickly access devices, folders and files, and searches you have saved

● **Files and folders**

Within a window, the contents of a location are shown; this example shows the icon view

● **Status and information**

Shows information about the current location, such as the amount of free space when you are viewing a hard drive

● **Resize handle**

Drag this handle to change the size of a window

DOCK AND SIDEBAR

● **Devices**

Contains your iDisk (.Mac members), the Network folder, hard drives, CDs/DVDs, and iPods that your MacBook can access

● **Shared**

Computers and other resources being shared on a network

● **Places**

Files and folders you can open by clicking them

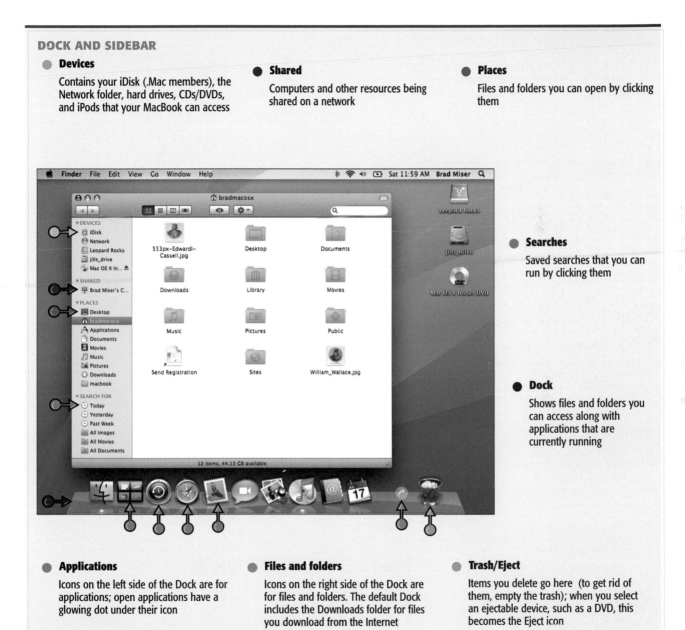

● **Searches**

Saved searches that you can run by clicking them

● **Dock**

Shows files and folders you can access along with applications that are currently running

● **Applications**

Icons on the left side of the Dock are for applications; open applications have a glowing dot under their icon

● **Files and folders**

Icons on the right side of the Dock are for files and folders. The default Dock includes the Downloads folder for files you download from the Internet

● **Trash/Eject**

Items you delete go here (to get rid of them, empty the trash); when you select an ejectable device, such as a DVD, this becomes the Eject icon

Point and Click, Double-click, or Right-click

To tell MacBook what you want to do, point the onscreen arrow to the object that you want to work with by sliding a finger over the trackpad.

The number of times and how you click the trackpad button determines what happens to what you are pointing at.

Point and Click, Double-click, or Right-click

POINT AND CLICK

① Slide your finger on the track pad until the arrow points at the icon of a file or folder.

② Click the trackpad button once.

The object is highlighted to indicate that it is now selected.

DOUBLE-CLICK

① Slide your finger on the trackpad until the arrow points at a file's or folder's icon.

② Click the trackpad button twice.

Whatever you were pointing at opens. For example, if you were pointing at a document, it opens in the associated application. If you pointed to a folder, it opens and you see its contents.

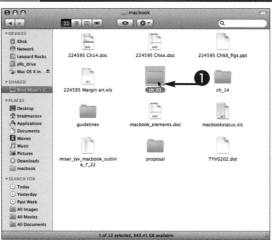

POINT, CLICK, AND DRAG

① Slide your finger on the track pad until the arrow points at something you want to work with, such as a file's or folder's icon.

② Press the trackpad button down and hold it.

The object at which you were pointing becomes attached to the arrow and remains so until you release the trackpad button.

3 Drag your finger on the trackpad to move the object while you hold the trackpad button down.

4 When you get to a different location, release the trackpad button.

The object is moved or copied to the new location.

Note: If you drag something to a different volume it is copied there. If you move it to a different location on the same volume, it is moved there.

RIGHT-CLICK (Ctrl -CLICK)

1 Point to an object on the desktop or even the desktop itself.

2 Press and hold the Ctrl key.

3 Click the trackpad button.

A contextual menu appears.

Note: It is called a contextual menu because the commands appearing on it depend on what you point to.

4 Choose a command on the resulting menu by pointing to it and clicking the trackpad button once.

Note: Clicking the right button on a mouse does the same thing as Ctrl -click; even though MacBook doesn't come with a mouse and uses a trackpad, right-click is still the common way to refer to this function.

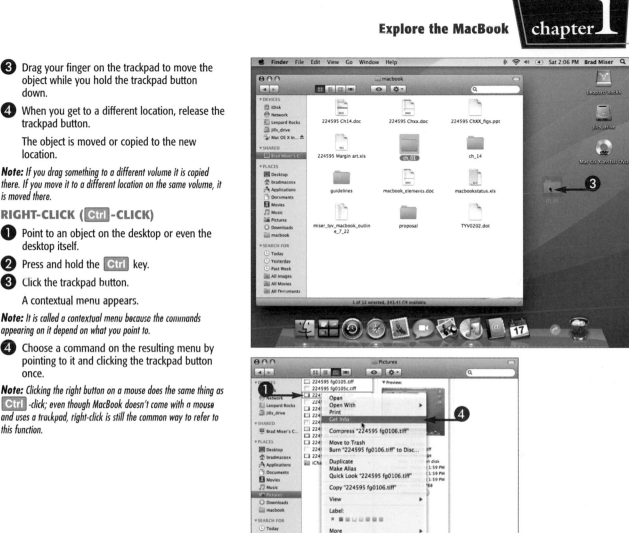

 TIPS

Why do things I click stick to the arrow?
You can configure the trackpad so you can drag things without having to hold the trackpad button. When this setting is on and you click something, it gets attached to the arrow. When you move the arrow, the object moves too. To disable this, open the System Preferences application, open the Trackpad pane of the Keyboard & Mouse pane, and uncheck the Dragging check box.

Nothing happens when I double-click things to open them. Why?
Two clicks have to happen within a certain amount of time to be registered as a double-click. You can configure the amount of time this takes by using the Trackpad pane of the Keyboard & Mouse pane of the System Preferences application.

As you use MacBook, you work with data. Underlying all this data is the need to store and organize it. The major data storing and organizing items thatMacBook uses are described in this section.

Hard Disk

Hard disks are the physical means MacBook uses to store data. The general concept is that data is stored on a magnetic disk accessed via a read/write head. MacBook has one internal hard drive that contains the software it needs to runapplications you install, and documents you create. You can connect external hard disks to MacBook through its USB or FireWire ports to expand the storage room available. Hard drives come in various storage capacities, such as 160GB, and operate at different speeds (faster is better). Hard disks are represented on MacBook with icons, each under a different name. Hard disks are also called hard drives.

Volume

A volume is an area of disk space created using software rather than a physical device. A hard drive can be partitioned into multiple volumes, where each volume acts like a separate hard disk. A volume performs the same task as a hard disk, which is to store data. In fact, when you work with a volume, you might not be able to tell the difference. You can also access volumes being shared with you over a network. Application installers often appear as volumes that you use as if they were a hard disk. Volumes are used to organize data in different ways and to represent various resources with which you work.

Discs

CDs and DVDs serve many purposes. Examples abound, including listening to audio CDs, watching DVD movies and TV shows, and installing applications on CD or DVD. You can also put your own data on CD or DVD, such as burning audio CDs with iTunes, creating DVDs with iDVD, and backing up your data on DVD. MacBook has a slot-loading disc drive located on its right side; to use a disc, simply insert it into the slot.

Folders

Like manila folders in the physical world, folders on MacBook are a means to organize things, such as files and other folders. Mac OS X includes many folders by default. You can create, name, delete, and organize folders in any way you see fit (mostly any way — there are some folders you cannot or should not change). You open a folder in a Finder window to view its contents.

Files

A file is a container for data. Files can contain many different kinds of data. For example, some files are documents, such as text documents you create with a word processor. Files are also images, songs, movies, and other kinds of content. Files make up the operating system that runs MacBook; you typically do not interact with system files directly. Files have names that include file name extensions, such as .jpg and .doc (which can be hidden), and are represented by icons in Finder windows and e-mail attachments.

Sleep, Log Out, Restart, or Shut Down

When your work with MacBook is complete for the day, there are several ways to stop using MacBook. Most of the time, you either put MacBook to sleep or log out. During sleep, activity continues and everything you had open remains open, but MacBook goes into low-power mode; you can wake it up to quickly get back to whatever you were doing. When you log out, all open documents and applications close and you return to the Log Out screen, but MacBook continues to run.

Restart shuts it down and then starts it again; you most typically use this during troubleshooting. Shut Down turns MacBook off.

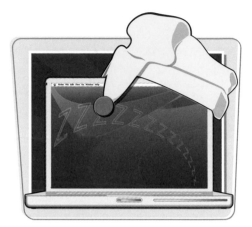

Sleep, Log Out, Restart, or Shut Down

SLEEP OR LOG OUT

1 Open the Apple menu by pointing to it and clicking.

2 Scroll down by dragging on the trackpad until **Sleep** or **Log Out** *Account Name* (where *Account Name* is your user account name) is highlighted.

3 Click the trackpad button.

If you selected **Sleep**, MacBook's display goes dark, its hard drive stops, and the Sleep indicator light pulses.

Note: You can put MacBook to sleep even faster by closing its lid.

If you selected **Log Out**, the Log Out confirmation dialog box appears.

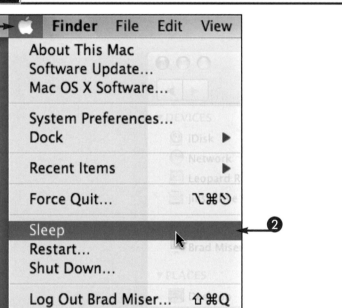

Finder	File	Edit	View

About This Mac
Software Update...
Mac OS X Software...

System Preferences...
Dock

Recent Items

Force Quit...

Sleep
Restart...
Shut Down...

Log Out Brad Miser...

4 Click **Log Out**.

All applications and documents close, and the Log In screen opens.

Note: A faster way to log out is to press ⌘+Shift+Q.

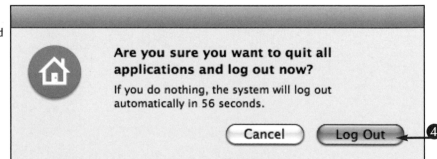

Are you sure you want to quit all applications and log out now?

If you do nothing, the system will log out automatically in 56 seconds.

Cancel   Log Out

RESTART OR SHUT DOWN

1 Open the Apple menu by pointing to it and clicking.

2 Scroll down the trackpad until **Restart** or **Shut Down** is highlighted.

3 Click the trackpad button.

Depending on which option you chose, the appropriate confirmation dialog box appears.

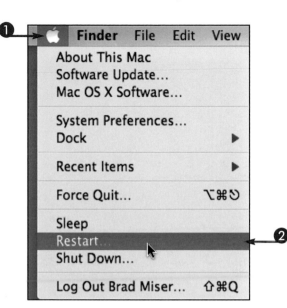

❶
 🍎 **Finder** File Edit View

About This Mac
Software Update...
Mac OS X Software...

System Preferences...
Dock ▶

Recent Items ▶

Force Quit... ⌥⌘⏏

Sleep
Restart... ← ❷
Shut Down...

Log Out Brad Miser... ⇧⌘Q

4 To restart MacBook, click **Restart**.

MacBook shuts down and then starts up again.

5 To shut down MacBook, click **Shut Down**.

MacBook turns off.

Note: You can also perform the tasks in this section by pushing the Power button. The dialog box that appears contains Restart, Sleep, and Shut Down buttons. Click a button to perform that action.

Are you sure you want to restart your computer now?

If you do nothing, the system will restart automatically in 59 seconds.

(Cancel) (Restart) ← ❹

 TIPS

Should I turn my MacBook off?
In most cases, no. It is usually better to just put it to sleep. When you want to use it again, wake MacBook up and it is ready in just a few seconds. Starting it up again can take several moments. If you will not be using MacBook for an extended period of time, it is better to shut it down so the battery does not get drained.

When should I log out instead of shutting my MacBook down?
If you leave your MacBook in a place where other people can get to it, you probably do not want to leave it running in case someone decides to see what he can do with it. You can shut it down. However, if automatic login is turned on, someone can simply turn MacBook on and start using it. To prevent someone from using MacBook, log out. Everything you had open closes and you return to the Login screen. When you want to use it again, you can quickly log back in. Later, you can learn how to set MacBook so it automatically locks to protect it when you aren't actively using it.

User Name
davidc
Password
****

Look Through Mac OS X Finder Windows

Everything you see on MacBook's desktop is viewed through some type of window (in fact, the desktop itself is a window). As you learn to use your MacBook, you will want to know how to make the most of each kind of window. The windows with which you will spend most of your time are the Finder, application, and document windows.

Understand Finder, Application, and Document Windows

Like windows in the physical world, windows on MacBook enable to you to view objects onscreen, such as folders, files, and documents.

In Mac OS X, most windows have common elements that are the same no matter what application you are using. In some cases, particularly with games and utilities, you might not see document windows when you run an application; instead, you see windows specific to the functions of those applications.

Understand Finder, Application, and Document Windows

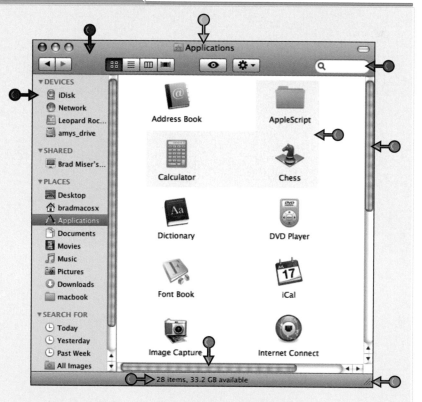

FINDER WINDOWS

● **Title**

Shows the name of the folder you are currently viewing

● **Toolbar**

Contains tools to control windows, move among them, change views, and perform actions

● **Search tool**

Enables you to search for files or folders

● **Files and folders**

The contents of the folder you are viewing appear within the main part of Finder windows

● **Sidebar**

Contains icons for locations; click an icon to view its contents in the window or open it if it is a document

● **Status**

Displays status information for what you are viewing, such as available disk space

● **Scroll bars**

Enable you to move up or down or left or right within a window to see all of its contents

● **Resize handle**

Drag this handle to change the size and shape of a window

APPLICATION WINDOWS

● **Document title**

The name of the document being shown in the window or the application's

● **Window controls**

Enable you to close, minimize, or maximize the application

● **Toolbar**

Provides buttons for specific actions in the application

● **Application-specific tools**

The main window of the application presents the tools and actions for which you can use it

DOCUMENT WINDOWS

● **Document title**

The name of the file being shown in the window

● **Scroll bars**

Enable you to move up or down or left or right within a window to see all of its contents

● **Application-specific tools**

Most applications provide tools in their windows that are specific to windows they create

Open, View, and Scroll in Windows

To work with documents, files, and folders, open a window that shows what you want to work with. You can scroll within an open window to view its contents.

OPEN WINDOWS FROM THE DESKTOP

1 Find the icon for the folder or file you want to open.

Note: *You can learn a lot more about finding items on MacBook later in this book. For now, use any icon you see on the desktop.*

2 Double-click a folder or file icon.

A window showing the contents of the file or folder opens.

OPEN WINDOWS FROM THE DOCK OR SIDEBAR

1 Find the icon for the folder or file you want to open on the Dock or on the Sidebar.

2 Click the icon once.

The icon's window opens.

24

OPEN WINDOWS WITH KEYBOARD COMMANDS

1 Find the icon for the folder or file you want to open.

2 Click the icon once.

The icon is highlighted to show you that it is selected.

3 Press ⌘+O.

The icon's window opens.

Note: There is yet another way to open a window for an icon. Point to the icon, press and hold the Ctrl key, and click. On the resulting menu, choose Open.

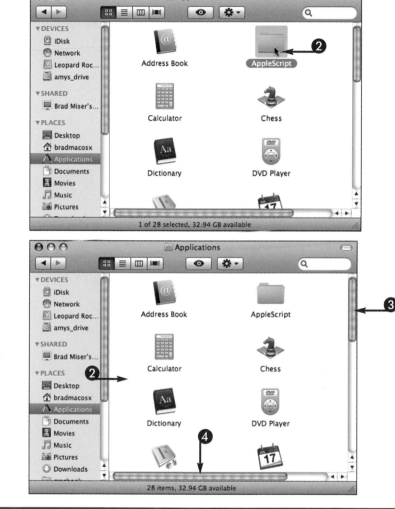

VIEW AND SCROLL WINDOWS

1 Open a window using one of the techniques you learned in the previous tasks.

2 View the icons within the window.

Note: You can tell if everything within a window is shown by the scroll bars, or lack thereof. If a window does not have scroll bars, you are seeing everything that window contains.

3 Drag the vertical scroll bar to move up or down the window.

4 Drag the horizontal scroll bar to move to the left or right within the window.

Note: You can also scroll by clicking the arrow buttons that appear at one end of each scroll bar.

TIPS

Why are scroll bars different sizes?

The relative size of the scroll bar indicates how much of the window's content you are currently seeing. If the scroll bar almost fills its space, you are seeing most of the window's content. If the scroll bar is very small compared to its space, you are seeing a smaller part of the window's contents.

Can I use the keyboard to scroll in windows?

Yes, in several ways. If you press the Tab key, you jump from icon to icon. As you move to icons that do not appear on the screen, the window scrolls to show the icon you have moved to. You can press Shift+Tab to move in the opposite direction. You can also use the arrow keys in the same way. If you press and hold the fn key while you press one of the arrow keys, you scroll by an entire window in the direction of the arrow key your press.

Minimize, Resize, Move, or Close Windows

As you use MacBook, you work through many windows. Some you leave open and others you close. Some you want to hide or minimize. Developing good window-management skills makes you a much more effective MacBook user.

When you are done working with a window, close it. If you want to leave a window open but do not want it taking up desktop space, minimize (shrinking the window and moving it onto the Dock) it. You can also resize open windows and move them around the desktop.

MINIMIZE WINDOWS

1. Click the **Minimize** button (⊙).

   ● The window shrinks and moves to the Dock.

2. To restore the window, click its icon on the Dock.

   The window returns to the size and position it was when you minimized it.

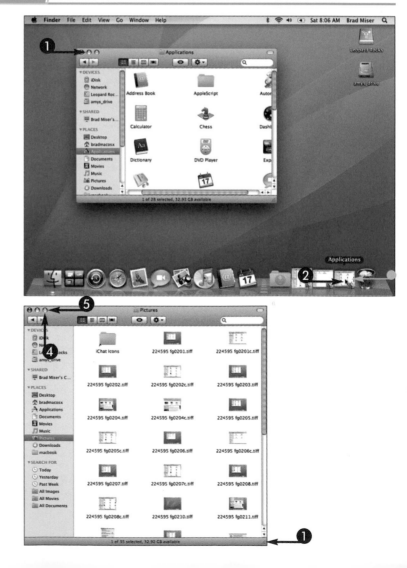

RESIZE WINDOWS

1. Click the **Resize** handle located in the lower right corner of the window.

2. Keep the trackpad button pressed down and drag until the window is the size and shape you want it to be.

3. Release the trackpad button.

4. To make the window as large as it can be on the screen, click the Maximize button (⊙).

   The window increases to its maximum size.

5. To return the window to its previous size, click (⊙) again.

MOVE WINDOWS

1 Point to the window's title bar.

2 Press and hold the trackpad button.

3 Drag the window on the desktop.

4 When it is in the location you want, release the trackpad button.

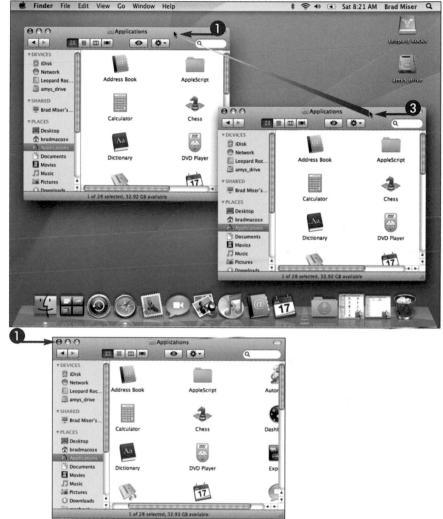

CLOSE WINDOWS

1 Click the **Close** button ().

The window closes. If you close a document window and you have not saved changes, a prompt appears.

TIPS

Can I use keyboard commands to manage windows?

To close a window using the keyboard, press ⌘+W. To minimize a window, press ⌘+M. To hide a window, press ⌘+H.

What is the purpose of the Window menu?

Most applications provide a Window menu that enables you to work with the application's windows. This menu typically includes a selection for each window that is open within that application; choose the window you want to view and it jumps to the front. You can also cycle through all the application's open windows and choose the Minimize command to minimize an open window.

View Finder Windows in Icon View

The Icon view is one that is most synonymous with Mac computers. Icons are pleasing to look at and visually indicate what kind of object they represent, such as a file or folder.

The Icon view is not the most useful one, but it is pretty.

View Finder Windows in Icon View

1. Open a window using one of the methods you learned earlier.

2. Click the **Icon view** button (🔡).

   The objects in the window are shown as icons.

3. Click **View** and then **Show View Options**.

   The View Options dialog box appears.

4. To have the folder always open in Icon view, check the **Always open in Icon View** check box.

5. Drag the Icon size slider to increase or decrase the size of icons.

6. Drag the Grid spacing slider to decrease or increase the space between icons.

7. Click on the **Text size** drop-down menu and choose the size of the text for icon labels.

8. To have icon labels appear at the bottom of icons, click **Bottom**, or click **Right** if you want labels to appear on the right side of icons.

9. To show additional information about items, check the **Show item info** check box.

10. To show a preview of items within the icon, check the **Show icon preview** check box.

11. Use the Arrange by pop-up menu to choose how items are arranged.

12. Click **White** to show the white background.

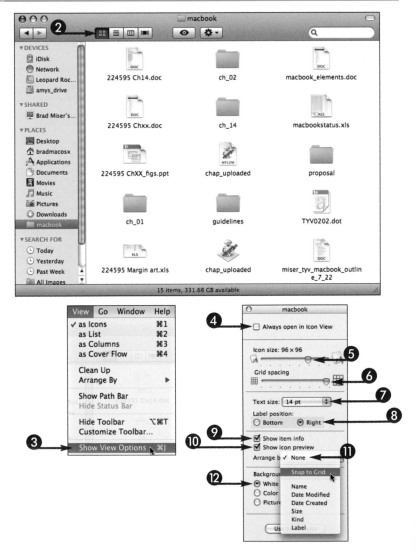

⑬ Click **Color** to use a different color for the background.

⑭ Click the color button.

The Color Picker appears.

⑮ Use the Color Picker to choose the color you want for the background.

⑯ When you have the color you want, click **OK**.

The Color Picker closes and you move back to the window.

⑰ To use an image as the background, click **Picture**.

The Select button appears.

⑱ Click **Select**.

The Select a Picture dialog box appears.

⑲ Use the dialog box to move to and select the file you want for the background.

⑳ When you have selected the file you want to use, click **Select**.

The dialog box closes and the image is applied as the background to the window.

㉑ To have every window you open in Icon view use these settings by default, click **Use as Defaults**.

㉒ Close the View Options dialog box by clicking its **Close** button (⊙).

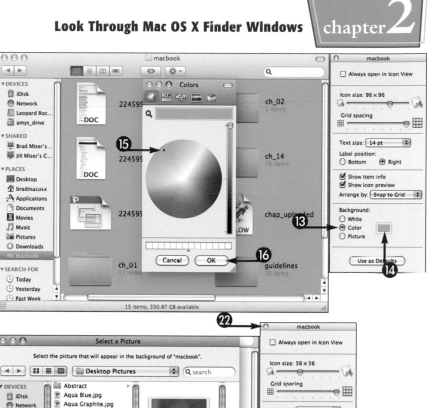

View Finder Windows in List View

The Icon view is pretty, but it does not provide a lot of information about the files and folders you see. Even if you make the icons small, they take up a lot of room, making it hard to see all the contents of a Finder window.

List view may not look as nice as Icon view, but it does provide a lot more information. Plus, you can more easily sort windows so the items appear in the order you want.

View Finder Windows in List View

① Open a window using one of the methods you learned earlier.

② Click the **List view** button (▤).

The objects in the window are shown in a list.

③ Choose **File** and then **Show View Options**.

The View Options dialog box appears.

④ If you want the window to always open in List view, check the **Always open in List View** check box.

⑤ Choose the icon size for the view by clicking the larger or smaller icon button.

⑥ Use the **Text size** pop-up menu to choose the text size for the List view.

⑦ Check the check boxes for each column you want to see.

⑧ If you want relative dates to be displayed, such as Yesterday or Today, check the **Use relative dates** check box.

⑨ If you want the sizes of folders to be displayed, check the **Calculate all sizes** check box.

⑩ If you want to see previews in the icons for each item, check the **Show icon preview** check box.

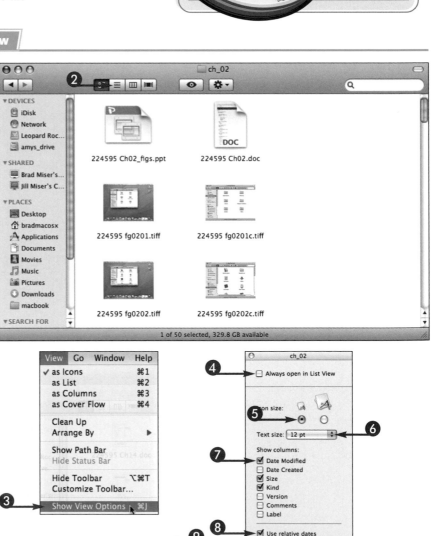

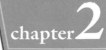

⓫ If you want other windows to use these settings by default, click **Use as Defaults**.

⓬ When you are done making changes, click (◉).

The dialog box closes and you see the window reflecting changes you made.

⓭ To change the order in which columns appear in the window, click a column heading that you want to move.

⓮ Move the column to the left or right.

⓯ Release the trackpad button.

The column settles in to its new location.

⓰ To open the contents of a folder, click its expansion triangle (▶ changes to ▼).

The folder expands so you can see the folders and files it contains.

⓱ Click (▼) to collapse a folder again.

How do I expand all the folders within a window at the same time?

Press and hold the Option key while you click a folder's expansion triangle. The folder expands along with all the other folders in the window and all the folders contained within those folders. Press and hold the Option key and click one of the expansion triangles to collapse all the folders again.

How do I tell where a folder is when I view its window?

Click **View** and then **Show Path Bar**. A bar appears at the bottom of the window that shows you the path from the startup disk to the location of the current folder.

View Finder Windows in Column View

The Column view is best for navigating quickly around MacBook. This view allows you to see the contents of folders along with the locations of those folders. You can click any folder's icon to immediately see the contents of that folder in the same window.

As you learn to use MacBook, get comfortable with the Column view so you can use it to quickly move to any location.

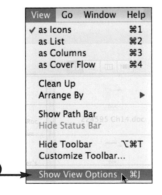

---

1 Open a window using one of the methods discussed earlier.

2 Click the **Column View** button (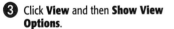).

The objects in the window are shown in columns.

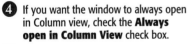

3 Click **View** and then **Show View Options**.

The View Options dialog box appears.

4 If you want the window to always open in Column view, check the **Always open in Column View** check box.

5 Use the **Text size** pop-up menu to choose a text size for the labels shown in the Column view.

6 If you want to see an icon for each item, check the **Show icons** check box.

7 If you want to see a preview of items within their icons, check the **Show icon preview** check box.

View	Go	Window	Help
✓ as Icons			⌘1
as List			⌘2
as Columns			⌘3
as Cover Flow			⌘4

Clean Up
Arrange By ▶

Show Path Bar
Hide Status Bar

Hide Toolbar ⌥⌘T
Customize Toolbar...

3 → Show View Options ⌘J

⑧ If you want to see a preview of a file you select, check the **Show preview column** check box.

⑨ Use the **Arrange by** pop-up menu to determine how items in the window are listed.

⑩ When you are done making changes, click (○).

⑪ Select a location on the Sidebar to view it.

⑫ Click a folder to see its contents.

● As you move through the folder hierarchy, columns shift to the left so that you always see the last column opened.

⑬ Click a file.

You see information about the file in the far right column.

⑭ To change the width of a column, drag its Resize handle (॥) to the left or right.

The column resizes immediately.

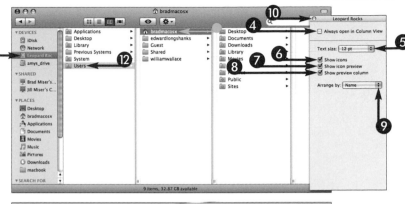

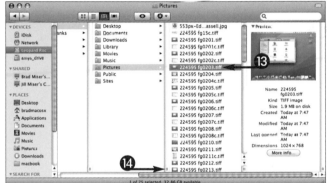

TIPS

How do I resize all the columns at once?
Press and hold the Option key while you drag one column's Resize handle. All the columns are resized at the same time.

How do I tell the difference between a folder and a file?
In Column view, folders always have a right-facing triangle at the right edge of their column. Files do not have this arrow.

THEATRE OF DIONYSOS

ATHENS ▶ TOWER OF THE WINDS

GATE OF ATHENA

33

View Finder Windows in Cover Flow View

Cover Flow view is modeled after the iPod interface on iPhones.

The easiest way to think about the Cover Flow view is to visualize a stack of CDs that you flip through to see each CD. A Finder window in Cover Flow view behaves similarly. You can flip through the various folders and files to browse them in the top part of the window. In the bottom part of the window, you see the items in List view.

View Finder Windows in Cover Flow View

① Open a window using one of the methods discussed earlier.

② Click the **Cover Flow View** button (▥).

The objects in the window are shown in columns.

③ Click **View** and then **Show View Options**.

The View Options dialog box appears.

④ If you want the folder to always open in Cover Flow view, check the **Always open in Cover Flow** check box.

⑤ Configure the rest of the settings just like the List view.

⑥ To browse the contents of the item quickly, drag the scrollbar to the left or right.

As you drag, each item flips by. The item currently selected is the one directly facing the screen.

⑦ To jump to a specific file or folder, click its icon.

It becomes selected and moves to the center of the flow view.

⑧ To make the Cover Flow part of the window larger or smaller, drag its Resize handle up or down.

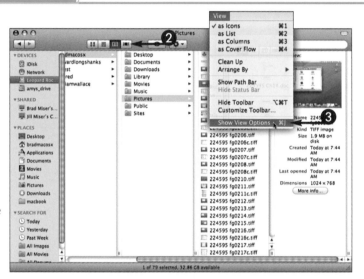

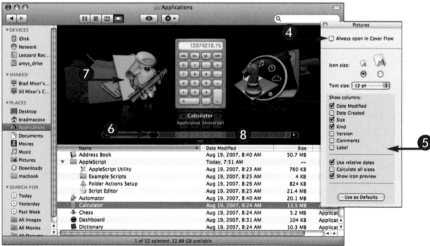

Configure the Sidebar

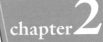

The Finder's Sidebar makes it easy to get to specific locations on MacBook. It comes with a number of default locations, but you can add items to or remove them from the Sidebar so that it contains the items you use most frequently.

The Sidebar is organized into sections. *Devices* includes volumes and devices mounted on MacBook, such as hard drives, an iDisk, iPods, and so on. *Shared* include those you are accessing on a network. *Places* contains folders and files. *Search For* presents saved searches.

Configure the Sidebar

① To remove an item from the Sidebar, drag it from the Sidebar.

● The item disappears in a puff of smoke.

Note: When you remove something from the Sidebar, it is not removed from the computer. The item remains in its current location on MacBook; it is just no longer accessible from the Sidebar.

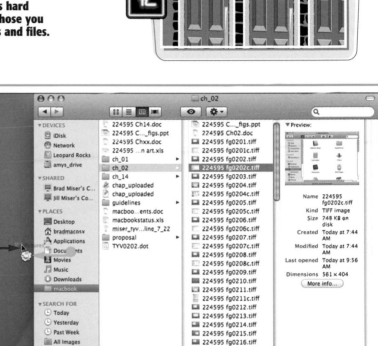

② To add something to the Sidebar, drag it from a Finder window or desktop onto the Sidebar.

③ When the item is over the location where you want to place it, release the trackpad button.

The item's icon is added to the Sidebar and you can use it just like the default items.

④ To change the order of items in the Sidebar, drag them up or down the list.

⑤ To collapse or expand sections of the Sidebar, click their expansion triangles (▶ changes to ▼).

Use the Action Pop-up Menu and Quick Look

The Action pop-up menu is a powerful element of Finder windows, though you might not think so to look at it. This menu contains a list of contextual commands that you can use.

The Finder's Quick Look command enables you to view the contents of a file or group of files without actually opening them. This can save time, especially when you are looking for specific files on the desktop.

Use the Action Pop-up Menu and Quick Look

USE THE ACTION POP-UP MENU

① Open a Finder window.

② Click the **Action** pop-up menu (⚙️▾).

The list of available commands appears.

③ Choose the command you want to use.

The action you select is performed.

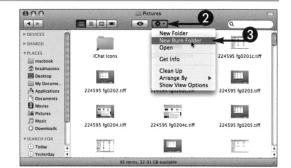

USE QUICK LOOK

① Open a Finder window containing files you want to view.

② Select the files you want to view.

Note: To select multiple files at the same time, press and hold the ⌘ key while you click each file.

③ Click the **Quick Look** button (👁).

The Quick Look window appears.

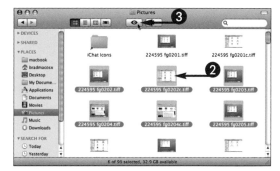

④ Use the controls in the Quick Look window to view the files.

Note: The controls you see depend on the kind of files you are viewing. For example, if you selected images, you can click the Play button to see those images in a slideshow.

⑤ To see Quick Look in full screen, click the **Full Screen** button.

⑥ When you are done with Quick Look, click its **Close** button.

As discussed earlier, the toolbar that appears at the top of the Finder window contains buttons that you can use to access commands quickly and easily. It includes a number of default buttons. However, you can configure the toolbar so it contains the buttons you use most frequently.

Configure the Finder Window Toolbar

① Open a Finder window.

② Click **View** and then **Customize Toolbar**.

The Toolbar Customization sheet appears.

③ To remove a button from the toolbar, drag its icon from the toolbar onto the desktop.

When you release the trackpad button, the button disappears in a puff of smoke.

④ To add a button to the toolbar, drag it from the sheet and drop it on the toolbar at the location in which you want to place it.

When you release the trackpad button, the button is added to the toolbar.

⑤ To change the locations of buttons on the toolbar, drag them from the current location to the new one.

⑥ When you are finished customizing the toolbar, click **Done**.

The Customization sheet closes and you see your customized toolbar.

CHAPTER

3

Manage the Desktop with the Dock, Exposé, Spaces, and the Dashboard

You will be spending a lot of time on MacBook's desktop. To work efficiently, you need to be able to access your items quickly. And you need to keep the many windows you open organized. Mac OS X includes several features that you can use to work with your desktop effectively.

Explore the Dock, Exposé, Spaces, and the Dashboard

Mac OS X includes the Dock, Exposé, Spaces, and the Dashboard to help you use your MacBook more effectively from the desktop.

The Dock is a bar containing many icons.

Exposé is a feature that helps you manage your open windows quickly and efficiently.

Spaces allows you to create groups of applications and windows and switch between them easily.

Explore the Dock, Exposé, Spaces, and the Dashboard

EXPLORE THE DOCK

● **Application icons**

Application icons can be stored on the Dock for easy access; icons for all open applications are also shown.

● **Running applications**

Applications that are open are marked with a blue dot in their reflection.

● **Dividing line**

On the left side of this line are application icons; on the right are folder and file icons, minimized windows, and the Trash.

● **Files and folders**

File and folder icons can also be placed on the Dock for easy access.

● **Minimized windows**

When you minimize a window, it shrinks and moves onto the Dock.

● **Trash**

The holding place for files you delete from MacBook.

EXPLORE EXPOSÉ

● **Thumbnail windows**

When you activate Exposé, all open windows are shrunk.

● **Window in focus**

Click a window to make it active.

EXPLORE SPACES

● **Spaces Manager**

When you activate Spaces, the desktop is hidden and the spaces available to you are shown.

● **Spaces**

Each space includes a collection of applications; when you move into a space, you can use the applications it's associated with.

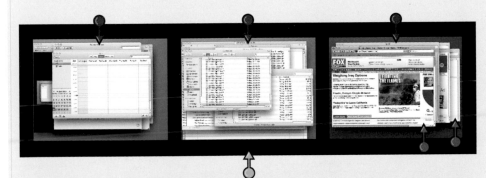

● **Applications**

Each space can have many applications included in it.

EXPLORE THE DASHBOARD

● **Dashboard**

When activated, the Dashboard fills the desktop and presents the active widgets.

● **Active widgets**

To have widgets appear when you activate the Dashboard, you install them on it.

● **Available widgets**

You can add widgets that are installed on MacBook to the Dashboard by dragging them onto it.

Use and Configure the Dock

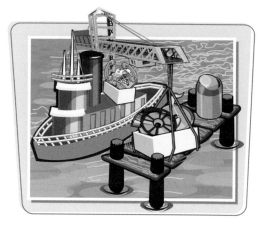

The Dock is a very useful part of Mac OS X. As explained earlier, the Dock has a number of functions; you can also customize the way it looks and works to suit your preferences.

USE THE DOCK

1 Point to an icon on the Dock.

● Its name appears above the icon.

2 Click the trackpad button.

3 To open a Dock icon's menu, point to the icon, press and hold the **Ctrl** key, and click.

Note: You can also open a Dock icon's menu by pointing to it and holding the trackpad button down for a second or two.

4 Choose the command you want to use from the menu.

CONFIGURE THE DOCK

1 Point to the dividing line so that the pointer becomes a horizontal line with arrows on the top and bottom.

2 **Ctrl** +click the line.

The Dock menu appears.

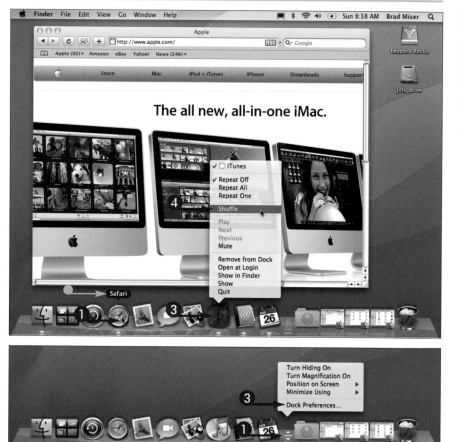

3 Choose **Dock Preferences**.

The Dock pane of the System Preferences application appears.

④ Drag the **Size** slider to the left or right to make the default size of the Dock smaller or larger.

⑤ If you want icons to be magnified when you point to them, check the **Magnification** check box and drag the slider for more or less magnification.

⑥ To position the Dock on the left, bottom, or right side of the desktop, click **Left**, **Bottom**, or **Right**.

⑦ On the **Minimize using** pop-up menu, choose **Genie Effect** to see windows get "sucked" onto the Dock when you minimize them.

⑧ To have icons bounce while their applications are opening, check the **Animate opening applications** check box.

⑨ To automatically hide the Dock when you are not pointing to it, check the **Automatically hide and show the Dock** check box.

Note: When the Dock is hidden, position the pointer over its location and it pops up so you can use it.

⑩ Press ⌘+Q to close the System Preferences application.

The Dock behaves according to your settings.

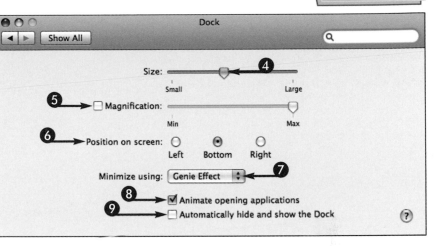

 TIPS

How can I configure the Dock without using the System Preferences application?

Open the Dock menu by ctrl+clicking the dividing line. On the Dock menu, use the commands to configure the Dock, such as Turn Magnification Off to stop the magnification effect, or the Position on Screen commands to change the Dock's location. You can also use the Dock command on the Apple menu.

What happens when I add folder icons to the Dock?

Folder icons on the Dock make accessing the folders and files they contain easy. When you click a folder's icon, a preview window appears showing the folder's contents. You can click an icon to work with one of the items, such as a document icon to open it. You can also click the Show in Finder button to open the folder in a Finder window. By default, the Dock contains the Downloads folder that is the default location for files you download from the Web, but you can add any folder to the Dock to make it instantly accessible.

Manage Open Windows with Exposé

Exposé greatly helps with the screen clutter that is inevitable as you use MacBook. It has three modes. You can hide all open windows to show the MacBook desktop; you can reduce all open windows to thumbnails so that you can quickly jump into a window you want to use; or you can create thumbnails of all the open windows within a specific application for quick access.

Manage Open Windows with Exposé

HIDE ALL OPEN WINDOWS WITH EXPOSÉ

① Open as many windows as you want, including those from the Finder, and from applications.

② Press the F11 key on MacBook's keyboard.

● All the windows are moved off MacBook's screen, leaving an uncluttered desktop for you to work on.

Note: To return the desktop to its cluttered state, press F11 again or click one of the edges of the windows that you see at one of the edges of the desktop.

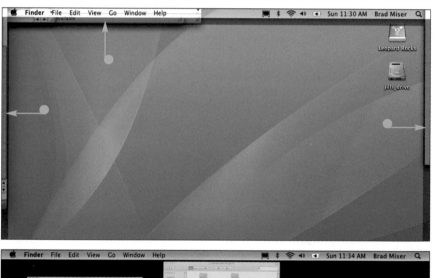

SHOW THUMBNAILS OF ALL OPEN WINDOWS WITH EXPOSÉ

① Open as many windows as you want, including those from the Finder, and from applications.

② Press the F9 key on MacBook's keyboard.

● All windows are shrunk down so that they all fit on the desktop.

③ Point to a window.

● The window is highlighted in blue, and the window's name pops up.

④ Click a window to move into it.

The window becomes active and moves to the front so you can use it.

SHOW ALL OPEN WINDOWS FOR AN APPLICATION WITH EXPOSÉ

1 Open multiple documents within the same application.

2 Press the F10 key on MacBook's keyboard.

All windows for the application are shrunk down so that they all fit on the desktop.

3 Point to a window.

● The arrow changes to the pointing finger, the window is highlighted in blue, and the window's name pops up.

4 Click a window to move into it.

The window becomes active and moves to the front so you can use it.

CONFIGURE EXPOSÉ

1 From the Apple menu, choose **System Preferences**.

The System Preferences application appears.

2 Click the **Exposé & Spaces** icon.

The Exposé & Spaces pane appears.

3 To cause an Exposé action when you point to a corner of the desktop, use the pop-up menus located next to each corner of the desktop thumbnail.

4 To change the keyboard shortcut for using Exposé with all open windows, open the **All windows** pop-up menu.

5 Choose the function key you want to use for this Exposé command.

6 Use the Application windows and Desktop pop-up menus to configure the keyboard shortcuts for those actions.

7 Press ⌘+Q.

The System Preferences application quits and the new keyboard shortcuts for Exposé take effect.

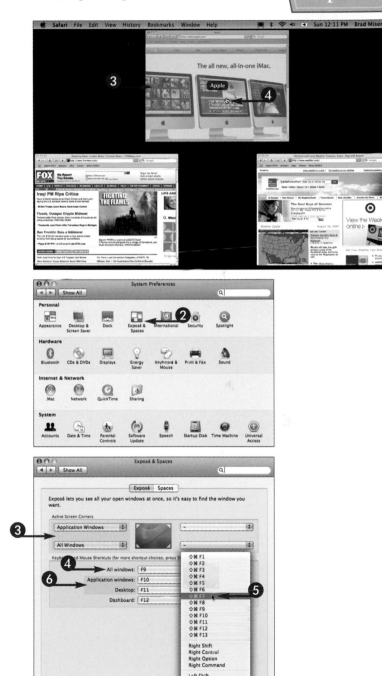

Create and Use Desktop Spaces

Spaces is a great way to create collections of applications and their windows so that you can jump between sets easily and quickly.

CREATE AND CONFIGURE DESKTOP SPACES

1 From the Apple menu, choose **System Preferences**.

The System Preferences application appears.

2 Click the **Exposé & Spaces** icon.

The Exposé & Spaces pane appears.

3 Click the **Spaces** tab.

The Spaces pane appears. At the top of the pane are thumbnails of the spaces you will be configuring.

4 Check the **Enable Spaces** check box.

5 Click the **Add** button (`+`).

The Applications sheet appears. By default, the Applications folder, where most applications are stored, is shown.

6 Click the application you want to add to the space.

7 Click **Add**.

The sheet closes. On the Spaces pane, you see the applications added to the space.

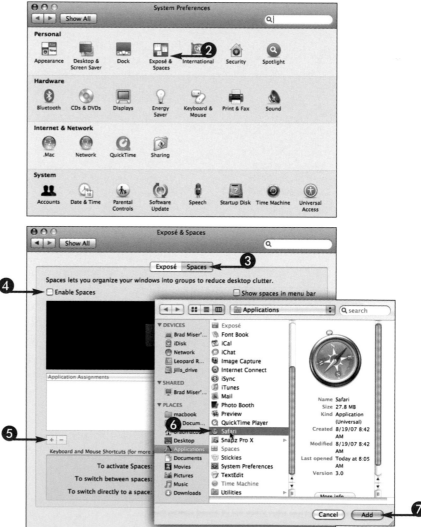

8️⃣ Repeat steps **5** to **7** until you have added all the applications you want to include in spaces.

9️⃣ To add two more spaces in a row, click the **Add** button (⊕).

A new space appears in the row.

🔟 To add two more spaces in a column, click (⊕).

A new space appears in the column.

1️⃣1️⃣ Repeat steps **9** and **10** until you have created all the spaces you want to manage.

Note: To delete spaces, click the Remove button (minus sign inside a circle) next to the Rows or Columns text.

1️⃣2️⃣ Open the **Space** menu for the first application on the list.

1️⃣3️⃣ Choose the number of the space in which you want to include that application or choose **Every Space** to include it in all spaces.

After you make a selection, the space number is shown on the menu for that application, and the space's icon at the top of the window is highlighted.

1️⃣4️⃣ Repeat steps **12** and **13** until you have added all the applications to the spaces in which you want them to be available.

1️⃣5️⃣ On the **To activate Spaces** menu, choose the keyboard shortcut you want to use to activate Spaces; the default is F8.

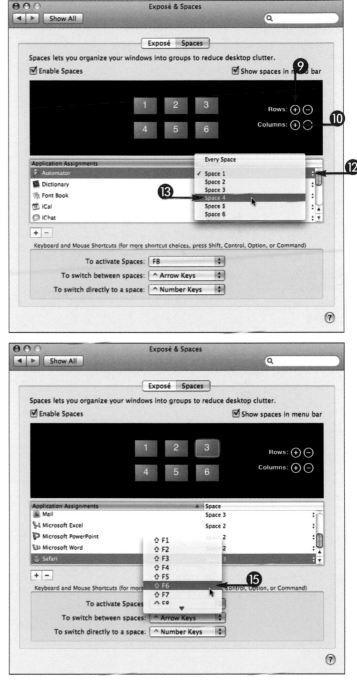

continued

Create and Use
Desktop Spaces *(continued)*

For example, if you have several Internet applications you use, create an Internet space. To use your Internet applications, just open that space and the windows are all in the positions you last left them. You can have as many spaces as you need.

Create and Use Desktop Spaces *(continued)*

16 On the **To switch between spaces** pop-up menu, choose the modifier keys you want to use with the arrow keys to jump to your space.

17 To set the modifier key you use to jump directly to a space by its number, open the **To switch directly to a space** pop-up menu and choose the modifier key you want to use.

18 Press ⌘+Q.

The System Preferences application quits and you are ready to use your spaces.

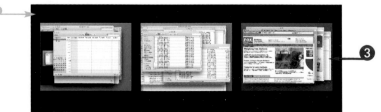

USE DESKTOP SPACES

1 Open the applications associated with your spaces.

2 To display all your different spaces, press the Spaces activation key (the default is F8).

● The desktop is hidden and the Spaces Manager appears. Within each space, you see the windows that are open in that space.

3 Click a space to move into it.

The applications associated with that space appear.

4 To jump directly to a space, press the keyboard shortcut for switching directly to a space, which by default is `Ctrl` +*spacenumber*, where *spacenumber* is the number of the space you want to move into.

The applications associated with that space appear.

5 To move between spaces without using a spaces number, press the keyboard shortcut for switching between spaces, which by default is `Ctrl` +*arrowkey*, where *arrowkey* is one of the arrow keys on the keyboard.

● The Spaces Manager palette appears. Each box on the palette represents one of your spaces.

TIPS

How can I access Spaces using a menu?
On the Spaces pane of the System Preferences application, check the **Show spaces in menu bar** check box. The Spaces menu becomes available on the menu bar; it is indicated by the number of the space you are currently using. Open the menu and choose the space number you want to work with. That space opens.

What happens when I click the Dock icon for an application that is not part of the space I am using?
If an application is available in only one space, when you open it from any source, such as the Dock or the Finder, you switch into the space associated with that space. You cannot add the Finder to a space, but it is associated with the space under which a Finder window is currently open; when you click the Finder's Dock icon, you jump into that space and can use that Finder window or open others as needed.

Use and Configure the Dashboard

The Dashboard is an easy way to access widgets, which are small applications that provide very specific functionality. Mac OS X includes a number of useful widgets by default.

USE THE DASHBOARD

①   Press F12.

● The desktop moves into the background and the Dashboard appears, displaying the widgets already on the Dashboard.

② If a widget is informational, such as a weather widget, view the information it provides.

③ If the widget needs input, click the widget to make it active.

Many widgets require configuration to provide useful information to you.

④ Point to the widget you want to configure.

The Info button (a lowercase *I*) appears.

⑤ Click the **Info** button.

Note: Many widgets require an Internet connection.

The widget moves into configuration mode.

⑥ Use the widget's configuration tools to change its settings.

⑦ Click **Done**.

The widget returns to its normal mode and reflects the changes you made.

CONFIGURE THE DASHBOARD

① Open the Dashboard.

② To change the location of widgets, drag them around the screen.

When you release the trackpad button, the widget is saved in its new location and appears in that spot each time you open the Dashboard.

③ Click the **Add Widget** button.

The Dashboard moves into configuration mode. A bar of available widgets appears at the bottom of the screen and a Close button is added to each widget.

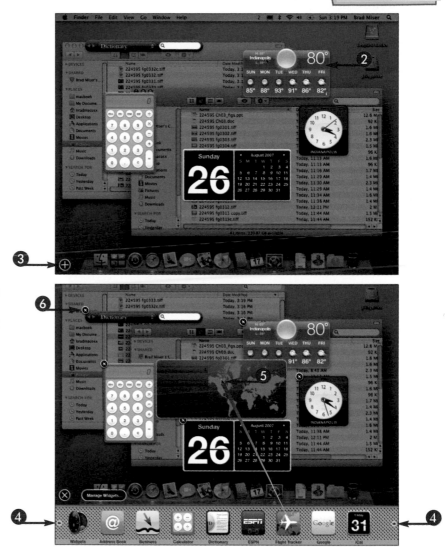

④ Browse the available widgets by clicking the scroll arrows.

⑤ To add a widget to the Dashboard, drag it from the bar and place it on the Dashboard.

When you release the trackpad button, the widget is installed on the Dashboard and starts to work.

⑥ To remove a widget from the Dashboard, click its **Close** button.

The widget is removed from the Dashboard, but remains installed so you can add it again later if desired.

continued

Because widgets are easy to create, there are thousands of them available for you to download, install, and add to your Dashboard.

Use and Configure the Dashboard *(continued)*

FIND AND INSTALL MORE WIDGETS ON THE DASHBOARD

1 Open the **Dashboard**, click the large plus sign at the bottom left of the screen, and then click the **Manage Widgets** button.

2 Click **More Widgets**.

Your Web browser opens and takes you to the Dashboard Widgets page on Apple's Web site.

3 Use the Web page to browse or search for widgets.

Note: Details about using Safari to browse the Web are provided in Chapter 8.

4 When you find a widget you want to install, click its **Download** button.

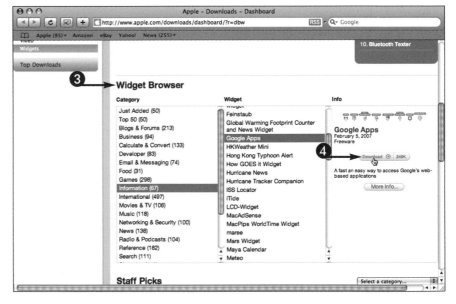

The widget is downloaded to your MacBook. When the process is complete, you are prompted to install the widget.

⑤ Click **Install**.

The Dashboard opens and you see the widget you are installing.

⑥ Click **Keep**.

The widget is added to the Dashboard.

⑦ Locate the widget on the screen and configure it.

TIPS

What if I want widgets to show information for more than one location or situation?
You can have as many copies of the same widget on your Dashboard as you want. For example, if you want to track the weather in five locations, add five copies of the weather widget to your Dashboard and configure one for each area you want to track.

What is the iTunes widget for?
Some applications include a widget that you can use to access that application more quickly and conveniently than opening it directly. The iTunes widget enables you to control the music playing in iTunes from the Dashboard. Many other applications have similar widgets that are typically installed with the application; usually you are prompted to install the widget along with the application.

CHAPTER

4

Work on the Mac Desktop

Birdwatching Weekly   John Simpson

Building a birdhouse is an excellent way to tell your feathered friends that they are welcome visitors to your yard. However, many people don't realize that the kind of birdhouse that you build can definitely affect the kinds of visitors that you attract. To ensure that you don't get a yardful of pigeons when you were expecting chickadees, there are a few important questions that you should ask when you plan your birdhouse. For example, what species of birds travel through your area? Are there particular species that you want to visit your yard? Are there other animals that may also be attracted by your tiny condo?

264

Much of the time you are using MacBook, you will be working on its desktop. The desktop is provided and controlled by the Finder application. This application enables you to do many things, including moving around the folders and files on MacBook, opening files and folders, creating folders, and finding information you need.

Being able to use the desktop effectively goes a long way toward getting the most out of MacBook. You can get your desktop organized the way you want it, understand important information about what is there, and also save folders and files on CDs and DVDs.

Go
Places

The Mac desktop provides many ways to get to specific folders that you want to view. Two of the most useful of these are the Sidebar and the Go menu. Starting from the Sidebar and using the Column view, you can quickly get to any location on the desktop. With the Go menu, you can easily jump to many locations that you commonly visit.

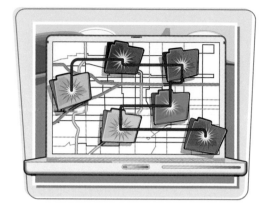

Go Places

GO PLACES FROM THE SIDEBAR WITH COLUMN VIEW

① Open a new Finder window by pressing ⌘+N.

Note: *For information about working with Finder windows, see Chapter 2.*

A new Finder window appears.

② Click the **Columns view** button.

③ Select the starting point, such as your Home folder or a disk.

④ Click the first folder you want to view.

● The contents of that folder appear in the rightmost column.

⑤ Click the next folder you want to move into.

● Its contents appear in the rightmost column.

Note: *In Column view, folders have a right-facing arrow at the end of the column; files do not.*

⑥ Keep selecting folders until you get to the specific folder or file in which you are interested.

Note: *You can always select one of the other views (Icon or List) after you have moved into a folder if you prefer to see windows in one of those views.*

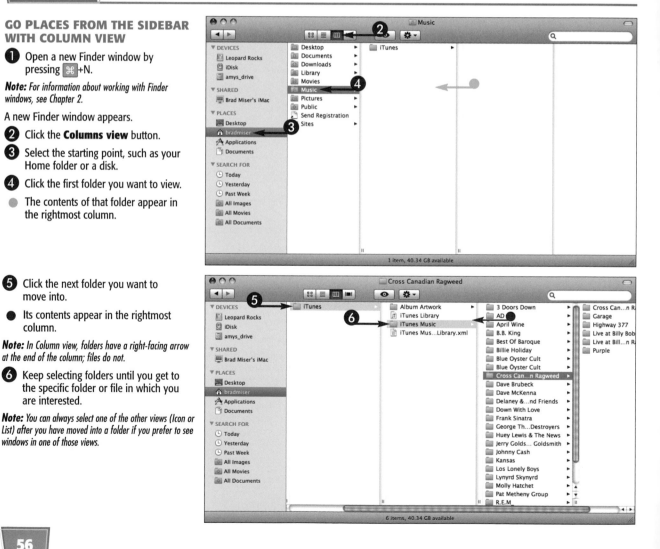

GO PLACES WITH THE GO MENU

① Open the **Go** menu in the Finder toolbar menu.

② Choose the location to which you want to move.

● A Finder window opens showing the location you selected.

How can I go places with the keyboard?

The standard folders on MacBook's desktop all have keyboard combinations that you can press to jump to them. The following list shows the location and keyboard combination (in parentheses): Computer (Shift+⌘+C), Home folder (Shift+⌘+H), Desktop (Shift+⌘+D), Network folder (Shift+⌘+K), iDisk (Shift+⌘+I), Applications folder (Shift+⌘+A), or Utilities folder (Shift+⌘+U).

How do I make it even easier to move to a folder I use all the time?

Drag the folder onto the right end of the Dock and drop it anywhere on the right side of the dividing line. The folder is installed on the Dock and you can open it by clicking its icon and choosing **Show in Finder** on the pop-up menu. (See Chapter 3 for more details.)

Return to Where You Have Been Before

As you work on the desktop, you will probably want to move back to items that you have used recently. Of course, you can always move back to a location in the same way you got there originally, such as by using the Sidebar or Go menu.

However, Mac OS X maintains two recent lists that you can use to quickly move back to places you have been by selecting them on menus.

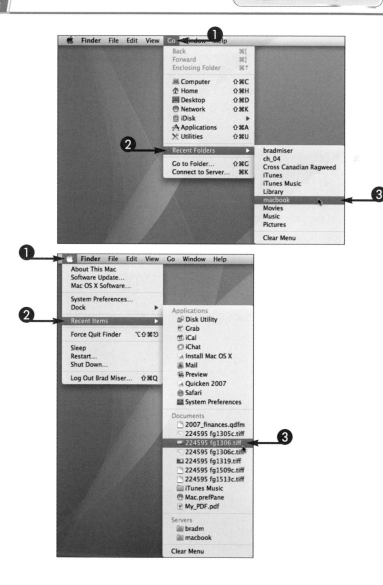

Return to Where You Have Been Before

RETURN TO PREVIOUS FOLDERS

1. Open the Go menu.
2. Choose **Recent Folders**.
3. Select the folder you want to open.

   The folder you selected opens in a Finder window.

RETURN TO PREVIOUS APPLICATIONS, DOCUMENTS, OR SERVERS

1. Open the Apple menu (changes to).
2. Choose **Recent Items**.
3. Choose the application, document, or server you want to access.

   The item you selected opens.

Note: If you want to remove all the items from either recent list, choose the **Clear Menu** command. The items are removed. The next time you go to an item, it is added to the appropriate menu again.

Open Files and Folders

To work with a folder or file, you must open it. There are many ways to open either of these, and what happens when you open something depends on whether you open a file or a folder.

When you open a file, the application associated with that file launches, and you see the contents of the file, such as an image or a text document. When you open a folder, you see a Finder window showing the files and folders within the folder you opened.

Open Files and Folders

OPEN A FILE

1 Double-click a file's icon, select its icon and press ⌘+O, select its icon and press ⌘+Down Arrow, or Ctrl+click its icon and choose **Open** on the file's contextual menu.

The file you selected opens.

Note: Files can be many different things such as documents, applications, preferences, and so on. Basically, a file is anything that is not a folder.

OPEN A FOLDER

1 If you are viewing the Finder window in Icon or List view, either double-click the folder's icon, select it and press ⌘+O, select its icon and press ⌘+Down Arrow, or Ctrl+click its icon and choose **Open** on the file's contextual menu.

You see the contents of the folder you selected.

Move or Copy Folders and Files

As you work on the desktop, you will want to move folders and files to organize them in the way that works best for you. You can move folders or files to any location on the desktop, such as within folders in your Home folder.

At times, you might want to copy files or folders. For example, you might want to have two versions of a document, or you might want to make a copy of a file or folder for backup purposes.

Move or Copy Folders and Files

MOVE FOLDERS AND FILES

1 Open a Finder window so it shows the folder or file you want to move.

2 Open a second Finder window and go to the location in which you want to store the folder or file.

3 Drag the folder or file icon from its current location to the new location.

4 When the pointer is over the new location, release the trackpad button.

The folder or file is moved from the first location and stored where you dropped its icon.

Note: If the second Finder window is located on a different volume (such as a different hard disk) than the folder or file is currently stored on, the file is copied instead of moved when you drag and drop its icon.

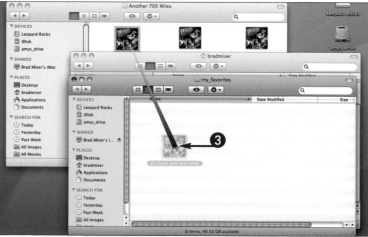

COPY FOLDERS AND FILES

① Open a Finder window so it shows the folder or file you want to copy.

② Select the icon of the folder or file you want to copy.

③ Press ⌘+C, choose **Copy** from the Edit menu, or press and hold the ⌃Ctrl key, press the trackpad button, and choose **Copy** from the contextual menu.

Note: You can also copy a file or folder by pressing and holding the Option key while you drag its icon.

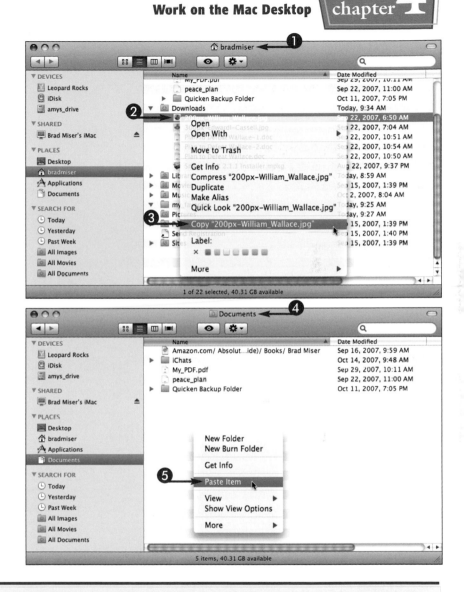

④ Open the location in which you want to place the copy of the folder or file.

⑤ Press ⌘+V, choose **Edit, Paste**, or press and hold the ⌃Ctrl key, press the trackpad button, and choose **Paste Item** from the contextual menu.

A copy of the folder or file is made in the location you selected.

TIPS

How can I move or copy multiple folders or files at the same time?

Press and hold the ⌘ key and click the icon of each folder or file you want to move to select each of them. To select files and folders that are contiguous, press and hold the Shift key, click the first icon, and then click the last icon. You can then drag all the files and folders in the group at the same time.

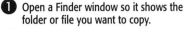

What's an alias?

An alias is a pointer to a folder or file. You can open the item to which an alias points by opening the alias. Aliases are useful when you want to access a folder or file from many locations but have only one version of that folder or file. To create an alias, select a folder or file and choose **File, Make Alias**. An alias is created; it has the same name as the original item with the word *alias* appended to its name, and its icon has an arrow to indicate that it is a "pointer" file.

Create Folders

As shown earlier, you can use folders to organize files and other folders. Mac OS X includes a number of folders by default that you can use to organize your own files and folders. These are located in your Home folder and include Documents, Movies, and Music.

Create Folders

① Open a Finder window showing the location in which you want to create a new folder.

② Press Shift+⌘+N, choose **File**, **New Folder**, or press and hold the **Ctrl** key, press the trackpad button, and choose **New Folder** from the contextual menu.

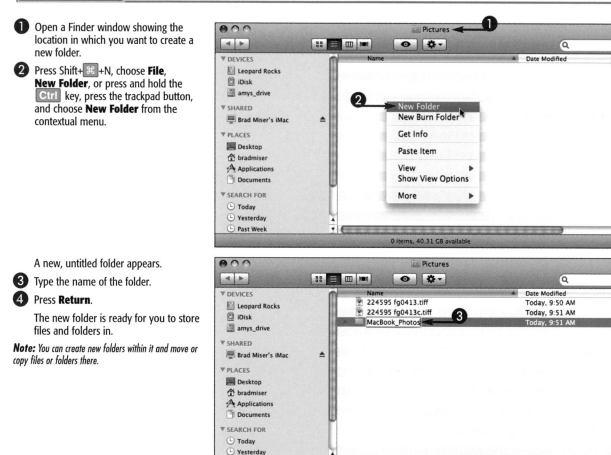

A new, untitled folder appears.

③ Type the name of the folder.

④ Press **Return**.

The new folder is ready for you to store files and folders in.

Note: You can create new folders within it and move or copy files or folders there.

Create Smart Folders

A smart folder is smart because instead of manually placing items within it, you define a set of criteria and the items that meet those criteria are placed within the folder automatically.

Create Smart Folders

① Open the folder in which you want to store the smart folder.

② Choose **File**, **New Smart Folder** or press Option+⌘+N.

A new smart folder window appears.

③ Click the areas of MacBook that you want to be searched for the smart folder.

④ Click the **Add Condition** button (⊕).

A new condition appears.

⑤ Choose the attribute you want to include on the first pop-up menu.

⑥ On the second pop-up menu, select the operand.

⑦ Enter the text for which you want to search.

⑧ Click the **Add Condition** button ⊕.

A new, empty condition appears.

● As you enter conditions, files and folders that meet those conditions appear in the window.

⑨ When you are done adding conditions, click **Save**.

The Save sheet appears.

⑩ Enter the name of the folder in the **Save As** field.

⑪ Choose the Save location.

⑫ Click **Save**.

Whenever you open the smart folder, you see all the files and folders that currently meet its criteria.

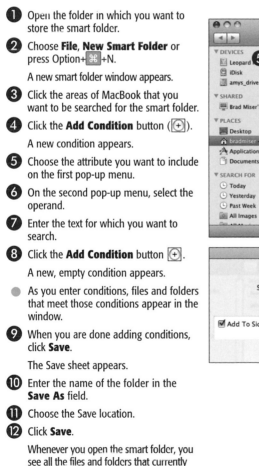

Rename Files and Folders

You can change the name of files or folders as you need to. Like when you create them, you can change the names to be just about anything you want, up to 255 characters.

When you change the name of files, you should usually avoid changing the filename extension (everything after the period in the name) because this extension is an important way that Mac OS X associates documents with applications. However, you can change the part of the name before the period to what you want it to be.

Rename Files and Folders

1 Select the folder or file whose name you want to change.

2 Press **Return**.

● The name becomes highlighted to indicate that you can change it.

Note: If your user account does not have write permissions for a folder or file, you cannot change its name.

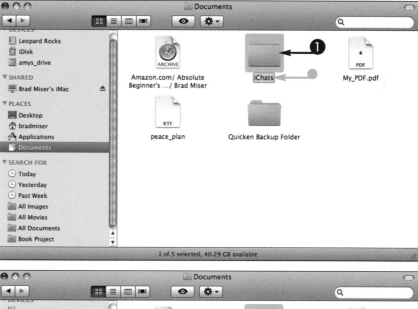

3 Type the new name of the folder or file.

4 Press **Return**.

The new name is saved.

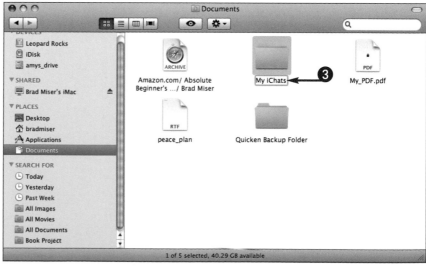

Compress Files and Folders

Folders and files take up disk space. You can compress them to reduce the space they consume.

This is even more useful when you move these files over a network, especially when you e-mail files as attachments. Not only do compressed files move more quickly, you can include all the relevant files in one compressed file to make them easier for the recipient to work with.

Compress Files and Folders

① Open a Finder window showing the files and folders you want to compress.

② Select the files and folders you want to include in the compressed file.

Note: *Press and hold the* ⌘ *or Shift keys to select multiple items.*

③ Hold the **Ctrl** down, click the selected items and choose **Compress X Items**, where **X** is the number of items selected.

The files and folders are compressed and a file called Archive.zip is created.

Note: *To learn how to attach files to e-mail messages, see Chapter 9.*

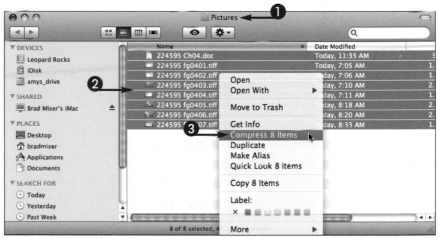

EXPAND COMPRESSED FILES

① Go to and double-click the compressed file.

The Archive Utility launches and expands the file. It stores the uncompressed files in a folder with the same name as the compressed file.

② Open the expanded folder to work with the files and folders it contains.

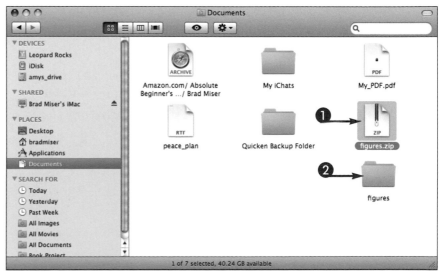

Delete Files and Folders

When you decide you no longer need files or folders, you should remove them from MacBook. Not only do you get rid of clutter, making what you do value easier to find and work with, but you conserve disk space.

Delete Files and Folders

① Select the files or folders you want to delete.

② Drag the files or folders from their current location onto the Trash icon on the Dock.

③ When the Trash icon is highlighted, release the trackpad button.

The items are placed in the Trash folder and the Trash icon now looks like it contains crumpled-up papers.

④ To delete Trash's contents forever, **Ctrl** +click the Trash icon.

Its contextual menu appears.

⑤ Choose **Empty Trash**.

A warning prompt appears.

⑥ Click **OK**.

All the files or folders in the Trash are deleted; the icon becomes empty again.

Note: *To disable the prompt when you empty the Trash, choose **Finder Preferences**. Click the **Advanced** tab and uncheck the **Show warning before emptying the Trash** check box. The Trash is emptied immediately when you choose the **Empty Trash** command.*

Eject Disks and Discs

Because MacBook has only one disc slot, you must obviously remove the current CD or DVD before you can insert another one. This is called ejecting the disc. There are a number of ways to do this, and none of them are challenging.

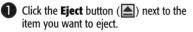
Eject Disks and Discs

EJECT WITH A CONTEXTUAL MENU

1 **Ctrl** +click the disk's or disc's icon that you want to eject.

2 Choose **Eject** *discname* where *discname* is the name of the disk or disc you selected.

If you selected a CD or DVD, it ejects from MacBook.

If you selected a hard drive, its icon disappears from the Sidebar; you can safely disconnect it from MacBook.

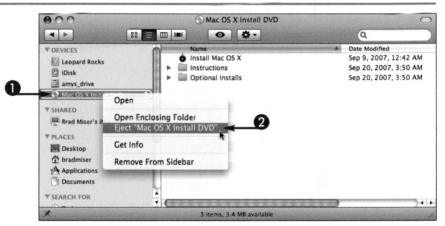

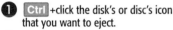

EJECT WITH THE EJECT BUTTON

1 Click the **Eject** button (⏏) next to the item you want to eject.

If you selected a CD or DVD, it ejects from MacBook.

If you selected a hard drive, its icon disappears from the Sidebar; you can safely disconnect it from MacBook.

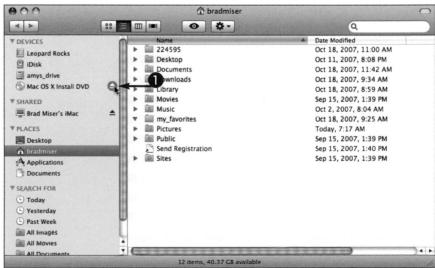

Find Files, Folders, and Other Information

Over time, you might not remember where all your e-mail, Web, and other information is. Mac OS X includes Spotlight, which enables you to search MacBook, and any computers you can access on your network, to find the information you need.

FIND FILES AND FOLDERS WITH FINDER

1 Open a Finder window.

2 Type the information for which you want to search in the Search bar.

● As you type, the window switches to search mode.

3 Select the area you want to search by clicking its button.

4 To see where a folder or file is located, select it.

● The path to the file or folder is shown at the bottom of the window.

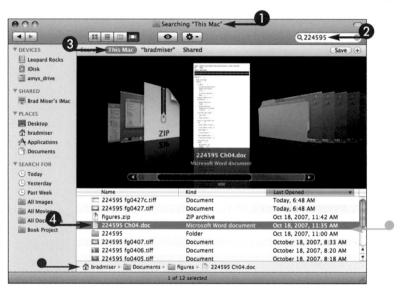

5 To make your search more specific, click the **Add** button (+).

A second search condition bar appears.

6 Choose the attribute you want to search on in the first pop-up menu.

7 Configure the search using the tools that appear.

As you add more conditions, the search results become more specific.

Note: If you click the **Save** button, you can save the search as a smart folder.

FIND INFORMATION WITH SPOTLIGHT

1 Click the **Spotlight** icon located in the upper left corner of the desktop (changes to Q).

Note: *You can also start a Spotlight search by pressing* ⌘ *+Spacebar.*

The Spotlight bar appears.

2 Type the information for which you want to search.

● As you type, Spotlight searches MacBook to locate information that relates to your search.

3 Continue typing to make your search more specific.

4 Point to a found item to see more information about it.

5 To open one of the found items, click it.

continued

There are several ways to search for information on MacBook. You can start using the Search tool in Finder windows. Then, try Spotlight on the desktop, which you can fine-tune to suit your search preferences.

● The source of that information appears.

⑥ To return to the search results, press ⌘+Spacebar.

The Spotlight results window appears and you can view other items in the results or you can change the search criterion.

Note: *To clear a Spotlight search, click the **Clear** button, which is the X located at the right end of the Spotlight bar.*

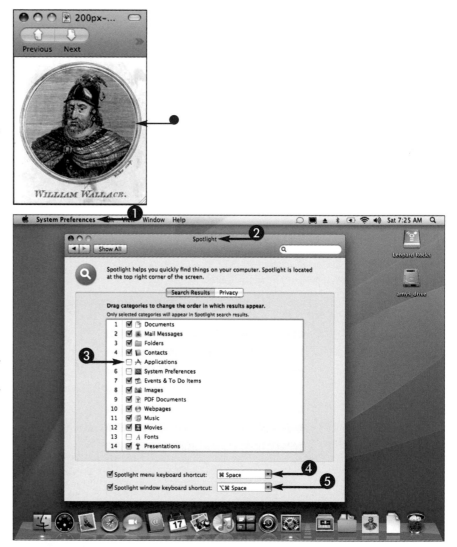

CONFIGURE SPOTLIGHT

① Open the **System Preferences** application.

② Click the **Spotlight** icon.

The Spotlight pane appears.

③ Uncheck the check box for any category of items that you do not want to be included in Spotlight searches.

④ To change the keyboard combination that activates Spotlight, use the first pop-up menu.

⑤ To change the keyboard combination for the Show All command (see the Tip at the end of this section), use the last pop-up menu.

6 Click the **Privacy** tab.

7 Add folders or volumes to the list using the Add button (+).

8 Exclude folders or volumes from Spotlight searches by dragging them from the desktop into the Spotlight window.

9 Quit the System Preferences application.

The next time you search with Spotlight, your preferences are used in the search.

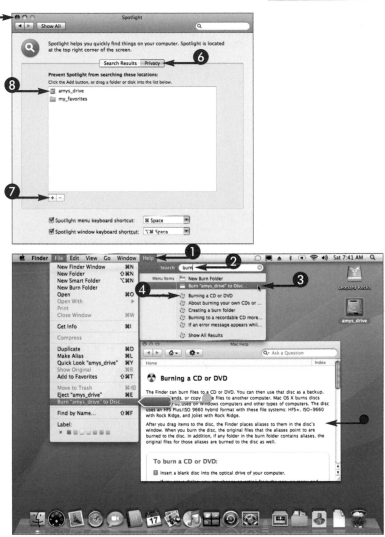

FIND HELP

1 Click **Help** in the Finder toolbar menu.

The Help Search tool appears.

2 Type the information related to the help you need.

As you type, the Mac's Help system is searched.

3 To see where a menu item is, point to it.

● The menu opens and a large pointer points to the menu item.

4 To read a help topic, click it.

● The Help window opens and you see the help topic you selected.

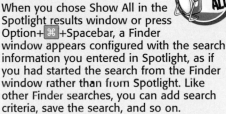

What does the Show All choice in the Spotlight results window do?

When you chose Show All in the Spotlight results window or press Option+⌘+Spacebar, a Finder window appears configured with the search information you entered in Spotlight, as if you had started the search from the Finder window rather than from Spotlight. Like other Finder searches, you can add search criteria, save the search, and so on.

Do all applications use the Mac's help system?

All applications are supposed to provide a Help menu that you can use to get help. Apple applications use the help system provided by Mac OS X so that you can use the same tools to find help in any of these applications. Some non-Apple applications also use the Mac OS X help system, but others (such as Microsoft Office) implement their own help systems that work a bit differently. No matter what application you happen to be using, start a search for help from its Help menu.

Get Information about Files and Folders

As mentioned earlier, you can choose the specific information you see in some of the views, such as the List view. However, what you see in Finder windows is just part of the information about these items.

To see more detail about any file or folder, you can use the Finder's Get Info command. This command opens the Info window that provides lots of detailed information about what you have selected.

① In a Finder window, select a file or folder you want to get information about.

② Choose **Get Info** from the File menu in the Finder toolbar, or press ⌘+I.

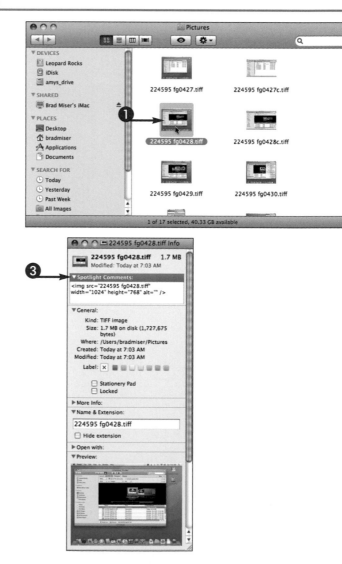

The Info window appears.

③ Click a section's expansion triangle to see the information it contains.

④ Scroll down the window to see all of the sections available for the selected item.

⑤ Expand the **Open with** section.

⑥ On the **Open with** pop-up menu, choose the application in which you want to the document to open.

⑦ If you want all documents of the same type to open in that application, click **Change All**.

The next time you open the document, the application you selected is used.

⑧ When you are done viewing or changing information, close the Info window.

Note: You can leave the Info window open as long as you want, and you can have many Info windows open at the same time, which makes comparing items easy.

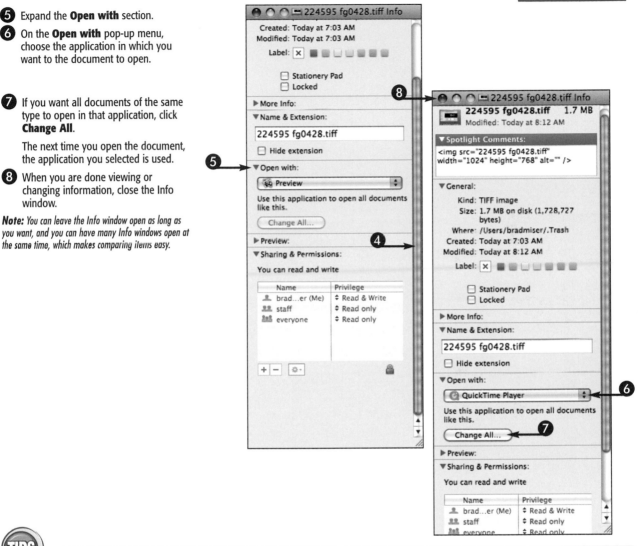

What are Spotlight Comments?

The Spotlight Comments section appears at the top of the Info window. You can enter text in this field to associate that text with an item. When you search using Spotlight, the information you enter in the Spotlight Comments section is included in the search. For example, you could type a keyword into the Spotlight Comments field for all the files relating to the same project. When you perform a Spotlight search for that keyword, all the files and folders are found based on the keyword you entered.

How about the Sharing & Permissions section?
This section shows the security settings for the selected item. You see each person or group who has access to the item along with the permissions they have. You can use the controls in this section to change the access people or groups have to the item. First, click the Lock icon and enter an administrator username and password. Second, use the pop-up menus to change privileges and the Add or Remove buttons to add people or groups to the list.

All MacBooks include a drive you can use to burn your own CDs; most MacBooks also enable you to burn DVDs. You may have many reasons to burn files and folders from the Finder to CDs or DVDs, such as to transfer them to someone else or to safeguard copies of important folders and files for future use.

Burn a CD or DVD

CREATE AND ORGANIZE A BURN FOLDER

1 Open a Finder window showing the location in which you want to create a burn folder.

2 From the File menu, choose **New Burn Folder**.

● A new burn folder is created; its name, Burn Folder, is highlighted and ready for you to edit.

3 Type the name of the burn folder and press Return.

The new name is saved.

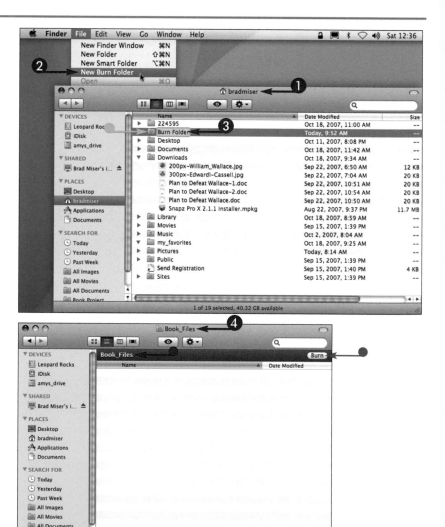

4 Open the burn folder in the Finder window.

● At the top of the window, you see the folder's name.

● You also see the Burn button that indicates it is a burn folder.

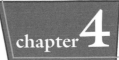

⑤ Open a new Finder window so that you have two windows on the desktop.

⑥ In the second window, go to the first folders or files you want to burn to a disc.

⑦ Drag the folders or files from the second window onto the burn folder's window.

Aliases are created in the burn folder for each file or folder that you move there.

⑧ Organize the files and folders in the burn folder as you want them to be organized on the disc.

Note: *In the Burn window, you can create new folders and place the dragged files and folders into them.*

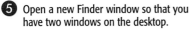

continued

There are several ways to burn folders and files onto disc. One of the most useful is by creating a burn folder. You can place and organize folders and files within a burn folder and then burn the folder onto a disc.

BURN A DISC

① Open the burn folder you want to place on a disc.

② Check the minimum disc size for the folder by looking at the status bar at the bottom of its window.

Note: *To determine if your MacBook can burn DVDs in addition to CDs, check its documentation. If it has a SuperDrive, it can burn single-layer and dual-layer DVDs.*

③ Click **Burn**.

● The insert disc prompt appears.

The prompt also tells you how much disc space you need to burn the disc.

④ Insert a blank CD or DVD.

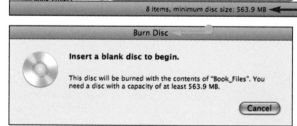

The burn dialog box appears.

5 Enter the name of the disc you are burning.

6 On the **Burn Speed** pop-up menu, choose the speed at which you want the disc to be burned.

Note: In most cases, leave the setting as Maximum Possible. If the burn process fails, try a slower burn speed.

7 Click **Burn**.

MacBook starts the burn process and you see the Burn progress window.

Note: You can use MacBook for other tasks while the disc is burning.

When the process is complete, the progress window disappears and the disc is mounted.

8 Open a Finder window.

9 Select the disc you burned.

● You see the contents of the disc, which looks exactly like the burn folder.

10 Eject the disc (⏏).

Note: You can make copies of the disc by repeating the burn process. When you are done, you can delete the burn folder.

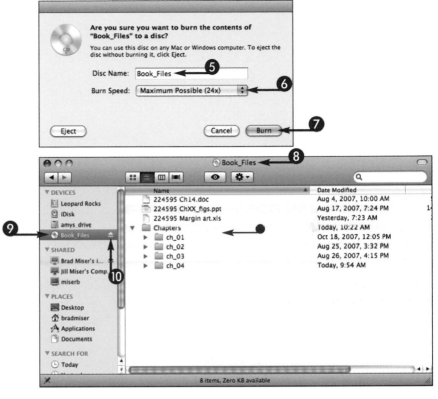

TIPS

What other applications can I use to burn CDs or DVDs?

You can use iTunes to create audio CDs or to back up your iTunes Music Library onto CD or DVD. Using iDVD, you can create DVDs that play in a standard DVD player just like those you might rent or buy. From iPhoto, you can burn photos to disc to archive them or make them easy to share. Each of these applications provides its own burn commands, typically located on the File menu or on the application's toolbar.

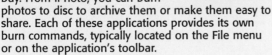

How can I create my own application installation discs?

You can use the Disk Utility application to burn disk images onto a CD or DVD; this is especially important when you download applications that you have purchased so that you can reinstall the application if you ever need to. Launch Disk Utility and select the disk image you downloaded. Choose the **Burn** command and follow the prompts to burn the disk image to a CD or DVD. Should you ever need to install the application again, you can do so from the disc you create.

CHAPTER 5

Work with Mac Applications

MacBook comes with many applications installed by default, including Safari for Web browsing, Mail for e-mail, iTunes for music and video, and iPhoto for your digital photos. You can also install many other applications as you use MacBook to provide even more functionality.

Whether you install them yourself or they came installed on MacBook, there are some general things you need to know about applications that apply no matter what applications you use.

Understand Applications

Although every application is different from the others, all applications share fundamental concepts that apply to each of them. Understanding these fundamentals will help you use a wide variety of applications on your MacBook.

Applications

The reason computers work so well is that they are very good at following repetitive instructions that adhere to very specific syntax and logic rules. An application is a collection of programming statements, more commonly called *code*, that are constructed according to a specific programming language. Applications separate us from the detailed code so that we can control what the application does by interacting with menus and graphical elements of the user interface, instead of having to re-create the lines of code each time we want to do something. Applications are created for many purposes, from running the MacBook (Mac OS X is a very complex application) to providing the weather at a glance through a simple Dashboard widget (a specific kind of application delivered through the Dashboard).

Documents

Most applications, but certainly not all of them, work with documents. In MacBook lingo, a document is much more than just a text file; documents can certainly contain text, but they can also be images, e-mails, and songs. Basically, a document is the content an application works with. So, for a text processor such as Microsoft Word, a document can include text and graphics. A graphics application, such as Photoshop, uses images as documents. The songs and video stored within iTunes can also be considered documents. If you open or save something with an application, that something can be called a document.

Windows

Chapter 2 talked about the various kinds of windows you see on MacBook. As that chapter mentioned, applications provide windows through which you view documents or controls and functions when an application doesn't work with documents (such as a game). An application's windows are whatever you see when you open and use that application. Most applications allow you to have many documents open at the same time, with each appearing in a separate window.

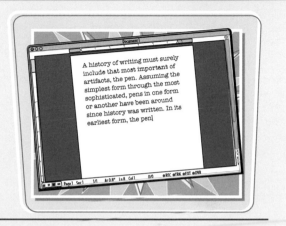

Standard Menus

Applications contain commands that you use to perform actions. For example, when you want to save changes you have made, you use the Save command. Commands are organized into logical collections on menus. When you open a menu, you can see and choose the commands it contains. Mac OS X applications are supposed to support a set of standard menus that have the same or similar commands; these include the application menu (which has the name of the application), File, Edit, Window, and Help. These menus also contain a set of standard commands; for example, the application menu always contains the Preferences command. Applications can and usually do have more menus than just the standard menus that are part of Mac OS X design specifications. Some applications, mostly games, do not include standard menus at all.

Application Preferences

Not everyone uses applications in the same way, and we all have our own preferences. Because of this, applications include preferences that enable you to configure various aspects of how the application looks and works. You can use preferences to enable or disable functions, change the appearance of the application's windows, and so on. In effect, these commands enable you to tailor the way they work to your preferences, thus the name for this type of command.

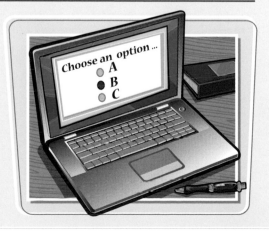

Install Applications

To be able to use applications on MacBook, you must install them. There are two ways you do this. Some applications include an installer program; to install the application, you open the installer and follow the onscreen instructions. Other applications use a drag-and-drop installation method that requires you to drag a folder or file onto MacBook's hard drive.

Install Applications

INSTALL APPLICATIONS WITH AN INSTALLER

① Download the application's installer from the Internet or insert the CD or DVD it came on.

In most cases, the installer starts automatically; if so, skip step **2**.

Note: *When you download an installer, by default it is stored in the Downloads folder on the Dock. Go there to access the installer.*

② Double-click the application installer's icon to launch it.

The installer starts running.

③ Read the information on the first screen of the installer.

④ Continue reading the information presented on each screen of the installer and providing the required input, such as clicking **Continue**, to complete the installation process.

Eventually, you move to the Install screen.

⑤ Click **Install**.

You are prompted to authenticate yourself as an administrator.

⑥ Enter your user name.

⑦ Enter your password.

⑧ Click **OK**.

The installer runs and presents progress information in its window. When the process is done, you see the Complete screen.

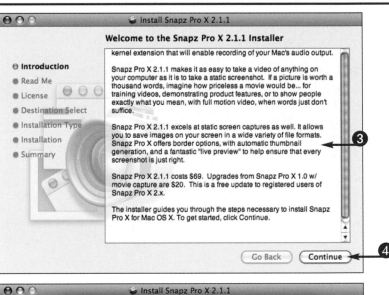

INSTALL APPLICATIONS WITH DRAG AND DROP

1. Download the application from the Internet or insert the CD or DVD it came on.

   In most cases, the files are provided as a disk image, which usually mounts on MacBook automatically. If so, skip step **2**.

2. Double-click the disk image file; its file name ends in .dmg.

   The disk image is mounted on MacBook.

3. View the files in the disk image; typically, they are organized into a folder and explain what you need to do.

4. From the File menu, choose **New Finder Window**.

   A new Finder window appears.

5. Click **Applications** in the Sidebar.

   The Applications folder is shown in the window.

6. Drag the application folder from the disk image window onto the Applications window and release the trackpad button.

   The application is copied into the Applications folder and is ready for you to use.

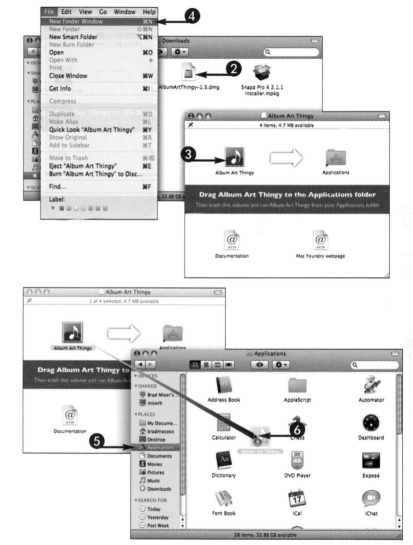

What is the Customize button in the Install window for?

Most installer applications include a Customize button that enables you to customize the application's installation. If your MacBook is very low on disk space, you might want to take a look at the customization options to see if you can skip features or resources you do not need.

Where should I install an application?

In most cases, the answer is in the Applications folder on MacBook's startup drive. You can install applications in other locations, but you need to make sure everyone who needs that application has the security to get to the location in which you install it, such as within your Home folder.

Launch and Control Applications

The first step in using an application is to open, or launch, it. There are many ways to do this, and as you use MacBook, you will no doubt develop your preferred method.

Once applications are running, there are a number of ways to control them.

Launch and Control Applications

OPEN APPLICATIONS FROM THE DOCK

① Click an application's icon on the Dock.

Note: The first time you open an application, you see a warning dialog box; this is intended to prevent you from opening applications unintentionally that might harm your computer, such as viruses.

● The icon bounces to show you it is opening.

When complete, the application's windows appear and it is ready for you to use.

Note: You can also install applications on the Sidebar by dragging their icons there.

OPEN APPLICATIONS FROM THE DESKTOP

① Click the desktop so you see the Finder menu bar.

② From the Go menu, choose **Applications**.

The Applications folder appears in a Finder window.

③ Scroll in the window until you see the application you want to open.

④ Double-click the application's icon or press ⌘+O.

The application opens and is ready for you to use.

Note: If an application is not installed on the Dock, its icon appears on the right or bottom side of the Dock when it is running. When you quit the application, its icon disappears from the Dock.

OPEN APPLICATIONS FROM DOCUMENTS

1 Find a document in a Finder window.

2 Double-click the document's icon.

The application with which the document is associated opens and you see the contents of the document you opened.

Note: *Chapter 6 explains how to have applications open automatically when you log in to your user account.*

SWITCH APPLICATIONS

1 Open applications as you need to use them; you do not need to close one application to open another one.

2 Press ⌘+Tab.

The Application Switcher appears. Here you see an icon for each application that is currently running.

● The application with which you are currently working is highlighted in the white box.

3 Click the application you want to move into or press Tab or Shift+Tab (while holding the key down) until the application you want to use is highlighted and release the trackpad button.

The application you selected becomes active and you can use it.

TIPS

An application does not appear to be doing anything and I see a spinning wheel on the screen.
Occasionally, an application hangs and stops working even though its windows remain on the screen. Let some time pass to see if the application starts working again. If it does not, open the Apple menu and choose **Force Quit**. The Force Quit window appears. Select the application that is having problems and click **Force Quit**. Click **Force Quit** again in the resulting dialog box. The application is forced to quit. You lose any unsaved changes in the application's open documents, so only do this as a last resort. Restart MacBook after normally quitting all other applications.

I have opened a lot of applications and do not want to quit all of them one by one. Is there a faster way?
Log out of your user account by pressing Shift+⌘+Q and clicking the **Log Out** button. When you log out, all open applications are closed. The next time you log in, you start with a "clean slate" of applications.

Remove Applications

If you no longer need an application, you can remove it from MacBook. You do not have to do this if MacBook's hard drive has lots of room, because the disk space an application requires is the only downside of leaving it on your MacBook. So, if your disk has lots of room, you can just leave the application installed in case you ever need it again. Or, you can get rid of it if you are sure will not use it again.

Like installing applications, there are two ways to remove an application from MacBook.

Remove Applications

REMOVE APPLICATIONS WITH AN UNINSTALLER APPLICATION

1 If the application included an uninstaller application, locate it; you can usually find these in the application's folder.

2 Double-click the uninstaller.

The application launches.

3 Read the information in the window and click **Continue**.

4 Continue following the onscreen instructions.

● When the uninstall is complete, you see the completion screen, which is sometimes confusing because it says the installation is complete.

5 Click **Close** or **Quit**.

REMOVE APPLICATIONS WITH DRAG AND DROP

 Click the desktop so you see the Finder menu bar.

2 From the Go menu, choose **Applications**.

The Applications folder appears in a Finder window.

3 Scroll in the window until you see the application you want to remove.

4 Drag the icon to the Trash. When the Trash icon is highlighted, release the trackpad button.

The application is moved into the Trash. The next time you empty the Trash, it is deleted from MacBook.

 TIPS

I want to keep an application I do not use on my MacBook, but documents I open still open in that application. What can I do?

You can stop MacBook from opening an application by changing the association between documents and that application. Change the association for the file that opens in the unwanted application, and then click the **Change All** button to change all documents associated with it. You might have to do this several times if the application is associated with several different types of documents.

If I remove an application and then decide I need it again, what do I do?

The answer depends on how you obtained the application. If you received it on CD or DVD, you can reinstall it from the original discs (you must also reapply any patches). If you downloaded the application from the Internet, you must have the original files you downloaded to reinstall it; sometimes these continue to be available at the Web site, but sometimes they are not. You should always keep a backup of any software you download from the Internet in case you ever need to reinstall it.

Save
Documents

As you make changes to a document, you need to save those changes to keep them. This sounds simple, and it is, but many people do not regularly save their work. If an application quits before you save changes, you lose all the work you have done. So, get in the habit of saving documents frequently and often.

SAVE EXISTING DOCUMENTS

① Open the document and work with it using its associated application.

② From the File menu, choose **Save** or press ⌘+S.

Note: The first time you save a document, you use the Save As command instead; see the next section for details.

The document is saved in its current state, and the new version replaces the previous version you saved.

File	Edit	View	Insert	Format	Font	Tools	Table	Window
Project Gallery...								⇧⌘P
New Blank Document						224595 Ch05.doc		⌘N
Open...								⌘O
Close								⌘W
Save	②							⌘S
Save As...								
Save as Web Page...								
Versions...								

SAVE NEW DOCUMENTS

① Open the application with which you want to create a new document.

② From the File menu choose **New Document**, where *Document* is the kind of document the application creates, such as Document, Presentation, Image, and so on.

An empty document appears in a new window.

③ From the File menu choose **Save As** or press Shift+⌘+S.

Note: The first time you save a document, you can use the Save or Save As command because they do the same thing. When you want to rename a document or save a new version, you can use the Save As command.

File	Edit	View	Insert	Format	Tools	Slide
Project Gallery...						⇧⌘P
New Presentation				Presentation1		⌘N
Open...						⌘O
Close						⌘W
Save						⌘S
Save As...						⇧⌘S
Save as Web Page...						

The Save As dialog box appears.

④ Click the **Show Details** button.

Save As: Presentation2.ppt ◀——④

Where: 🗀 macbook

Format: PowerPoint Presentation

Description

The default format for PowerPoint 2004. This format is shared by PowerPoint 97 through PowerI 2003 for Windows, and PowerPoint 98 through PowerPoint 2004 for Mac.

Learn more about file formats

☑ Append file extension

(Options...) (Compatibility Report...) ⚠ Compatibility check recommended

(Cancel) (Save)

The dialog expands so you see more details.

⑤ In the Save As box, enter a name for the file; you should leave the file name extension, which is everything after the period, as it is.

⑥ Choose the location in which you want to save the file; this works just like a Finder window in Columns view and the Open dialog box.

⑦ Use the other controls, such as the Format pop-up menu, to change how the file is created.

⑧ Click **Save**.

The document's file is created in the location you set and you are ready to get to work.

Save As: my_presentation.ppt ◀——⑤

◀ ▶ | 🔳 ☰ ▥ | 🗀 ch_05 | 🔍 search

SHARED
🖥 Brad Mi...

PLACES
🗀 My...
🗀 macbook
🏠 bradma...
🖥 Desktop

🗀 ch_01
🗀 ch_02
🗀 ch_03
🗀 ch_05 ⑥
🗀 ch_14
chap_uploaded

224595 Ch05.doc
224595 fg05_figs.ppt
224595 fg07c.tiff
224595 fg08c.tiff
224595 fg0501.tiff
224595 fg0501c.tiff
224595 fg0502.tiff

Format: PowerPoint Presentation ◀——⑦

Description

The default format for PowerPoint 2004. This format is shared by PowerPoint 97 through PowerI 2003 for Windows, and PowerPoint 98 through PowerPoint 2004 for Mac.

Learn more about file formats

☑ Append file extension

⑦ ——▶ (Options...) (Compatibility Report...) ⚠ Compatibility check recommended

(New Folder) (Cancel) (Save) ◀——⑧

 TIPS

Can my documents be saved automatically?

Many applications, such as Microsoft Word, have preference settings that can be configured to save your documents periodically, for example, every 5 minutes. Open the application's Preferences dialog box and look for the save preferences. Set them to a frequent amount of time.

My hard drive crashed. Can I recover my saved document?

It depends on what kind of failure your disk had. In some cases, the documents and other data can be restored. In other cases, you are out of luck. You should always keep important documents backed up so you can recover them if needed.

Personalize Your MacBook

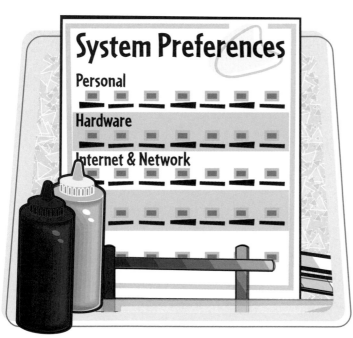

There are many ways to make MacBook your own using the built-in capabilities that Mac OS X provides.
Starting with Finder, you can change many aspects of how MacBook looks and works to tailor it to your personal preferences. This makes it work better for you because MacBook adapts to the way you work, instead of you having to adapt to the way it works.

Set Finder Preferences

Finder is the application that controls MacBook's desktop, how files and folders are managed, and many other aspects of the way MacBook works. Like all the other applications you use, Finder also has a set of preferences you can configure to change the way it looks and works.

Like other applications, you change Finder preferences using its Preferences command. The resulting dialog box has several tabs that you use to configure specific aspects of how Finder works.

Set Finder Preferences

① From the Finder menu, choose **Preferences**.

The Finder Preferences window appears.

Note: A faster way to open the preferences for any application, including the Finder, is to press ⌘ *+,.*

② Click the **General** tab.

③ Check the **Hard disks**, **CDs, DVDs, and iPods**, or **Connected servers** check boxes if you want any of these to show up as an icon on the desktop (they are always available within Finder windows).

④ Use the pop-up menu to choose the default location for new Finder windows.

⑤ If you always want folders to open in a new window rather than inside the current one, check the **Always open folders in a new window** check box.

⑥ If you want folders to spring open when you drag icons onto them, check the **Spring-loaded folders and windows** check box.

⑦ Click the **Labels** tab.

Note: You can associate files and folders with labels to help you identify and organize them more easily on the desktop.

⑧ Enter a name for each label in the box next to its color.

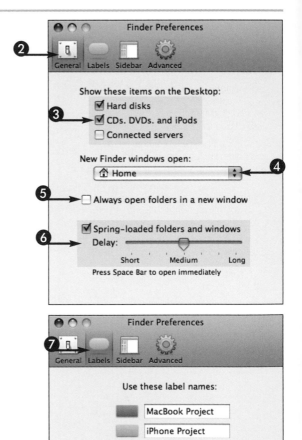

9 Click the **Sidebar** tab.

10 Check the box next to each item you want to appear in the Sidebar or uncheck the box next to each item you do not want to appear in the Sidebar.

Note: When you uncheck an item's check box, it is still available in Finder windows, you just do not see its icon on the Sidebar.

11 Click the **Advanced** tab.

12 If you always want filename extensions to be shown, check the **Show all file extensions** check box.

13 To be warned when you change a file-name extension, check the **Show warning before changing an extension** check box.

14 If you want to have to confirm emptying the Trash, check the **Show warning before emptying the Trash** check box.

15 If you want the Trash to be emptied securely, making it harder to recover, check the **Empty Trash securely** check box.

16 Click .

The Finder Preferences window closes.

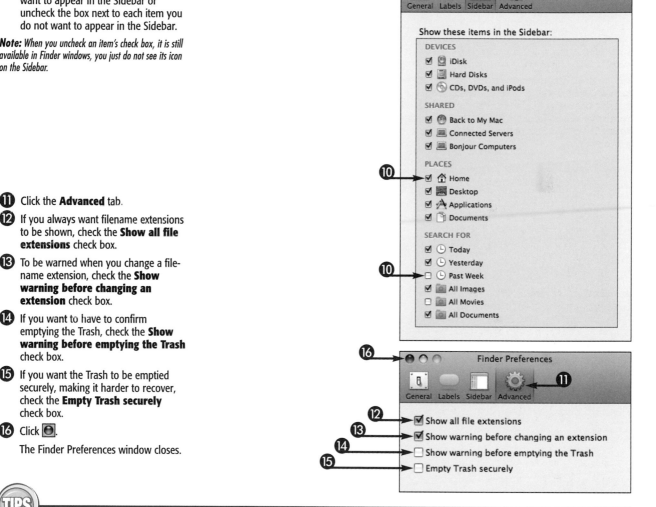

Which folders can I use as my start folder for new Finder windows?

The initial location is your Home folder, but you can choose any folder you want. On the New Finder windows open pop-up menu, choose **Other**. In the resulting dialog box, select the folder you want to be the default, and then click **Choose**. Each time you open a new Finder window, you move to that folder automatically.

How do I associate labels with folders and files?

Open a Finder window showing the folder or file you want to label. Press ⌘+I. The Info window opens. Expand the General section if needed. Click the label color that you want to apply. The selected file or folder is marked with that color. You can then search for files and folders by their labels.

Explore the System Preferences Application

The System Preferences application is used to configure many different aspects of how MacBook looks and works. In fact, most of the personalization you do is done with this application.

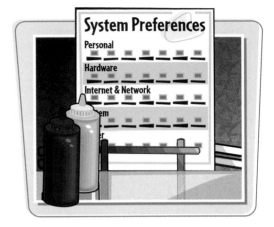

The System Preferences application is a single application that is organized in many different panes; each pane uses to configure a specific aspect of MacBook. You open the pane you want to use to configure a specific area. For example, you use the Dock pane to configure the Dock and the Network pane to connect MacBook to a network.

Explore the System Preferences Application

OPEN AND USE SYSTEM PREFERENCES

① From the Apple menu, choose **System Preferences**.

The System Preferences application opens and you see all of the panes it offers.

② Click an icon.

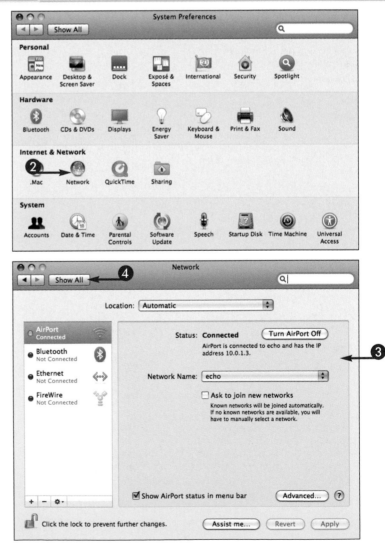

The pane associated with that icon appears.

③ Use the controls on the pane to make changes to the way MacBook works.

④ When you are done with the pane, click **Show All**.

The open pane closes and you see all the icons again.

SHOW PANES ALPHABETICALLY

① From the View menu, choose **Organize Alphabetically**.

● The panes are organized alphabetically instead of by category.

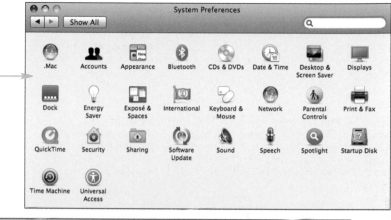

SEARCH FOR A PANE

① To search for a pane, type text in the Search box.

● As you type, panes that meet your search are highlighted.

② Click the icon you want to use.

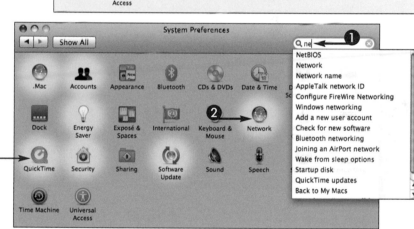

TIPS

I cannot make some changes in the System Preferences application, but I can make others. Why?
In order to make changes to various, but not all, settings using the System Preferences application, you must be logged in under an administrator user account or verify that you are an administrator. The easiest way to tell is to look at the Lock icon located in the lower left corner of a pane. If you do not see the Lock icon, any user can change the pane. If the Lock is "locked," click it to verify you are an administrator by entering you user name and password. If the Lock is "unlocked," you are verified as an administrator and can make changes.

Why do I see a section called Other in my System Preferences application?
Some software you install, especially when it is associated with a hardware device, includes a pane installed on the System Preferences application that you use to configure that software or hardware. All of these additions to the default panes are organized in the Other category.

Change the Desktop's Appearance

Using the Appearance pane, you can configure the color of buttons, menus, and windows along with the color used when something is highlighted to show that it is selected. You can also configure how scrolling in Finder windows works.

While not directly related to appearance, you also use the Appearance pane to determine how many items are stored on Recent menus. You can also control how font smoothing works.

CHOOSE FINDER COLORS

① Open the System Preferences application and choose the **Appearance** pane.

② On the Appearance menu, choose **Blue** to see the default button, menu, and window colors.

③ On the Highlight Color pop-up menu, choose the color you want to be used to show when a file or folder is selected on the desktop.

④ From the Highlight Color pop-up menu, choose **Other**.

The Color Picker appears.

⑤ Click the type of color picker you want to use, such as the Crayon.

The controls for the picker you selected fill the window.

⑥ Use the controls to configure the color you want to use.

⑦ Click 🔵.

The color you configured is shown on the Highlight Color menu and is used to highlight items on the desktop.

CONFIGURE SCROLL TOOLS

1 Open the System Preferences application and choose the **Appearance** pane.

2 Click the **At top and bottom** radio button if you want scroll arrows to be at the corners of windows; click **Together** if you want them placed together in the lower right corner of windows.

3 Click **Jump to the next page** if you want to move to the next or previous page when you click above or below the scroll bar. Click **Jump to here** if you want to move to a location on the window relative to where you click.

4 If you want scrolling to be smoother when you use a mouse, check the **Use smooth scrolling** check box.

5 If you do not want to be able to minimize a window by double-clicking its title bar, uncheck the **Minimize when double-clicking a window title bar** check box.

SET RECENT ITEMS AND FONT SMOOTHING

1 Open the System Preferences application and choose the **Appearance** pane.

2 On the **Number of Recent Items** pop-up menus, choose the number of items you want remembered on Recent menus.

Note: *Most applications also have a recents list; the System Preferences application setting impacts only Mac OS X.*

3 To determine when font smoothing is applied, use the **Font smoothing style** pop-up menu.

4 To determine the point size at which font smoothing is turned off, use the bottom pop-up menu.

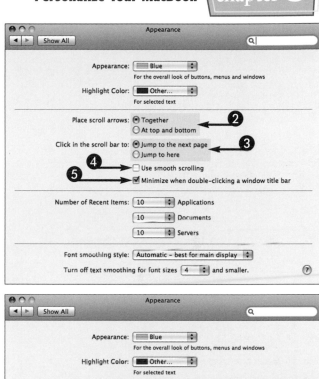

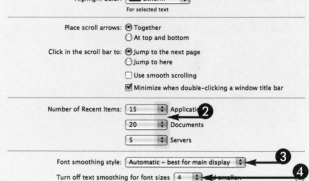

 TIP

Which Color Picker mode is the best?
Each mode offers different ways to choose colors. The easiest to use is the Crayon mode because you can simply choose colors by clicking a crayon. The other modes offer more control and specificity. For example, you can use the Color Wheel mode to select any color in the spectrum by dragging the intensity bar up or down and then clicking in the wheel to choose a specific color. The other modes offer different tools. To add a custom color to a mode's palette, drag it from the sample box at the top of the window to the palette at the bottom; you can choose the color again by clicking it on the palette.

Set a Desktop Picture

As you use MacBook, you look at the desktop quite often. So why not look at something you want to see? That is where setting the desktop picture comes in; the desktop picture fills the background on the desktop and you see it behind any windows that are open.

While it is called a desktop picture, you are not limited to pictures. You can use just about any kind of graphic file as a desktop picture.

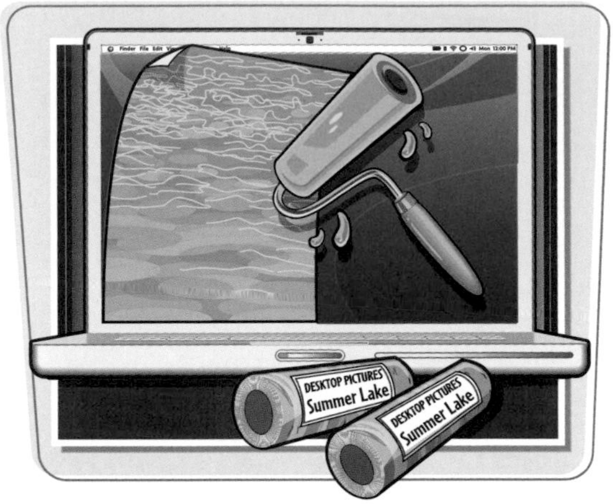

Set a Desktop Picture

SET A DEFAULT IMAGE AS THE DESKTOP PICTURE

1. Open the System Preferences application and choose the **Desktop & Screen Saver** pane.
2. Click the **Desktop** tab.

   The Desktop picture tools appear.
3. Choose a source of images in the left pane of the window, such as Apple Images.

   - The images in that source appear in the right pane of the window.
4. Click the image that you want to apply to the desktop.

   That image fills the desktop.

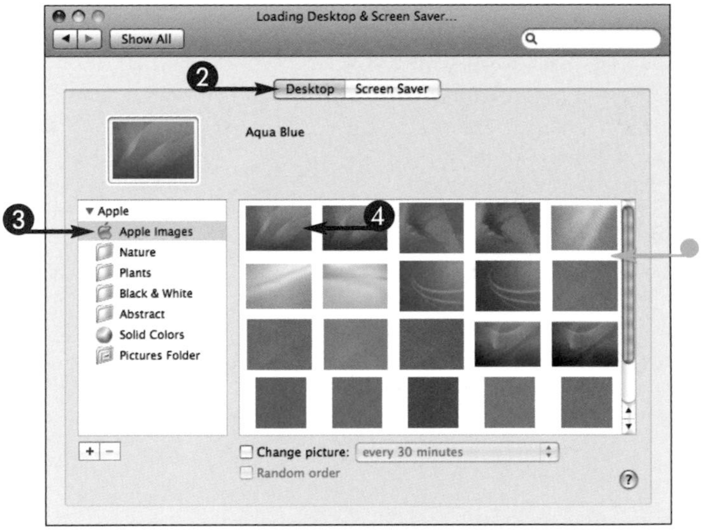

5. To have the image changed automatically, check the **Change picture** check box.
6. On the pop-up menu, choose how often you want the picture to change.
7. If you want images to be selected randomly instead of by the order in which they appear in the source, check the **Random order** check box.

   A new image from the selected source is applied to the desktop according to the timing selected.

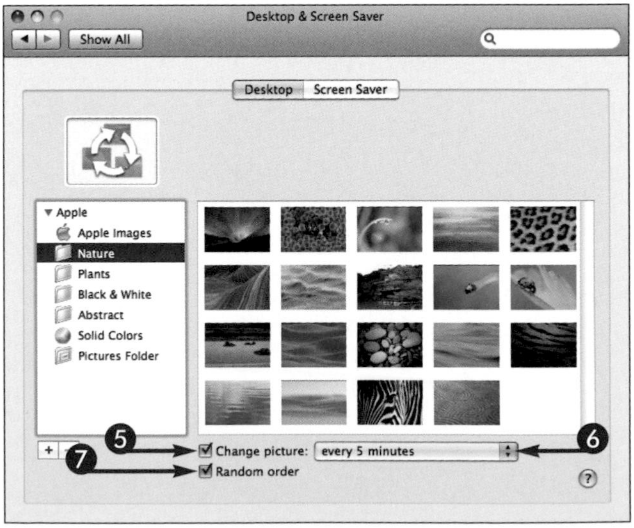

SET A PHOTO FROM YOUR IPHOTO LIBRARY AS THE DESKTOP PICTURE

1 Open the System Preferences application and choose the **Desktop & Screen Saver** pane.

2 Click the **Desktop** tab.

3 Scroll down the source list until you see the iPhoto Albums section.

4 Choose the photo album containing the photos you want to use on the desktop.

The images in the selected album appear in the right-hand part of the window.

5 Use the pop-up menu at the top of the window to choose how you want photos to be scaled to the screen; this example chooses the **Fit to Screen** option.

6 Click the **Color** button and use the Color Picker to choose the background color shown behind photos when they do not fill the desktop.

7 To have the image changed automatically, check the **Change picture** check box.

8 On the pop-up menu, choose how often you want the picture to change.

9 If you want images to be selected randomly instead of by the order in which they appear in the source, check the **Random order** check box.

A new image from the iPhoto album source is applied to the desktop according to the timing selected.

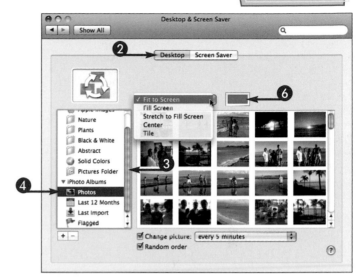

TIPS

What is the Picture Folder source?

By default, a number of applications store graphic files in the Pictures folder within your Home folder. If you choose this folder on the source list, you see all the images it contains; you can select images from this source just as you do from one of the other sources.

What if the location of the photos I want to use as the desktop picture does not appear on the source list?

You can choose any folder as a source of desktop pictures by clicking the Add (+) button located at the bottom of the source list. Use the resulting dialog box to move to and select the folder containing the images you want. After you click the Choose button, that folder appears as a source on the list.

Choose a Screen Saver

A screen saver does two things for you. One is that it prevents possible damage to your screen from having the same image on it for a long period of time. The other, and probably more important, purpose is to entertain you by displaying images that you choose on the screen.

When you are running on batteries, it is better to put MacBook to sleep when you are using it instead of showing the screen saver because that uses more power. The screen saver is more useful when you are running on the power adapter.

Choose a Screen Saver

CHOOSE AN APPLE SCREEN SAVER

1 Open the System Preferences application and choose the **Desktop & Screen Saver** pane.

2 Click the **Screen Saver** tab.

3 Choose the screen saver you want to use from the list in the Apple section in the left part of the window.

● You see the selected screen saver run in the right-hand part of the window.

4 Drag the slider to set the amount of idle time that passes before the screen saver activates.

5 If you want the time displayed on the screen saver, click the **Show with clock** check box.

Note: If you want a screen saver to be selected at random, check the **Use random screen saver** check box.

6 Click the **Options** button.

7 Use the tools on the Options sheet to configure the screen saver.

Note: Each screen saver has its own set of options, so what you see on the Option menu depends on the screen saver you select.

8 Click **OK**.

9 Click **Test**.

You see the screen saver in action.

10 Press a key or drag on the trackpad to move back to the System Preferences application.

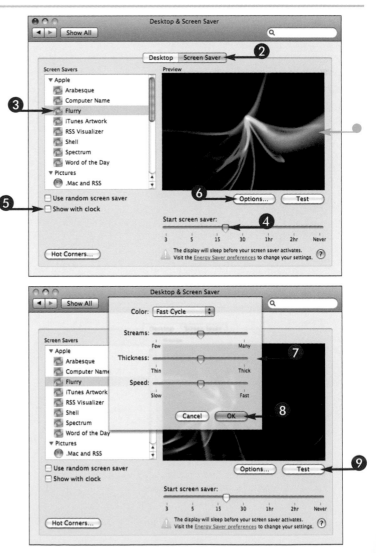

CREATE YOUR OWN SCREEN SAVER

1 Open the System Preferences application and choose the **Desktop & Screen Saver** pane.

2 Click the **Screen Saver** tab.

3 Scroll down until you see the options in the Pictures section.

4 Choose the source of images you want to use in the screen saver, such as an iPhoto photo album.

5 If you want the photos to appear as a collage, click the **Collage** button ().

6 If you want the images displayed in a mosaic, click the **Mosaic** button (▦).

● You see the selected images in the screen saver run in the right-hand part of the window.

7 Drag the slider to set the amount of idle time that passes before the screen saver activates.

8 If you want the time displayed on the screen saver, click the **Show with clock** check box

9 Click the **Options** button.

10 Use the tools on the Options sheet to configure the screen saver.

Note: *Each type of screen saver has its own set of options that appear in the Options menu.*

11 Click **OK**.

12 Click **Test**.

You see the screen saver in action.

13 Press a key or drag on the trackpad to move back to the System Preferences application.

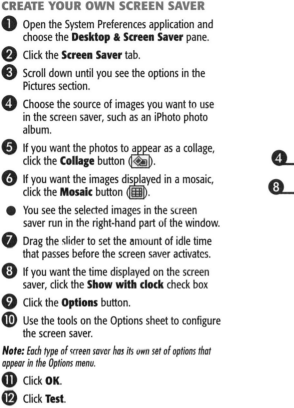

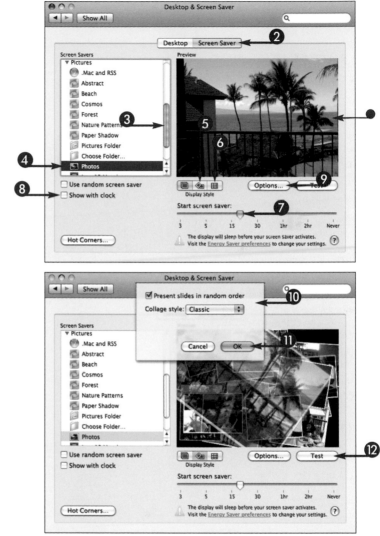

Why do I never see my screen saver?
The screen saver interacts with the settings on the Energy Saver pane, one of which is the amount of time that passes before the screen darkens to save energy (which also happens to be the best way to save the screen, too). If that time is less than the screen saver is set for, you do not see the screen saver before the screen goes dark; you see a warning saying so below the time slider on the Screen Saver pane. Reduce the time for the screen saver to be less than the time for the display to be darkened (see the next section).

Screen Darkens: 10 minutes
Screen Saver: 15 minutes

What are hot corners?
You can set a hot corner so that when you place the pointer in that corner, the screen saver activates. Click the **Hot Corners** button and then choose **Start Screen Saver** on the menu for the corner you want to be hot. When you move the pointer to that corner, the screen saver starts.

MacBook uses so little energy that it is unlikely that you can make any difference in your electric bill by changing how MacBook uses energy.

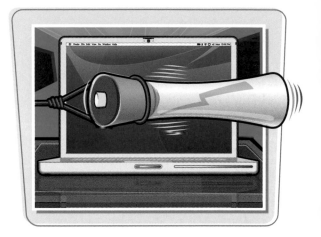

However, when you are running MacBook on battery power, saving energy is very important because the rate at which MacBook consumes battery power determines how long you can work.

Save Energy

① Open the System Preferences application and choose the **Energy Saver** pane.

② Click **Show Details**.

The pane expands so you see all of its controls.

③ On the **Settings for** pop-up menu, choose **Battery**.

④ You can choose one of the predefined configurations from the **Optimization** pop-up menu. For example, to maximize battery life, choose **Better Battery Life**.

The other controls on the pane are adjusted to match the settings you selected.

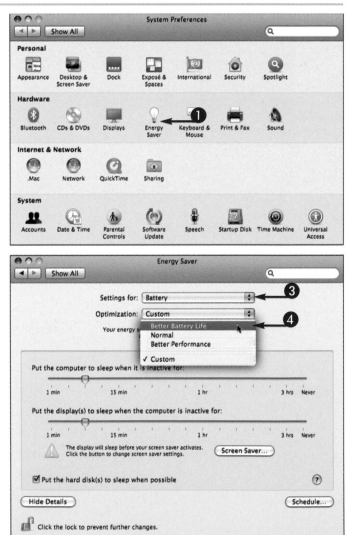

5 Drag the upper slider to set the idle time after which MacBook goes to sleep.

Note: As soon as you make a change, the setting on the Optimization pop-up menu becomes Custom to show that you are not using a default scheme anymore.

6 Drag the lower slider to set the amount of inactive time after which the display darkens.

7 To have the hard drives go to sleep when they are not being used, check the **Put the hard disk(s) to sleep when possible** check box.

8 Click the **Options** tab for more ways to manage MacBook's energy.

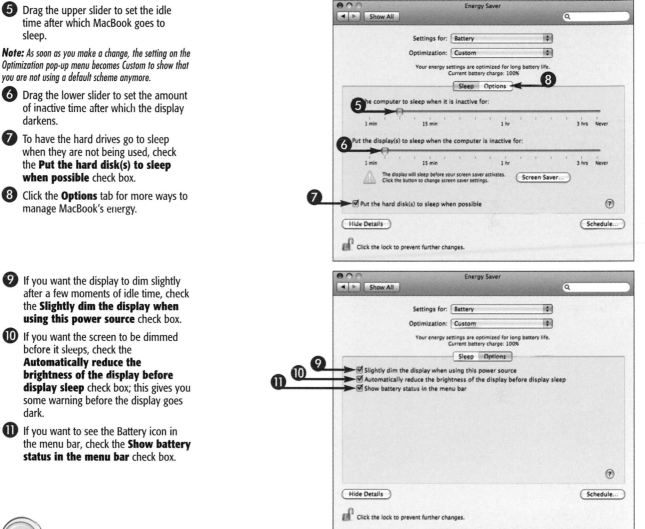

9 If you want the display to dim slightly after a few moments of idle time, check the **Slightly dim the display when using this power source** check box.

10 If you want the screen to be dimmed before it sleeps, check the **Automatically reduce the brightness of the display before display sleep** check box; this gives you some warning before the display goes dark.

11 If you want to see the Battery icon in the menu bar, check the **Show battery status in the menu bar** check box.

TIPS

What about running on the power adapter?

If you choose **Power Adapter** on the Settings for pop-up menu, you can configure energy settings when MacBook is running on the power adapter. These can be different than those you use while on battery power. MacBook knows when it is on battery and chooses the appropriate energy options automatically. When you choose Power Adapter, a different set of options appears on the Options tab.

What is the Schedule button for?

If you click the **Schedule** button on the Options tab, you can schedule MacBook to start or wake up at a specific time automatically. You can have it shut down or sleep at a specific time automatically, too.

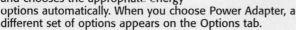

Configure MacBook's Screen

MacBook's screen is what you look at while you use it, so knowing how to configure the screen so it matches your viewing preferences is important. You can configure the display's resolution, number of colors, and brightness.

Although the physical size of MacBook's screen is fixed, the amount of information that can be displayed (its resolution) on it is not. That is because each pixel (short for picture element) that makes up the display's images can be larger or smaller. When pixels are larger, what is on the screen is shown on a larger, zoomed-in scale. When pixels are smaller, more content is displayed on the screen, but on a smaller, zoomed-out scale.

Configure MacBook's Screen

CONFIGURE THE MACBOOK'S SCREEN ON THE DISPLAYS PANE

1 Open the System Preferences application and click the Displays icon.

The Displays pane opens.

2 Click the **Display** tab.

3 Click a resolution.

● MacBook's screen updates to use that resolution. The current resolution is highlighted on the list.

4 Experiment with resolution settings until you choose the highest resolution that is still comfortable for you to see.

⑤ Drag the Brightness slider to the right to make the screen brighter or to the left to make it dimmer.

Note: *If you are running on battery power, keeping the screen dimmer lowers the amount of power you use, which extends the time you can work.*

⑥ To add a Displays menu to the menu bar, check the **Show displays in menu bar** check box.

CONFIGURE THE MACBOOK'S SCREEN ON THE DISPLAYS MENU

① Open the **Displays** menu (▭).

② To change the resolution, select the resolution you want to use on the list of recent resolutions.

③ To set the number of recent resolutions on the menu, choose *number* under **Number of Recent Items**, where *number* is the number of resolutions you want to see on the menu.

④ Choose **Displays Preferences** to open the Displays pane of the System Preferences application.

Color LCD

Display Color

Resolutions:
640 x 480
640 x 480 (stretched)
800 x 500
800 x 600
800 x 600 (stretched)
1024 x 640
1024 x 768
1024 x 768 (stretched)
1152 x 720
1280 x 800

Colors: Millions
Refresh Rate: n/a

Detect Displays

⑥ ☑ Show displays in menu bar

⑤ Brightness

---

① ▭ ✻ 📶 ◀) ▣ Tue 9:31 AM
Detect Displays

Color LCD
✓ 1024 x 768 (stretched), Millions
1152 x 720, Millions ②
1280 x 800, Millions

③ Number of Recent Items ▶
④ Displays Preferences...

TIPS

How else can I set screen brightness?

MacBook includes two keys you can use to change the screen's brightness. Press F1 to lower the brightness or F2 to increase it. These do the same thing as the Brightness slider on the Displays pane. Each time you press one of the keys, an indicator appears on the screen to show you the relative brightness level you have set.

What do the other controls on the Display tab do?

You can use the Colors pop-up menu to set the number of colors displayed on MacBook's screen; however, there is not really any reason to use less than Millions of colors (this control is used for older Macs that do not have enough graphics processing power to display millions of colors at all resolutions). The Detect Displays button  (and command on the Displays menu) is used when you connect MacBook to an external display or projector. The Color tab is used to configure a color profile for the display. You will not likely need to do this unless you are doing very precise color printing work, in which case, you configure a screen profile to match your printer output.

Configure the Keyboard and Trackpad

Obviously, using MacBook is a hands-on experience. Your primary inputs are through the keyboard and trackpad. You can configure both the keyboard and trackpad to suit your input preferences.

Like other areas, you use specific panes of the System Preferences application to change settings for either.

Configure the Keyboard and Trackpad

CONFIGURE THE KEYBOARD

1 Open the System Preferences application and click the **Keyboard & Mouse** icon.

2 Click the **Keyboard** tab.

The Keyboard pane opens.

3 Drag the **Key Repeat Rate** slider to the right to increase the number of times a letter or number repeats while you hold a key down, or to the left to lessen the rate.

4 Drag the **Delay Until Repeat** slider to the right to increase the amount of time you have to hold a key down for its letter or number to repeat, or to the left to shorten the time.

5 If you don't want to use the built-in functions for the function keys but instead want them to act as normal function keys, check the **Use all F1, F2, etc. keys as standard function keys** check box.

6 Click the **Modifier Keys** button.

7 Use the pop-up menus to choose the key presses associated with the various modifier keys.

Note: *If you get annoyed by accidentally hitting the Caps Lock key, you can disable it by choosing **No Action** on its pop-up menu.*

8 Click **OK**.

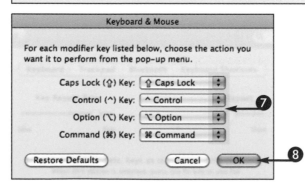

106

CONFIGURE THE TRACKPAD

1 Open the **System Preferences** application and click the Keyboard & Mouse icon.

2 Click the **Trackpad** tab.

The Trackpad pane opens.

3 Drag the **Tracking Speed** slider to cause the pointer to move more or less for the same amount of finger movement.

4 Drag the **Double-Click Speed** slider to increase or decrease the interval between clicks to register a double-click.

5 If you want to be able to scroll by dragging two fingers on the trackpad, check the **Use two fingers to scroll** check box.

6 Drag the **Scrolling Speed** slider to increase or decrease the speed at which the screen scrolls.

7 If you want to be able to scroll horizontally too, check the **Allow horizontal scrolling** check box.

8 To be able to zoom from the trackpad by dragging two fingers on it, check the **Zoom while holding** check box.

9 Click the **Options** button.

The **Options** drop-down menu appears.

10 To zoom continuously with the pointer, click **Continuously with pointer**.

11 To zoom only when the pointer reaches the edge of a screen, click **Only when the pointer reaches an edge**.

12 To keep the pointer at the center of the image on which you are zooming, click **So the pointer is at or near the center of the image**.

13 To smooth images while zooming, check the **Smooth images** check box.

14 Click **Done**.

15 To be able to tap the trackpad so it registers as a trackpad button, check the **Clicking** check box.

16 To be able to drag something using the trackpad, check the **Dragging** check box.

17 To lock a drag, check the **Drag Lock** check box.

18 To be able to "right-click" (same as Ctrl+click) from the trackpad, check the **Tap trackpad using two fingers for secondary click** check box.

19 To prevent accidental motions when you brush across the trackpad, check the **Ignore accidental trackpad input** check box.

20 If you use an external mouse and want to disable the trackpad when it is connected, check the **Ignore trackpad when mouse is present** check box.

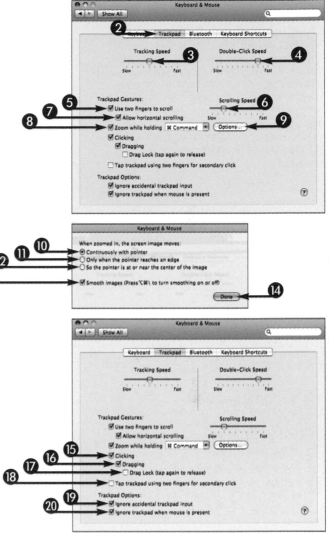
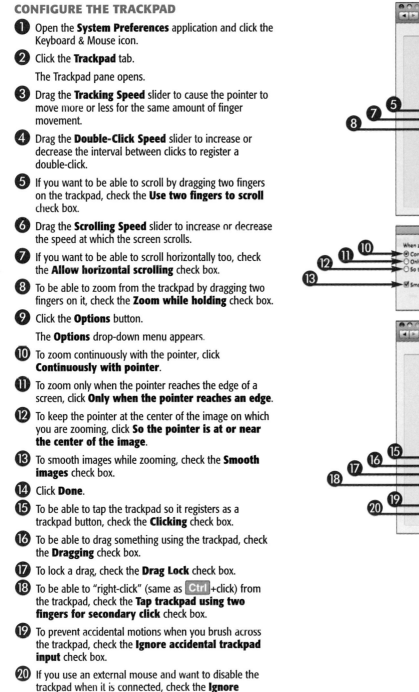

Control MacBook's Sound

From sound effects to music and movies, sound is an important part of the MacBook experience. Additionally, you will want to use sound input for audio and video chats, recording narration for movies, and so on.

The Sound pane of the System Preferences application is your primary stop for managing audio settings on MacBook.

Control MacBook's Sound

CONFIGURE SOUND EFFECTS

① Open the System Preferences application and click the Sound icon.

The Sound pane appears.

② Click the **Sound Effects** tab.

③ Click a sound on the alert sound list.

The sound plays.

④ Drag the **Alert volume** slider to make the alert sound louder or quieter.

⑤ To hear sound effects for system actions, such as when you empty the Trash, check the **Play user interface sound effects** check box.

⑥ If you want audio feedback when you change the volume level, check the **Play feedback when volume is changed** check box.

⑦ If you want to hear Front Row's sound effects, check the **Play Front Row sound effects** check box.

CONFIGURE SOUND OUT

① Open the System Preferences application and click the Sound icon.

The Sound pane appears.

② Click the **Output** tab.

③ Select the output device over which you want MacBook to play sound.

④ Drag the Balance slider to set the balance between the left and right speakers.

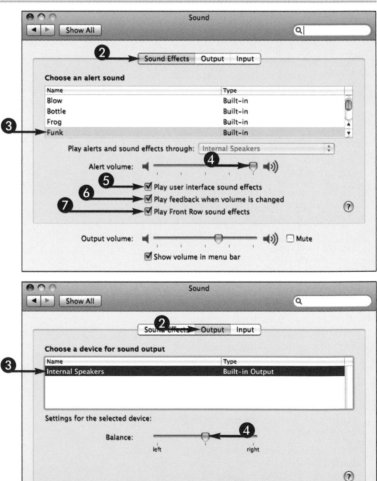

Control System Volume

① Open the System Preferences application and click the Sound icon.

The Sound pane appears.

② Drag the Output volume to the right to increase the volume or to the left to decrease it.

③ To mute all sounds, check the **Mute** check box.

④ To configure the Volume menu on the menu bar, check the **Show volume in menu bar** check box.

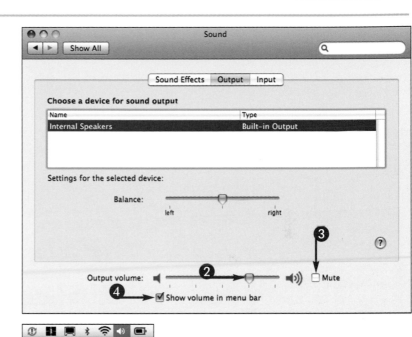

⑤ To set the volume using the menu, open it and drag the slider up to increase volume or down to decrease it.

CONFIGURE SOUND INPUT

① Open the System Preferences application and click the Sound icon.

The Sound pane appears.

② Click the **Input** tab.

③ Select the input device you want to use; for MacBook's internal microphone, choose **Internal microphone**.

④ Play the sound you want to input; if you are recording yourself or preparing for an audio chat, speak.

● As MacBook receives input, the relative volume of the input is shown on the **Input level gauge**.

⑤ Drag the **Input volume** slider to the left to reduce the level of input sound or to the right to increase.

⑥ Keep trying levels until the gauge looks about right.

⑦ If the area you are in is noisy, check the **Use ambient noise reduction** check box.

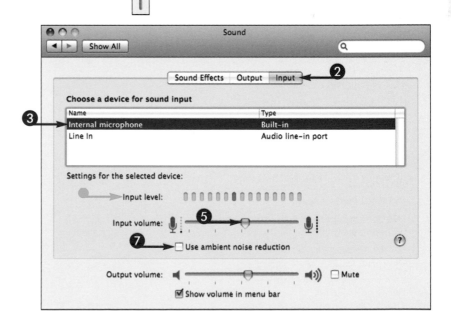

Create and Configure User Accounts

Mac OS X is a multiuser system; you can create user accounts for each person who uses MacBook. Each person then has a unique desktop, folders, files, and preferences, so MacBook is tailored specifically to each person who uses it.

CREATE A USER ACCOUNT

1 Open the System Preferences application and click the Accounts icon.

● The Accounts pane appears. In the accounts list on the left side of the window, you see the accounts that currently exist.

2 Click the **Add account** button (+).

The New Account sheet appears.

3 Choose the type of account on the **New Account** pop-up menu.

4 Enter a full user name for the account in the Name field. This can be just about anything you want, but it is usually the person's name.

Mac OS X creates a short user name based on what you enter.

5 Edit the short user name as needed.

Note: *This name is important because it appears in a number of places, such as the URL to that user's Web site on MacBook.*

6 Enter a password for the user (and skip to step **10**). If you click the key icon, Mac OS X helps you create one.

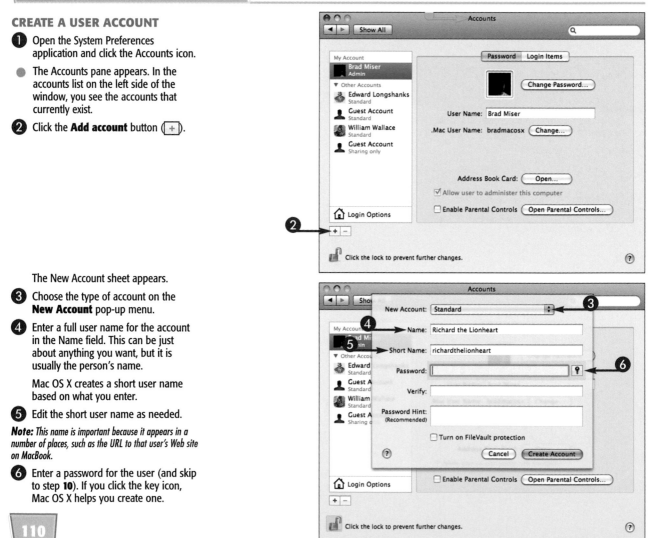

The Password Assistant appears.

⑦ Choose the type from the **Type** pop-up menu.

● Mac OS X generates a password for you. If there are tips related to the type you selected, you see them in the **Tips** box.

⑧ Drag the slider to the right to increase or decrease the length of the password.

● As you make changes, the **Quality** gauge shows you how secure the password is.

⑨ When you are happy with the password, click back in the **New Account** drop-down menu.

⑩ Re-enter the password in the **Verify** field

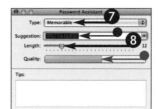

Note: *If you did not keep the Password Assistant open, you need to remember the password you configured to be able to type it in.*

⑪ If you want users to be able to access a hint when they cannot remember their password, type the hint in the **Password Hint** field.

⑫ If you want the user's data to be protected with FileVault, check the **Turn on FileVault protection** check box.

⑬ Click **Create Account**.

● The user account is created and appears on the list of accounts.

⑭ Click ⊝ to close the Password Assistant.

⑮ To associate an image with the user account, click the **Image well**.

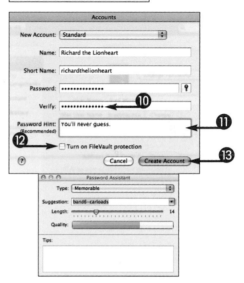

continued

Create and Configure
User Accounts *(continued)*

A Standard user account can access all the MacBook's resources, but cannot perform administrator tasks, such as installing applications; you should use this type for most users. An administrator account allows access to the administration tasks, many of which are discussed in this chapter.

Create and Configure User Accounts (continued)

16 Choose an icon from the pop-up menu and skip to step **21** or choose **Edit Picture**.

If you clicked **Edit Picture**, the Edit Picture sheet appears.

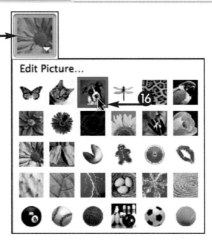

17 Drag an image file from the desktop onto the Image well.

● To use as a photo as a user account's icon, click the **Camera** icon (📷) and place the subject in front of MacBook's iSight camera.

After about three seconds the image is captured.

18 Drag the slider to the right to zoom in on the image of the user's icon or to the left to zoom out.

19 Drag the selection box until the part of the image you want to use is enclosed in the box.

20 Click **Set**.

The image is associated with the user account.

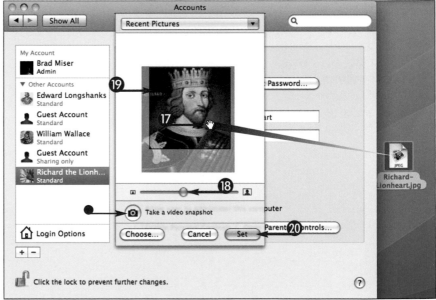

112

㉑ If the user has a .Mac account, enter the member name in the **.Mac User Name** field.

㉒ If you want the user to be able to administer MacBook, check the **Allow user to administer this computer** check box.

㉓ Provide the user name and password to the person who you want to be able to use MacBook.

CONFIGURE LOGIN ITEMS FOR A USER ACCOUNT

① Log in under the user's account (you can set login items for your own account in the same way).

② Open the System Preferences application and click the Accounts icon to open the Accounts pane.

③ Click the **Login Items** tab.

④ Drag the items that should open automatically from the desktop onto the pane; you can drag applications, documents, or folders onto the list.

⑤ Check the check box for any items you want to be hidden by default.

⑥ Log out of the user's account.

The next time the user logs in, the items you configured open automatically.

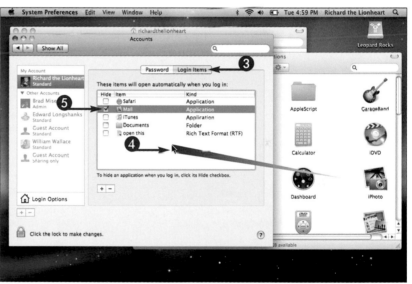

TIPS

Do I have to configure a password for a user account?

A user account does not have to have a password. If you leave the Password and Verify fields empty, you see a warning that not providing a password is not secure. If you are sure that is not a problem for you, clear the warning prompt and complete the user creation. The user is able to log in to MacBook without entering a password, which can mean that anyone who has access to the MacBook can use it.

******

What if a user forgets his or her password?

Open the Accounts pane, select the user's account on the list, and click Reset Password. Use the resulting sheet to configure a new password just as you do when you create an account. The user is able to log in with the new password.

password

Set Login Options

There are a number of ways you can configure the login process for MacBook. On the Login window, you can present a list of users so that to log in, a user clicks his or her user name and enters a password. Or, you can present an empty user name and password field and the user has to complete both to log in. There are also a number of other ways to configure the Login window by showing or hiding specific buttons. You can also disable or enable Automatic Login.

Fast user switching is another option, which allows multiple people to be logged into MacBook at the same time. Each user can quickly move back into his or her account because it is left open instead of each user logging out before another logs in.

Set Login Options

CONFIGURE AUTOMATIC LOGIN

① Open the System Preferences application and click the Accounts icon.

② Click **Login Options**.

The Login Options pane appears.

③ On the **Automatic login** pop-up menu, choose the name of the user you want to be automatically logged in.

④ Enter the user's password.

⑤ Click **OK**.

Each time MacBook starts or restarts, the user you selected is logged in automatically.

CONFIGURE THE LOGIN WINDOW

① Open the System Preferences application and click the Accounts icon.

② Click **Login Options**.

③ To show a list of users on the Login window, click **List of users**.

④ If you want to be able to restart MacBook, put it to sleep, or shut it down from the Login window, check the **Show the Restart, Sleep, and Shut Down buttons** check box.

⑤ If you want to be able to choose the language layout from the Login window, check the **Show Input menu in login window** check box.

⑥ To show a hint when users forget their password, check the **Show password hints** check box.

⑦ To have MacBook read the text in the Login window, check the **User VoiceOver at login window** check box.

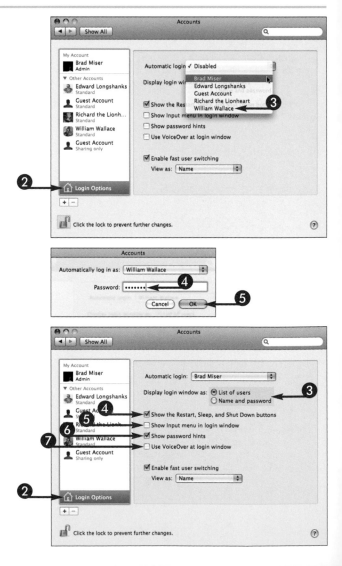

CONFIGURE AND USE FAST USER SWITCHING

1 Open the System Preferences application and click the Accounts icon.

2 Click **Login Options**.

3 Check the **Enable fast user switching** check box.

4 On the **View as** pop-up menu, choose **Name** to see the current user's user name at the top of the **Fast User** Switching menu.

The Fast User Switching menu ( ) appears on the menu bar.

5 Open the **Fast User Switching** menu ( ).

All the user accounts on MacBook are shown. The users that are currently logged in are marked with a check mark.

6 Choose the user to switch to.

7 Enter the user's password.

8 Click **Log In**.

The user is logged in and his or her desktop appears. The previous user remains logged in; select that user's account on the menu to move back to it.

What happens to running applications when another user logs in using fast user switching?

Because a user does not log out when another one logs in using fast user switching, the applications and processes running under a user account continue to run in the background even while another user is using MacBook

How I can leave myself logged in so my applications continue to work, but no one else can see or use what I am doing?

On the Fast User Switching menu, choose **Login Window**. The Login window appears, but you remain logged in. To start using MacBook again, choose your user account, enter your password, and click **Login**. You move back to where you left off.

Set and Configure MacBook's Clock

MacBook can help you by keeping track of the time and date for you. Obviously, you can use MacBook to see what time it is, but time and date are also important because MacBook stamps all the files and folders you use with the time and date they were created and when they were changed. Likewise, e-mails are also time and date stamped. The time and date that gets applied to these items are those that are configured on MacBook.

There are two basic ways to set MacBook's time and date: automatically using a timeserver, or manually. If you have an Internet connection, having MacBook set its clock automatically is a good idea.

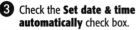
Set and Configure MacBook's Clock

CONFIGURE MACBOOK TO SET ITS CLOCK AUTOMATICALLY

1 Open the System Preferences application and click the Date & Time icon.

2 Click the **Date & Time** tab.

3 Check the **Set date & time automatically** check box.

4 On the pop-up menu, choose the timer server you want to use; if you live in the U.S., choose **Apple Americas/U.S.**

5 Click the **Time Zone** tab.

6 Click the time zone you want to set.

● The time zone you select is indicated by the light band on the map and next to the "Time Zone" text.

7 Open the **Closest City** pop-up menu and choose the city closest to your location.

If MacBook is connected to the Internet, it sets the time and date automatically.

CONFIGURE MACBOOK'S CLOCK

① Open the **System Preferences** application and click the Date & Time icon.

② Click the **Clock** tab.

③ If you want to see the clock on the menu bar, check the **Show date and time in menu bar** check box.

④ To see the time in the digital format, click **Digital**, or to see it in analog, click **Analog**.

⑤ If you want to see seconds in the time, check the **Display the time with seconds** check box.

⑥ To show the AM/PM indicator, check the **Show AM/PM** check box.

⑦ To show the day of the week, check the **Show the day of the week** check box.

⑧ To flash the colon between the hour and minutes at each second, check the **Flash the time separators** check box.

⑨ To use the 24-hour format, check the **Use a 24-hour clock** check box.

⑩ To hear an announcement of the time, check the **Announce the time** check box.

⑪ Use the pop-up menu to choose how often the time should be announced, such as **On the hour**.

⑫ Click **Customize Voice** and use the resulting sheet to select and configure the voice you want MacBook to use to announce the time.

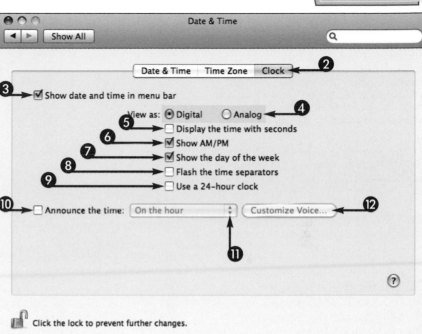

TIPS

What if I take MacBook to a different time zone?
You can leave MacBook in its previous time zone no matter where you are located. Of course, when you are in a different time zone than the one configured on MacBook, its time will not match the local time. If that bothers you, you can always change the current time zone using the previous steps.

What if the time and date are not in the right format?
Open the **International** pane of the System Preferences application. Click the **Formats** tab. Choose the region whose time and date format you want to use or click **Customize buttons** to configure a custom format.

Monday, August 11, 2008
August 11, 2008
Aug 11, 2008
8/11/08

Protect Users with Parental Controls

The phrase *parental controls* is a bit misleading. Although these can certainly be used to protect children from interactions on the Internet that might not be good for them, you can use the same tools to tailor any user's access to MacBook and the Internet.

You can also use Parental Controls to limit access to applications and system functions.

Protect Users with Parental Controls

① Open the System Preferences application and click the Parental Controls icon.

② Select the user account for which you want to configure Parental Controls.

③ Click **Enable Parental Controls**.

The Parental Controls tabs appear.

④ To limit the access of the user to specific applications, check the **Only allow selected applications** check box.

⑤ Uncheck the check box for the groups or individual applications you do not want the user to be able to use.

⑥ Use the check boxes at the bottom of the pane to allow or prevent access to system actions.

⑦ Click the **Content** tab.

⑧ To prevent profanity from appearing in the Mac OS X dictionary, check the **Hide profanity in Dictionary** check box.

⑨ To prevent access to adult Web sites automatically, click **Try to limit access to adult websites automatically**.

● Click the **Customize** button to open the Customize sheet on which you can allow or prevent specific Web sites.

⑩ To limit access to only specific Web sites, click **Allow access to only these websites**, click the **Add** button (｜＋｜), and enter the URLs of the Web sites you want to allow.

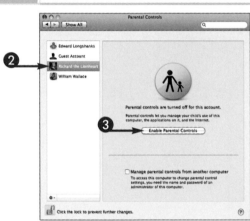

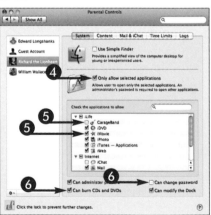

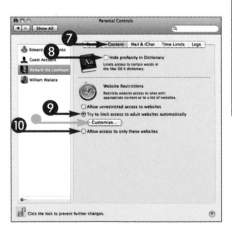

⓫ Click the **Mail & iChat** tab.

⓬ To limit e-mail, check **Limit Mail**.

⓭ To limit chats, check **Limit iChat**.

Note: The e-mail and chat controls work only with Mail and iChat.

⓮ Click (➕).

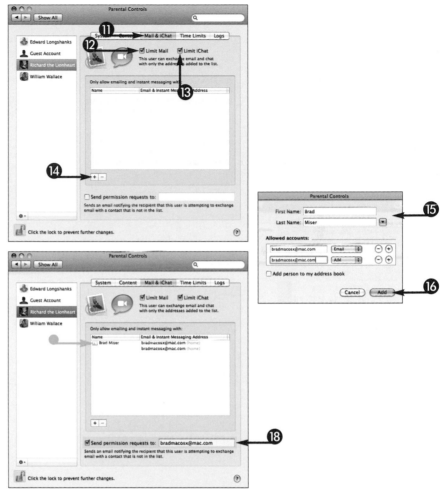

The Parental Controls drop-down menu appears.

⓯ Configure the drop-down menu for the person with whom you want to allow e-mail or chat interaction.

⓰ Click **Add**.

● The person is added to the allowed list.

⓱ Repeat steps **14** to **16** for each person with whom you want to allow interaction.

⓲ If you want to receive a permission e-mail when someone not on the list is involved in an e-mail exchange, check the **Send permission requests to** check box and enter your e-mail address.

 TIPS

What is the Time Limits tab for?

You can use the Time Limits tab to limit the amount of time the user can use MacBook. You can configure time on weekdays and weekends. You can also configure "bedtimes" during which the user is unable to access MacBook.

What is the Logs tab for?
On the Logs tab, you can view the user's activities, such as Web sites visited, Web sites blocked, applications used, and so on.

Connect to a Network and the Internet

A stand-alone MacBook is useful, but not nearly as useful as when it is connected to a local network, and, more importantly, to the Internet. Networking can be a complicated topic, and there are many technical details involved. The good news is that Mac OS X and MacBook manage most of these for you. In this chapter, you get a good foundation of networking knowledge and some examples of how to configure MacBook on a local network and on the Internet.

Understand Networking Concepts

MacBook and Mac OS X manage most of the details of networking for you, but there are a number of concepts that are helpful to understand as you create your own network.

Network

Simply put, a network is two or more computers and other devices connected together using cables or wireless connections. The purpose of a network is to enable the devices on it to communicate with each other. This is done in various protocols (which can be thought of as languages) to provide different services. For example, the Transmission Control Protocol/Internet Protocol (TCP/IP) is the basic "language" devices speak over the Internet. There are other protocols for a variety of services, such as file sharing, printing, and so on, but the data for all of these services are communicated over a network. Networks can be large or small, simple or complicated, but they all have the same basic purpose.

Internet

The Internet is the largest network possible because it literally spans the globe and millions upon millions of devices and people are connected to it. The Internet makes communication and information available way beyond anything that was possible before it came to be. Many services are available over the Internet, such as e-mail, searching the Web, chats, and file transfers. Connecting MacBook to the Internet is just about as important as being able to charge its battery.

Local Network

A local network, also known as a local area network or LAN, is a network that covers a defined physical space. LANs can be quite large, such as in a business or school, or fairly small, such as in a home. A LAN connects its devices together so they can communicate with one another and also connects to outside networks, most importantly, to the Internet. This chapter focuses on helping you create a small LAN, such as many people use in their homes. The principles of larger LANs are the same, but the details get much more complicated.

Ethernet

Ethernet is both a physical means of connecting devices together, for example, an Ethernet cable, and the protocol used to communicate over those physical means. Ethernet can support various communication speeds, and all of them are quite fast. MacBooks support the fastest current speed, which is called Gigabit Ethernet. In addition to their speed, Ethernet connections offer other benefits including simplicity and security. The primary downside to Ethernet is the need for a physical connection between the devices, which can involve long runs of cable.

Wi-Fi Network

Wi-Fi is a general term for a set of wireless communication standards and technologies that are defined in the Institute of Electrical and Electronics Engineers (IEEE) 802.11 specifications. Like Ethernet networks, Wi-Fi enables devices to communicate, but uses radio transmissions instead of physical wires to connect devices. This offers ease of configuration and makes it possible to move around while remaining on a network, which is especially useful for MacBooks. The downsides of Wi-Fi are that configuration is more difficult and Wi-Fi networks aren't as secure as Ethernet networks. But, the flexibility they provide more than makes up for the slightly more difficult configuration.

AirPort

AirPort is Apple's term for its implementation of Wi-Fi. All MacBooks, and other Macs for that matter, support AirPort. Apple also offers AirPort base stations that you can use to create your own Wi-Fi networks. Fortunately, AirPort technologies are based on the Wi-Fi standards so MacBook can access any Wi-Fi network, and other kinds of devices that support Wi-Fi can connect to AirPort networks.

Hub/Router/Access Point

All networks need a device that controls the flow of information among the various devices on the network. These devices are called hubs, routers, or access points. There are many kinds of these devices, and they all offer different sets of features and benefits. They can support Ethernet, Wi-Fi, or both kinds of networks. Because AirPort Base Stations offer lots of nice features and support is built in to Mac OS X, they are the focus of this chapter. However, MacBook can be used with other kinds of routers as well. Some of the key features are the ability to share an Internet connection among many devices and to shield those devices from Internet attacks.

Internet Service Provider

The Internet must be accessed via specific entry points. To do this, you need the services of an Internet Service Provider. The Internet Service Provider provides the means that you use to connect your network to the Internet via various technologies, such as cable, Digital Subscriber Line (DSL), or even satellite.

Internet Account

To access the Internet, you need an Internet account with an ISP. The cost of the account varies depending on the specific ISP you use. Typically, ISPs require you to have only one Internet account for your network, but you're responsible for everything connected to the modem on "your side," which is the device that communicates from your LAN to the ISP, while the ISP is responsible for ensuring that the signal to the modem is working. Depending on the type of Internet access you use, you might need a user name and password to connect to your account or it might be based on your physical location (such as with a cable connection).

IP Address

An IP address is the way devices on the Internet are identified. Put another way, to be able to connect to and use the Internet, a device must have an IP address. IP addresses include a set of four numbers with periods between each number as in 169.455.12.3. In most networks, you do not need to worry about the details of IP addresses because the hub/router uses Dynamic Host Control Protocol (DHCP) to automatically assign addresses to devices as they are needed. You just need to be able recognize when a device has a valid IP address and when it does not, which is not difficult.

Internet Services and Applications

The reason to connect devices to the Internet is to be able to access the services that are delivered over it. To access these services, you use Internet applications. Obvious examples are Mail for email, and Safari for Web browsing. There are many kinds of services available on the Internet and many different applications to use each of those services, but it's likely that you will end up using just a few of them. Because Mac OS X includes powerful and easy-to-use Internet applications, they are a good place to start.

Internet Dangers

While the Internet offers amazing capabilities, they do not come without a risk. Unfortunately, just like in the physical world, there are many people on the Internet who want to hurt other people. The dangers of Internet life include the annoying, such as pornography and spam, to the truly dangerous, such as viruses, hacking, or identity theft. Fortunately with some basic precautions and common sense, you can protect yourself from most Internet dangers relatively easily.

Local Network Services

Similar to the Internet, you can take advantage of services that you can provide over your local network. These include file and printer sharing, local Web sites, and chatting. Configuring and using local network services are pretty straightforward because these services are built in to Mac OS X.

Obtain an Internet Account

In order to connect your network or MacBook itself to the Internet, you must have an Internet account. There are different kinds of Internet accounts, mostly based on differences in how the connection is made. The most common high-speed technologies for homes are cable and DSL. Satellite connections are also available. To get an Internet account, you must know the options available and then choose the option that works best for you.

If your location has cable TV service available, contact the provider to see if Internet access is available what the cost is. Also check to see if there are any limitations about the number of devices you can connect to it.

Obtain an Internet Account

DETERMINE THE KIND OF INTERNET ACCOUNTS AVAILABLE

① If you have access to a computer that is connected to the Web, move to dsl.theispguide.com.

② Use the tools to search for DSL access in your location.

③ Contact DSL providers that serve your area to get details about their services, such as cost, limitations on the number of devices you connect, and so on.

Note: Make sure you have potential providers check your actual phone number to make sure DSL is available. DSL availability in your area does not guarantee service at your location.

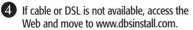
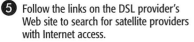

④ If cable or DSL is not available, access the Web and move to www.dbsinstall.com.

⑤ Follow the links on the DSL provider's Web site to search for satellite providers with Internet access.

Note: When you contact a potential provider, ask if Macintosh is supported. Although you do not really need formal support, because Macs work with standard technologies, Mac support can be a factor when you choose a provider.

CHOOSE, OBTAIN, AND INSTALL AN INTERNET ACCOUNT

1 Compare your options.

If you have only one option for a broadband connection, the choice is made for you.

2 If you have a choice between cable and DSL, consider which is best for you.

● DSL offers steadier performance than cable, but is typically slower. However, because DSL is delivered via a standard phone line you probably have phone jacks in more locations making the installation of a network easier.

3 Contact the provider you want to use to obtain an account and schedule installation.

The provider activates your account and if you choose to have the provider install the modem, schedules an appointment with you.

Note: *If the provider installs your modem, ask the technician not to install any software on MacBook. You do not need any special software to connect to the Internet and the applications many providers install are really just ways to get you to visit their home pages more frequently.*

 TIPS

What about dial-up Internet accounts?

Internet accounts that you access over a standard phone line and dial-up modems are available just about everywhere. Early in the Internet's life, these were the primary types of accounts that homes could use. However, dial-up accounts offer very low speed, are unreliable, and must connect each time Internet access is needed.

If I need an Internet account to connect, how come I can use Wi-Fi at public places without an account?

In public places, the organization that controls that place can make a wireless network available to you. Through that network, you can access the organization's Internet account. In some cases, you can do this for free. In others, you need to purchase access from the organization providing the network.

Set Up a Local Network

After you have a working Internet connection, you are ready to build a local network. You can include lots of devices on the network and support both wired and wireless devices. The heart of any network is the hub or router you use.

Set Up a Local Network

INSTALL AN AIRPORT EXTREME BASE STATION

1 Connect the output cable of the modem to the modem port on the base station.

2 Connect power to the base station.

3 Connect MacBook to the base station with an Ethernet cable.

CONFIGURE AN AIRPORT EXTREME BASE STATION

1 From the Desktop's toolbar menu, click **Go**.

2 Click **Applications**.

The Applications folder opens.

3 Scroll down to the Utilities folder, and click it to open it.

4 Double-click the **AirPort Utility** application.

The application opens with the base stations connected to MacBook displayed on the intro screen.

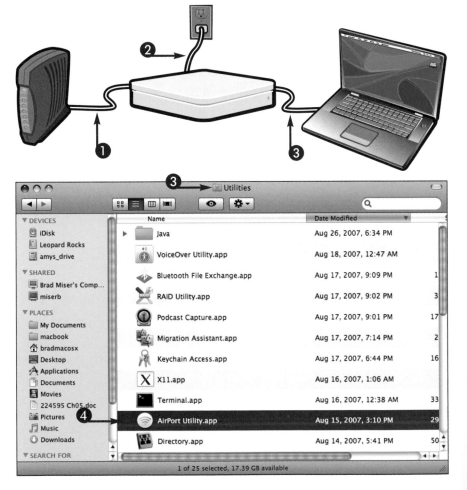

5 Select the base station.

6 Click **Continue**.

Note: *If you are configuring a base station that's already been configured once, you may be prompted to type its password between steps **5** and **7**.*

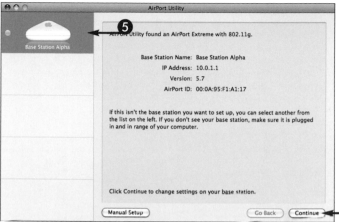

7 Select the **Create a new wireless network** radio button.

8 Click **Continue**.

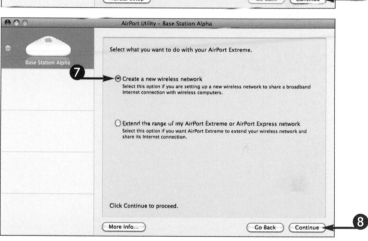

9 Type the name of the wireless network you are creating in the **Wireless Network Name** field.

10 Type a name for the base station you are configuring in the **Base Station Name** field.

11 Click **Continue**.

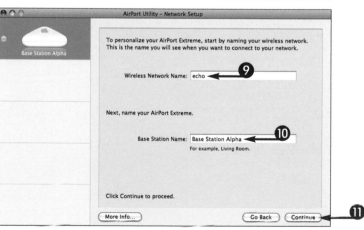

continued

Set Up a Local Network *(continued)*

The best hub choice for most Mac users is Apple's AirPort Extreme Base Station, because support for administering AirPort networks is built in to Mac OS X. Also, these base stations shield your network from Internet attacks. The rest of this chapter assumes the use of an AirPort Extreme Base Station. The steps to install other kinds of hubs are similar. They also assume that you have a working Internet connection and modem.

Set Up a Local Network *(continued)*

⑫ Choose the type of security you want to use.

You can select **WPA2 Personal (more secure)**, **128-bit WEP (more compatible)**, or **No security**.

Note: Choose WPA2 if your network consists only of Macintosh computers. Chose 128-but WEP if you have a mixture of PCs and Macs. The No Security option is not recommended.

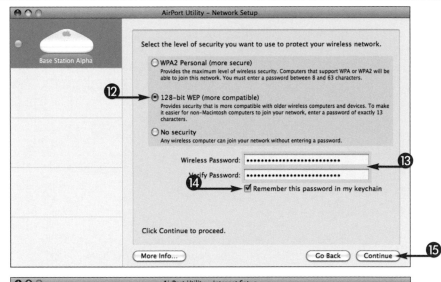

⑬ Type the password for the network you are creating in the two password fields.

⑭ Select the **Remember this password in my keychain** check box so that you do not have to type the password each time you connect to the network.

⑮ Click **Continue**.

⑯ Select the **I connect to the Internet with a DSL or cable modem using DHCP** option.

Note: If you connect to the Internet in some other way, choose one of the other options. The details of those options are beyond the scope of this chapter.

⑰ Click **Continue**.

⑱ Type an administrative password for the base station in both password fields. This is required to make any future changes to the base station.

⑲ Select the **Remember this password in my keychain** check box.

⑳ Click **Continue**.

A summary screen of the settings you have configured appears.

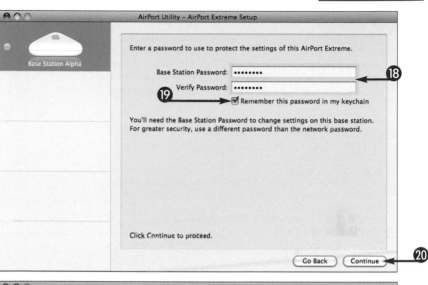

㉑ Review the settings to make sure they are correct.

㉒ Click **Update**.

The base station is configured and restarts. Once that process is complete, the wireless network is ready for use.

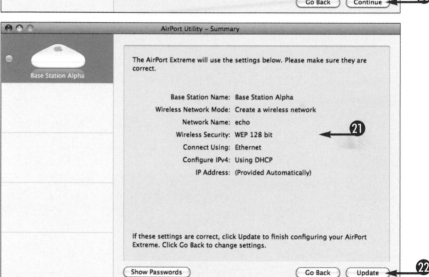

TIPS

What's the difference between an Extreme Base Station and an Express Base Station?

The most significant one is that you cannot have a wired network connected to an Express Base Station because it has only one Ethernet port, which is connected to the modem. Typically, you should use an Extreme Base Station for the primary hub on the network; you can add Express Base Stations to expand the range of the network as needed.

How do I expand the range of my network?

If the Extreme Base Station does not provide sufficient coverage of the area in which you use MacBook, you can chain base stations together using WDS. Use the AirPort Utility to connect to an Express Base Station and configure it to expand the existing network. You can do this by selecting Extend the range of my AirPort Extreme or AirPort Express network and following the onscreen instructions.

Protect MacBook from Internet Attacks

One of the great things about the Internet is that it connects you to an unlimited number of people and organizations. However, all that connectedness opens you up to various kinds of Internet attacks. The worst of these are attempts to steal your identity and to hack into your computers to steal the information they contain or to use them to launch attacks on other computers.

Fortunately, while the dangers of these attacks are very real, you can protect yourself with relatively simple techniques. An AirPort Extreme Base Station protects you from most attacks automatically. If you even connect MacBook directly to the modem, such as for troubleshooting, make sure you configure its firewall before doing so. And, you always need to be aware of viruses.

Protect MacBook from Internet Attacks

CHECK A BASE STATION TO ENSURE IT IS PROTECTING MACBOOK

1. Open the AirPort Utility application (see the section "Set Up a Local Network" for details).

2. Select the base station.

3. Click **Manual Setup**.

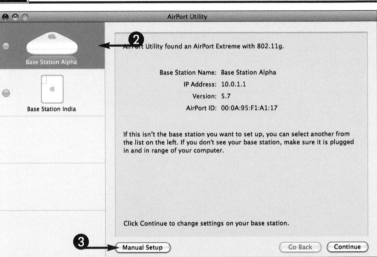

4. Click the **Internet** button.

5. Click the **NAT** tab.

6. Ensure the **Enable NAT Port Mapping Protocol** check box is checked, and quit the AirPort utility.

7. If the check box is not selected, select it and click **Update**.

   When NAT is active, the only IP address exposed to the Internet is the base station's. This shields all the devices connected to the Internet through the base station from Internet attacks.

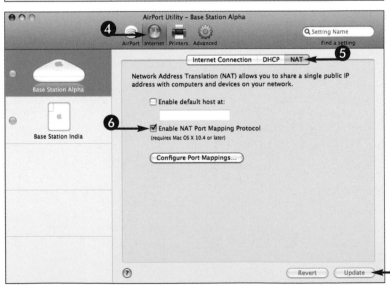

USE THE MAC OS X FIREWALL TO PROTECT MACBOOK

1 Open the System Preferences application and click the **Security** icon.

   The Security pane opens.

2 Click the **Firewall** tab.

3 Click **Block all incoming connections** to block all incoming connections to MacBook.

   This prevents anyone from accessing information on MacBook.

PROTECT MACBOOK FROM VIRUSES

1 Purchase and install an antivirus application, such as Norton AntiVirus for Macintosh.

2 Configure the antivirus application so that it updates its virus definitions and scans MacBook automatically (see the instructions for the particular application you use).

TIPS

Do I really need antivirus software?

To be as safe from viruses as possible, it's a good idea to install and use antivirus software. However, being smart about how you deal with the Internet can be almost as effective. Never open attachments to e-mail messages unless you are very sure of where they can from, especially if they are Office documents or applications. Download software only from reputable Web sites.

What else can I do with the Manual Setup options?

When you use the Manual Setup options in the AirPort Utility application, you can configure various aspects of a base station beyond the basics that the guided approach uses. Once you are comfortable with base station configuration, using the Manual Setup options is easier and faster than the guided approach.

Connect to the Internet with Ethernet

Because MacBook has Ethernet support built in, you can connect MacBook to the Internet by connecting it to a wired network over which an Internet connection is being shared.

There are two steps. You can connect MacBook to the network and then configure it to access the Internet over the network. This section assumes you are using an AirPort Extreme Base Station. If you have a different network configuration, the details might be slightly different.

Connect to the Internet with Ethernet

CONNECT MACBOOK TO AN ETHERNET NETWORK

1 Connect an Ethernet cable to one of the available ports on the Extreme Base Station.

2 Connect the other end to the Ethernet port on MacBook.

CONFIGURE MACBOOK TO ACCESS THE INTERNET OVER AN ETHERNET NETWORK

1 Open the **System Preferences** application.

2 Click the **Network** icon.

The Network pane appears.

3 Select Ethernet in the left part of the pane.

● The status should be Connected. If it isn't, the cable isn't connected correctly or the base station is not working.

4 On the Configure menu, choose **Using DHCP**.

5 Click **Apply**.

MacBook gets an IP address from the base station and should be able to access its Internet connection.

6 Quit the System Preferences application.

7 Open Safari by clicking its icon on the Dock.

8 If Safari doesn't move to a Web page automatically, enter a URL in the Address bar and press the Return key.

Safari moves to the Web site if MacBook is successfully connected to the network via Ethernet. If not, troubleshoot the problem.

Note: *See the section "Troubleshoot an Internet Connection" later in this chapter for information on troubleshooting connection problems.*

Note: *For detailed information about using Safari, see Chapter 8.*

Why use Ethernet when wireless is available?

Wireless connections are great for MacBook because you aren't tethered to one spot. However, the best wireless connection is not as fast as an Ethernet connection. So if you are "parked" in a location where an Ethernet connection is available, you get better performance if you use it instead of the wireless network.

Can I have more than one connection active at a time?

MacBook can have multiple connections to networks active at the same time. You can use the steps in this section to configure MacBook for Ethernet access and the steps in the next section to configure MacBook for wireless access.

MacBook chooses the connection to use at any point in time based on how you configure it and the connections available.

Connect to the Internet with AirPort

The whole point of having a MacBook is that you can move around with it. By connecting to an AirPort wireless network, you can connect to the Internet and a local network from any location that's covered by that network.

This section assumes your network uses an AirPort Extreme Base Station. If not, the steps you use to connect to a wireless network might be slightly different.

Connect to the Internet with AirPort

1 Open the System Preferences application.

2 Click the **Network** icon.

The Network pane appears.

3 Click **AirPort** in the left part of the window.

4 Click **Turn AirPort On** if it is not on already.

AirPort services start.

*Note: You might see a window that shows the available networks as soon as you turn AirPort on. Select the network you want to join and click **Join** or click **Cancel** to follow the rest of these steps.*

5 On the **Network Name** pop-up menu, choose the network you want to join.

6 Type the network's password.

7 Check the **Remember this network** check box.

8 Click **OK**.

You return to the System Preferences application window and the status of the network becomes Connected.

9 Select the **Show AirPort status in menu bar** check box.

10 Click **Apply**.

11 Quit the System Preferences application.

12 Open Safari and move to a Web page.

The Web page opens demonstrating that MacBook is connected to the network via AirPort.

If the Web page does not open troubleshoot the problem.

Note: See the section "Troubleshoot an Internet Connection" later in this chapter for information on how to troubleshoot connection problems.

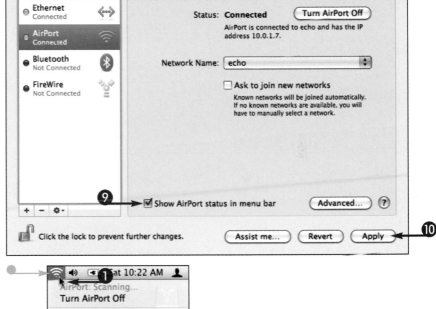

USE THE AIRPORT MENU

1 Open the AirPort menu (📶).

● You can determine signal strength by the number of waves at the top of the menu.

More waves mean a stronger and faster connection; one or two waves may result in slow or intermittent performance.

2 Choose another network you want to join by selecting it on the menu.

TIPS

How I connect directly to another Mac using AirPort?

Open the AirPort menu on the Finder menu bar and choose Create Network. Name the network, give it a password, and click OK. Other Mac users can connect to your network using the same steps you use to connect to a network provided by an AirPort Base Station.

I see only one or two waves and MacBook seems to lose its connection. What can I do?

The most likely cause is that MacBook is too far away from the base station. The most common solutions are to move MacBook closer to the base station so that the signal is stronger, or use WDS to add another base station to the network to expand its coverage.

Share Files on a Local Network

Just like services you access over the Internet, you can provide services over a local network. These include sharing files, printers, an Internet connection, Web sites, iTunes, and so on. Any computers that connect to the network, whether they use Ethernet or AirPort, can access any of the services you make available.

Share Files on a Local Network

SHARE FILES WITH OTHERS

① Open the System Preferences application.

② Click the **Sharing** icon.

③ Type a name for MacBook in the **Computer Name** field. This is the name others on the network choose to access MacBook.

④ Check the **File Sharing** check box.

File sharing starts.

⑤ To share specific folders, click the **Add** button (+).

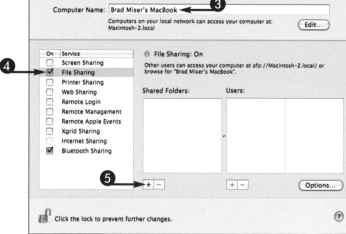

⑥ Select the folder you want to share.

⑦ Click **Add**.

● The folder appears on the Shared Folders list.

⑧ To allow everyone with whom you share files to access the folder, click **Everyone** in the User's list and choose the permission level from the pop-up menu that appears.

⑨ To configure more users, click (+) at the bottom of the Users list.

⑩ Choose the users for which you want to configure access on the list.

Note: *If the user with whom you want to share files isn't on the list, click **New Person** and create a user name and password for that person.*

⑪ Click **Select**.

The users appear on the list.

⑫ Repeat step **8** to configure the user's access to the shared folder.

⑬ Repeat steps **5** to **12** to share other folders and configure users to access your shared files.

continued

139

File sharing is one of the most useful local network services because you can easily share resources with multiple computers. You can configure MacBook to share files with others, and you can access files being shared with you.

Share Files on a Local Network *(continued)*

ACCESS FILES BEING SHARED WITH YOU

1 Move to the Desktop and open a Finder window.

● In the Shared section, you see all of the computers sharing files on the network.

2 Select the computer whose files you want to access.

MacBook connects to that computer.

Note: The Public folder in each user's Home folder is always available to everyone on the network.

3 Click **Connect As**.

④ To connect as a guest, click **Guest** and skip to step **9**.

⑤ To connect as a registered user, click **Registered User**.

⑥ Type the user name of the account under which you want to connect.

⑦ Type the password for the user name you typed in step **6**.

⑧ Check the **Remember this password in my keychain** check box.

⑨ Click **Connect**.

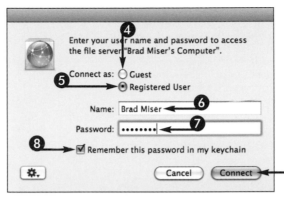

Enter your user name and password to access the file server "Brad Miser's Computer".

Connect as: ○ Guest
○ Registered User

Name: Brad Miser

Password: ••••••••

☑ Remember this password in my keychain

Cancel | Connect

● The Finder window appears listing the resources available to you based on the kind of access the user account you used has.

Brad Miser's Computer

Connected as: Brad Miser | Connect As...

Name	Date Modified
bradm	----
Macintosh HD	----
Mirror	----

DEVICES
iDisk
Leopard Rocks
amys_drive

SHARED
Brad Miser's Computer
iMac G5
macintosh
miserb

PLACES
My Documents
macbook
bradmacosx
Desktop
Applications
Documents
224595 Ch05.doc
Pictures
Music
Downloads

3 items

TIPS

When are the files I share available to others?

In order for people to access files you are sharing, MacBook must be awake and connected to the network. If it's configured to go to sleep automatically, people lose access to shared files when MacBook sleeps. Likewise, if MacBook is no longer connected to the network, its files aren't available.

How can I share files with Windows computers?

Move to the Sharing pane of the System Preferences application and turn File Sharing on by clicking its check box. Click **Options**. In the resulting sheet, select the **Share files and folders using SMB** check box. Select the check box next to each user with whom you want to share files, type the password for that user's MacBook Mac by typing **smb://ipaddress** where *ipaddress* is the current IP address for MacBook; this address is shown on the Sharing pane. You can also access files being shared by Windows computers.

Troubleshoot an Internet Connection

You can troubleshoot your Internet connection if you have problems with it. Fortunately, you probably will not need to do this very much. Networks are typically pretty reliable and once configured correctly, you usually can just keep using them. However, as in the real world, things in the virtual world do not always go according to plan.

More good news is that you can solve most network and Internet connection problems with a few simple steps.

Troubleshoot an Internet Connection

TROUBLESHOOT A NETWORK PROBLEM

1 Check lights to make sure the modem appears to be working.

If the modem appears to be working, move to step **2**.

If the modem does not appear to be working, move to step **7**.

2 Check the status of the AirPort Base Station.

If the status lights indicate the base station is working, move to step **3**. If not, move to step **8**.

3 Disconnect power from the base station and from the modem.

4 Wait about 20 seconds.

5 Connect power to the base station and then to the modem.

This often solves the problem.

6 Check the activity again.

If it was successful, you are done; if not, continue with the next steps.

7 If the power light is on but the connection light is not, contact the ISP to make sure service is available. It probably is not, in which case you need to wait until service is restored.

8 Remove power from the base station, wait 10 seconds, and connect it again.

9 Check the status lights.

If they do not appear to be working, the base station may have failed and you need to reset it.

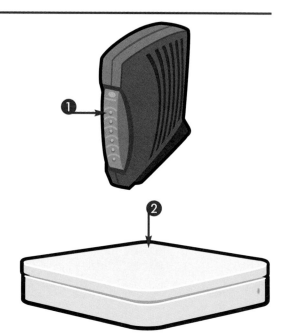

TROUBLESHOOT A MACBOOK PROBLEM

 Open the **Network** pane of the System Preferences application.

2 Check the status of the various connections.

If the status is **Not Connected** for a connection, you need to reconfigure that connection using steps shown in "Connect to the Internet with Ethernet" and "Connect to the Internet with AirPort" earlier in this chapter.

3 If the status is **Connected**, click **Apple menu**, and then click **Restart**.

4 After MacBook restarts, try the activity again.

Restarting when you have a problem is always a good thing to try; it is easy to do and solves lots of different issues.

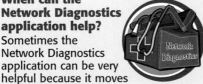

When can the Network Diagnostics application help?

Sometimes the Network Diagnostics application can be very helpful because it moves through each phase of troubleshooting to guide you along the way. When it finds a problem, it identifies it and provides some hints about how to solve it.

None of these steps helped. Now what?

While the steps in this section help with many problems, they certainly do not solve all problems. When they do not work, you have a couple of options. First, find a computer that can connect to the Internet and move to www.apple.com/support. Search for the specific problem you are having and use the results you find to solve it. Second, disconnect everything from your network and connect MacBook directly to the modem (ensuring the firewall is on first). If the connection works, you know the problem is related to the network; add devices one-by-one starting with the base station until you find the source of the problem. If the connection doesn't work, you need help from your ISP.

Surf the Web

With MacBook and its Safari Web browser, you're in a great position to take advantage of all the Web has to offer. Safari takes you way beyond basic Web browsing. Using its tabbed interface, you can easily open many Web pages at the same time. With its Autofill, you can complete Web forms easily because Safari remembers the common details for you. Of course, you can also download files and search for just about anything you can think of.

Safari is an elegant application, meaning that it offers lots of functionality and is a pleasure to use at the same time. Safari is organized well from the start, and you can set various preferences to tailor the way it works for you.

- **Back**

  Moves back to the previous page

- **Forward**

  Moves forward to the next page

- **Refresh or Stop Loading**

  Gets the current version of the page or stops loading a page (⟳ changes to ✕)

- **Create Web widget**

  Enables you to capture part of a Web page and put it on the Dashboard

- **Add Bookmark**

  Saves the current location as a bookmark

- **Address bar**

  Shows the current Web address (Uniform Resource Locator, aka URL)

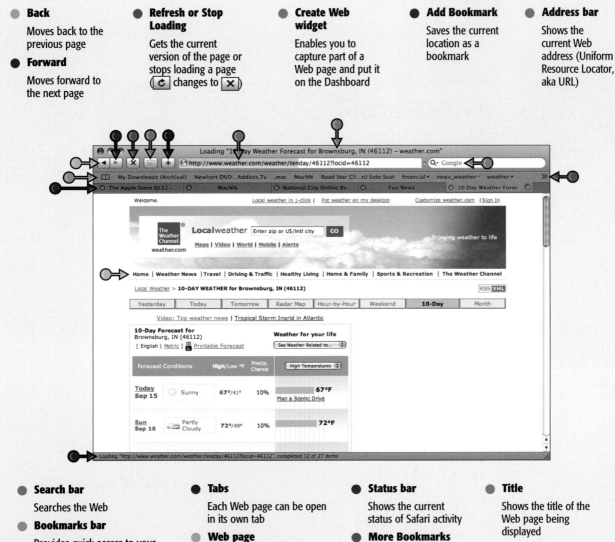

- **Search bar**

  Searches the Web

- **Bookmarks bar**

  Provides quick access to your favorite bookmarks

- **Tabs**

  Each Web page can be open in its own tab

- **Web page**

  Provides access to the information and tools on the Web page

- **Status bar**

  Shows the current status of Safari activity

- **More Bookmarks**

  Shows bookmarks that do not fit on the Bookmarks bar

- **Title**

  Shows the title of the Web page being displayed

Bookmarks mode

Enables you to view and organize your bookmarks

Collections

Special groups of bookmarks, such as those on the Bookmarks bar

Bookmarks

Shows individual bookmarks and folders containing bookmarks

Selected source

Select a source of bookmarks to see them on the list

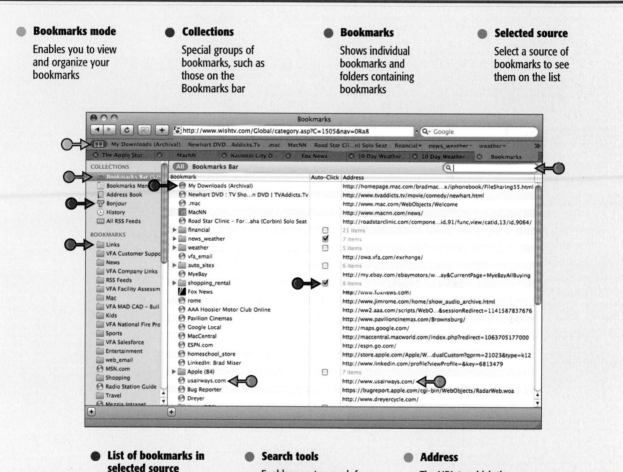

List of bookmarks in selected source

Show the bookmarks and folders of bookmarks in the selected source

Search tools

Enables you to search for bookmarks

Bookmark name

A descriptive name you can assign to bookmarks

Address

The URL to which the bookmark points

Auto-click check box

Enables you to open all the bookmarks in a folder with one click

The most basic task when you use the Web is to move to the Web site in which you are interested and then navigate within that site's pages. There are a number of ways to do this, and you will probably use all of them as you explore the Web for yourself.

MOVE TO A WEB SITE BY ENTERING A URL

1 Launch Safari by clicking its icon on the Dock (the compass icon).

Safari opens and you move to the current Home page.

2 Type the address of a Web site.

Note: *As you type in the Address bar, Safari tries to match what you type with a site you have visited previously and shows you the matches on a list under the Address bar. Click an address on the list to move to it.*

3 When you finish typing the address, press Return.

● Safari moves to the address and you see its content.

MOVE TO WEB SITES WITH A BOOKMARK

1 To use a bookmark on the Bookmarks bar, click the bookmark.

2 To access a bookmark on the Bookmarks menu, open the menu.

3 Choose the bookmark you want to use.

4 To move to any bookmark you have saved, click **Show All Bookmarks** under the Bookmarks menu.

Moving to a Web site by entering its URL address is the most powerful and is the method to use when none of the others are available to you. For most sites you use regularly, you need to type the URL only once. After that, you can move back to it with a bookmark or history.

Move to Web Sites *(continued)*

● The Web site is replaced by the Bookmarks window, which means Safari is in Bookmarks mode.

❺ Choose the location where the bookmark is saved.

❻ If the selected source includes folders, click their expansion triangles to view the bookmarks they contain.

❼ Double-click the bookmark you want to use.

Whichever method you used to access a bookmark, once you click it, its Web page fills the Safari window.

MOVE TO WEB SITES USING HISTORY

❶ Open the **History** menu by clicking on it on the Desktop toolbar.

Near the top of the window, you see a list of pages you've visited recently.

❷ If the page to which you want to return is on the list, select it.

❸ If the site is not on the list, select the folder for the time period in which you visited it.

❹ Select the site you want to visit on the resulting menu.

The site you selected opens.

MOVE TO WEB SITES USING A LINK

1 Click a link in an e-mail or document.

Safari opens and moves to the Web site.

MOVE THROUGH WEB PAGES

1 Click links to move to Web pages.

2 Click the **Back** button to move to a previous page.

3 Click the **Forward** button to move to a later page.

What is the https that Safari adds to the front of URLs?

Lots of Web sites deal with information that needs to be protected, such as bank accounts, shopping, and so on. These sites use Secure Socket Layer (SSL) technology to encrypt the data being sent between the Web page and Safari to protect it. These sites use the https protocol (Hyper Text Transfer Protocol Secure). You typically do not have to append https to sites to move to them; when you reach the part of the site that is secure, https is employed automatically.

Search
the Web

One of the most useful things to do on the Web is to search for information. And one of the best search engines is Google. Google searching is built into Safari to make Web searches fast and easy.

Search the Web

1 Type the information for which you want to search in the Search bar.

2 Press Return.

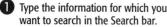

The search is performed and you see the Google results page.

3 Click a link to visit one of the search results.

That Web page appears.

4 View and use the Web page.

5 To return to the search results page, click the **SnapBack** button.

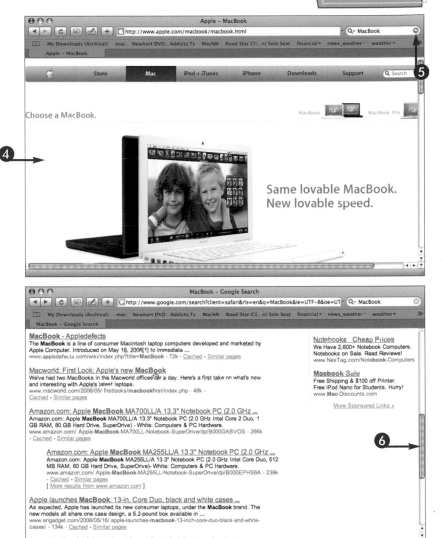

You return to the search results page.

6 Scroll the page to explore other results.

Note: When you get to the bottom of a search results page, you see how many pages are in the results. Click Next to move to the next page of results or click a page's number to jump to it.

TIPS

How can I repeat a previous search?
Safari remembers the most recent searches you have performed. To repeat a search, click the magnifying glass icon in the Search bar and choose the search that you want to repeat on the list.

Can I use any search page with Safari or do I have to use Google?
You can use any search page by moving to its URL. For example, to search with Yahoo!, enter **www.yahoo.com**. The search page appears and you can use its tool to search the Web. When you use Safari's Search bar, you search using Google only.

Download Files

There are all kinds of great files you can download from the Web. These include applications that you can run on MacBook (in fact, many applications you obtain are downloaded from the Web), images, PDF documents, and so on.

After you download a file, how you use it depends on the kind of file it is. Most applications are provided in a disk image file (file name extension .dmg), which mounts automatically. Some files, such as PDF documents, are downloaded as they are. Other files are archived so that you need to uncompress them before you use them.

Download Files

DOWNLOAD FILES FROM THE WEB

1️⃣ Move to a file that you want to download.

2️⃣ Click the file's download link.

The file begins to download, and the Downloads window appears.

● The Downloads window appears.

3️⃣ Monitor the progress of the download.

Note: You do not really have to monitor a file download because it downloads in the background. You can continue to do other things as it downloads.

When the download is complete, the file is ready for you to use.

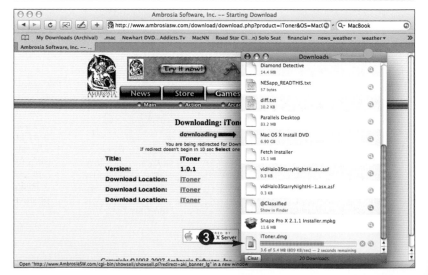

USE DISK IMAGES YOU HAVE DOWNLOADED

1 Open a Finder window.

2 Choose the disk image that you downloaded.

The contents of the disk image are shown just like a hard drive or other volume you select.

3 Run the application installer or install it with drag-and-drop.

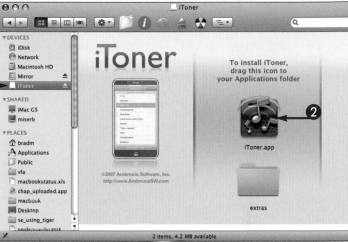

USE DOCUMENT FILES YOU HAVE DOWNLOADED

1 Open the **Downloads** folder, which is located in your Home folder.

Note: The Downloads folder has a default stack on the Dock. This has the icon of the most recent file you have downloaded. Click the icon and it expands to show the contents of the folder; click an icon to use it or click More in Finder to open the folder in a Finder window.

2 Find the downloaded document you want to use.

3 Double-click the document to open it.

It opens using the application with which it is associated.

Note: When you download a group of files that have been compressed using the ZIP format, they are uncompressed for you automatically. Instead of a single file, you see a folder with the ZIP file's name. Open that folder to see the files it contains.

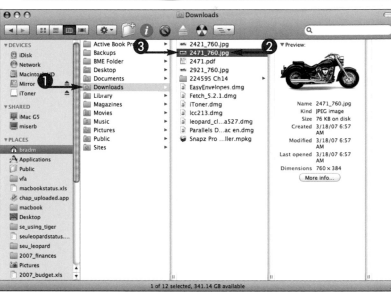

What is a SIT file?

These are files compressed with an older scheme first introduced by an application called StuffIt. When Mac OS X was introduced, support for the Windows standard compression (file extension .zip) was built into the OS, so most files you encounter these days are compressed as ZIP files. However, there are a few older files that might have .sit as their filename extension. If you come across one of these, you need to download and install the free StuffIt Expander application (do a Web search and you will find it) to be able to open SIT files.

What about FTP?

Some sites use FTP to provide files for you to download. The primary benefit of an FTP site is that files are usually downloaded faster than they are via HTTP. You can access FTP sites in Safari (their URLs start with ftp:// instead of http://) or you can use an FTP application, such as Fetch. Most FTP sites require you to have a username and password to be able to download files.

Browse the Web with Tabs

Often, you will want to have several Web sites open at the same time. Opening each of these in its own window works, but can result in screen clutter.

Safari's tabs enable you to open as many Web pages at a time as you want, while keeping all those pages in one window so you do not clutter up your desktop. Moving to a page is as simple as clicking its tab.

Browse the Web with Tabs

CONFIGURE SAFARI TO USE TABS

1 Press ⌘+,.

Safari Preferences opens.

2 Click the **Tabs** tab.

3 Check the top check box if you want to be able to press the ⌘ key when you click a link to open a Web page in a new tab.

4 Check the middle check box if you want to move to new tabs and windows when they are created.

5 Check the bottom check box if you want to confirm closing a window when it has multiple tabs open.

6 Review the keyboard shortcuts shown at the bottom of the window; these reflect the check boxes you checked or unchecked.

7 Close the **Preferences** window.

OPEN AND USE TABS

1 Open and move to a Web page.

2 Press ⌘+T.

A new tab appears.

3 Open a Web page in the new tab.

● The Web page fills the tab.

4 To open a link in a new tab, press and hold the ⌘ while you click the link.

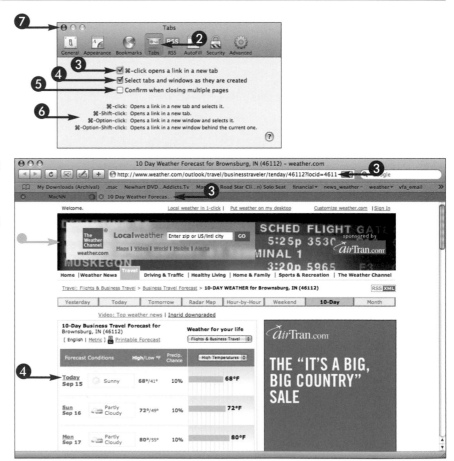

● A new tab opens and the destination page of the link is shown.

⑤ To move to a tab, click it.

The tab's Web page appears.

⑥ To close a tab, click its **Close** button (🔳).

The tab disappears.

TIPS

How can I move through open tabs with the keyboard?

Press ⌘+{ to move to the next tab, or press ⌘+} to move to the previous tab.

SHORT CUT

When should I open more windows instead of tabs?

Tabs are great because you can have many pages open in the same window. However, you can see only one page at a time. If you open multiple windows instead (press ⌘+N), you can arrange the windows so that you can see multiple windows at the same time. To convert a tab into a window, move to it and under the Window menu choose **Move Tab to New Window**.

Set and Organize Bookmarks

Earlier you saw how easy it is to move to Web sites by choosing a bookmark. Safari includes a number of bookmarks by default that you can use, but as you explore the Web, there will be lots of sites you visit regularly. You can create bookmarks for each of these sites so that it is simple to get back to them.

CREATE BOOKMARKS

1. Move to a Web page that you want to bookmark.

2. Press ⌘+D, choose **Bookmark** and then **Add Bookmark**, or click the **Add Bookmark** button.

● The Bookmark sheet appears.

3. Name the bookmark.

4. Open the pop-up menu.

5. Choose the location in which you want to store the bookmark.

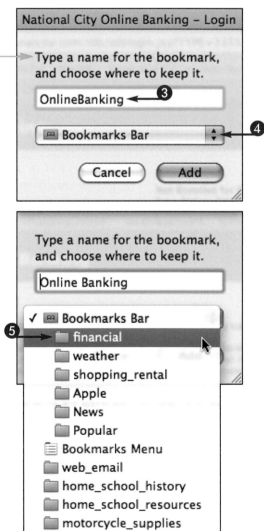

The location you selected is shown in the pop-up menu.

6 Click **Add**.

You can move back to the site at any time by clicking the new bookmark.

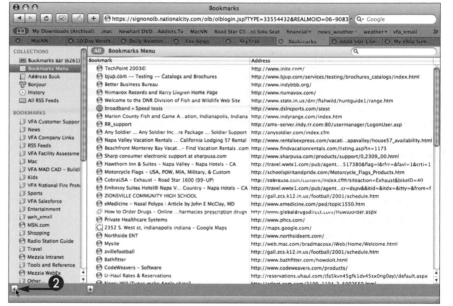

ORGANIZE BOOKMARKS

1 Press Option+⌘+B, or choose **Show All Bookmarks** from the Bookmarks menu.

Safari opens the Bookmarks window.

2 To create a new folder for bookmarks, click the **Add Folder** button (➕).

continued

Because you are likely to end up with many bookmarks, you need tools to keep them organized. Safari helps with that, too.

● A new untitled folder appears. The bookmarks list is empty because there are not any bookmarks in the folder.

❸ Type a name for the folder.

❹ Press Return.

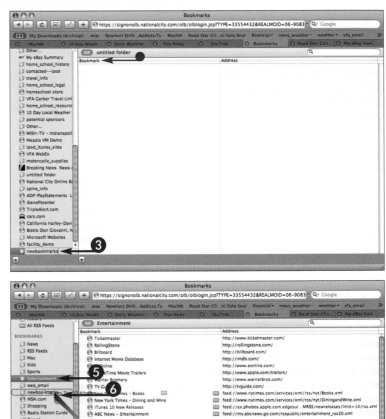

❺ Select the location containing bookmarks you want to move into the folder.

❻ Drag the bookmark from its current location onto the folder you want to contain it; when that folder is highlighted in blue, release the trackpad button.

❼ Repeat steps **5** and **6** to place more bookmarks in the folder.

⑧ Select the folder you created.

The bookmarks you placed in it appear on the list.

⑨ To create a folder within the selected folder, click (+).

⑩ Name the new folder and press Return.

⑪ Drag and drop bookmarks onto the nested folder to place them in it.

⑫ Drag bookmarks and folders up and down in the folder to change the order in which they appear.

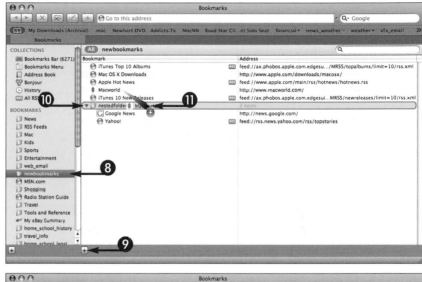

⑬ To add the bookmarks you use most frequently to the Bookmarks bar or Bookmarks menu, select **Bookmarks Bar** or **Bookmarks Menu**.

⑭ Drag bookmarks onto the list.

⑮ Organize the contents of the Bookmarks bar or Bookmarks menu just like other locations.

Note: *To delete a folder of bookmarks or bookmarks, select what you want to delete and press Delete.*

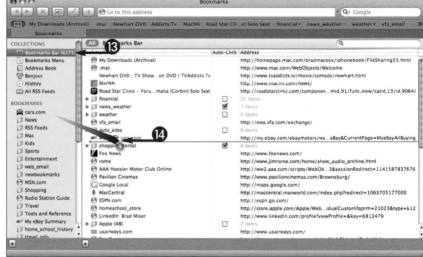

When should I bookmark a site?
Although there are some pages you use over long periods of time and for which you will definitely want to have bookmarks, there are others that are useful only in the short term. Bookmark these sites as you go so you can get back to the ones you need. When you are done, just delete the bookmarks you created to prevent Safari from becoming cluttered with bookmarks you no longer use.

Can I change the order in which folders are shown in the Bookmarks window?
To reorder folders in the Bookmarks section of the Source pane, drag them up or down until they are in the order you want.

Open Several Web Pages at the Same Time

You can have many Web pages open at the same time, which is useful. However, opening one tab after another is a bit of a pain. Wouldn't it be nice if there was a way to open lots of pages at the same time?

Using bookmarks, folders, and tabs, you can configure any collection of Web pages to open with a single click. First, prepare the folder containing bookmarks for the pages you want to open. Second, open those pages.

PREPARE A ONE-CLICK BOOKMARK FOLDER

① Set bookmarks for the pages you want to open.

② Choose **Show All Bookmarks** under the Bookmarks menu.

Safari moves into Bookmark mode.

③ Create a folder for your fast pages.

④ Add the bookmarks you want to open to the folder you created in step **3**.

⑤ Drag the bookmarks up or down the list so they are in the order in which you want them to open.

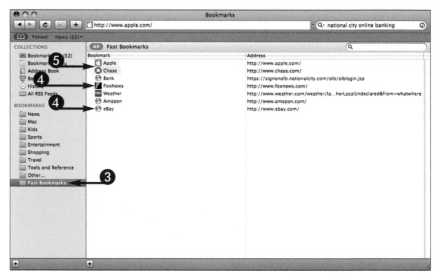

⑥ Select the **Bookmarks Bar** source.

⑦ Drag the folder you created in step **3** onto the bookmark list in the order in which you want it to appear on the Bookmarks Bar (the top of the window is the left end of the bar).

⑧ Check the **Auto-Click** check box.

● The folder you created appears on the Bookmarks Bar. At the right side of its name, you see a box, which indicates it is an auto-click folder.

OPEN LOTS OF PAGES WITH A CLICK

1 When you want to open all the bookmarks in the Auto-Click folder, click it on the Bookmarks Bar.

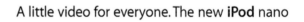

● Each bookmark in the folder opens in its own tab.

TIPS

Can I put other folders on the Bookmarks Bar too?
You can place any folder of bookmarks on the Bookmarks Bar. When you do, the folder becomes a menu showing the bookmarks it contains. Click the folder and it opens showing you the bookmarks it contains.

What if I do not want to open all the bookmarks in an Auto-Click folder at the same time?
Click the bookmark's name on the Bookmarks Bar and hold the trackpad button down. A menu appears showing you each of the bookmarks in the folder. Choose a bookmark to move to it.

Watch Movies on the Web

Movies are common on the Web. From trailers for the latest Hollywood productions to instructional videos, commercials, and other video content, there is a lot to watch. You can use Safari to view many of these movies through its embedded QuickTime player.

Watch Movies on the Web

1. Move to a site containing a movie you want to watch. For example, most movie Web sites have previews for you to watch.

2. Click the size of the movie you want to watch. Larger movies look better, but require more bandwidth to download.

Note: *If you are using a broadband connection, you can usually choose the largest size.*

● The movie opens, starts to download, and begins to play.

3. Use the **Volume** menu to change the volume.

4. Press **Pause** to pause it.

5. Drag the playhead to right to fast forward or to the left to rewind.

Note: *The shaded part of the timeline bar indicates how much of the movie has downloaded. You can watch only the part that has downloaded; if the connection slows down for some reason, the movie may stop. Just restart it when more of the movie has downloaded.*

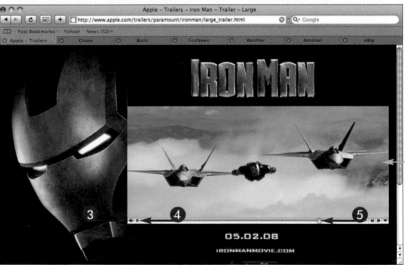

Use AutoFill to Quickly Complete Web Forms

As you use the Web, you will need to complete forms, such as when you are registering for an account on a Web site, shopping, and so on. Many of these forms require the same basic set of information, such as your name, address, and telephone number. Using Safari's AutoFill feature, you can complete the basic information with a single click.

AutoFill can also remember user names and passwords that you use to log into Web site so that you do not have to retype this information each time you want to access your account.

Use AutoFill to Quickly Complete Web Forms

CONFIGURE AUTOFILL INFORMATION

1 Press ⌘ +,

Safari Preferences opens.

2 Click the **AutoFill** tab.

3 To complete forms using the information on your card in Address Book, check **Using info from my Address Book card**.

Note: Your card is automatically populated with the information you entered when you registered MacBook. You can also edit your card by clicking the Edit button and using Address Book. See Chapter 14 for information about Address Book.

4 To have Safari remember user names and passwords for Web sites you access, check the **User names and passwords** check box.

5 To have Safari remember information for other forms, check the **Other forms** check box.

6 Close the Preferences window.

USE AUTOFILL INFORMATION

1 Move to a Web site that requires your information.

2 Choose **AutoFill Form** from the Edit menu on the Safari toolbar or press Shift+⌘+A.

● Safari completes as much information as it can based on the form and the contents of your Address Book card. The fields it completes are highlighted in yellow.

3 Manually complete or edit any of the fields AutoFill did not correctly fill in.

Create Your Own Web Widget

Chapter 3 explained how to use the Dashboard to access widgets that perform various functions. You can create your own widgets from any Web page and then access the widgets you create on the Dashboard.

When you create a widget, you capture part of a Web page. Because pages are constructed in different ways, the part of the page you capture might or might not work the way you expect. The only way to know is to try it. Fortunately, creating widgets is easy, so you are not wasting much time if it does not work the way you expect.

Create Your Own Web Widget

1 Move to a Web site containing information that you want to have on a widget.

2 Click the **Open this page in Dashboard** button ().

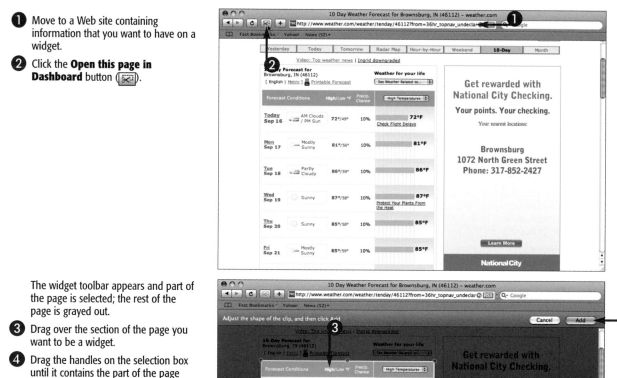

The widget toolbar appears and part of the page is selected; the rest of the page is grayed out.

3 Drag over the section of the page you want to be a widget.

4 Drag the handles on the selection box until it contains the part of the page you want to be a widget.

Note: Safari tries to capture functional blocks on a page. If a section of a page is selected automatically when you click it, you should use that section as is for best results.

5 Click **Add**.

● A widget is created, the Dashboard opens, and you see the new widget.

⑥ Click the **Info** button.

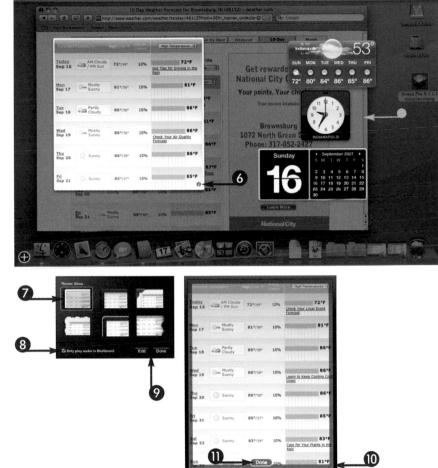

⑦ Choose a theme for the widget.

⑧ If the widget contains audio, check the **Only play audio in Dashboard** check box if you want that audio to only play when the Dashboard is open.

⑨ To adjust the area captured in the widget click **Edit** and move to step **10** or click **Done** and skip steps **10** and **11**.

⑩ Resize the widget using its resize handle.

⑪ Click **Done**.

You see the new widget with the theme and size you selected. You can manage widgets you create (such as changing locations on the Dashboard) just like the other widgets (see Chapter 3 for details).

Note: When you click a link on a Web page widget, the page that link points to opens in Safari.

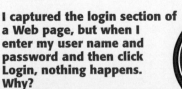

What happens if the Web page I captured changes?
If the Web page you have captured is reorganized, your widget might change, too. When you capture a widget, you capture it based on the area you select on the page. If the content in that area changes, your widget does, too. In that case, you need to recreate or edit the widget based on the new page layout.

I captured the login section of a Web page, but when I enter my user name and password and then click Login, nothing happens. Why?
Sometimes the underlying code related to a button is not physically in the area of the button that you capture as a widget. When that area is separated from the button on a widget, that button in the widget does not work. You can try capturing other parts of the page or just use AutoFill to make logging in easy.

Save or E-mail Web Pages

As you explore the Web, you will probably find Web pages you want to view again. Because the Web is always changing, there is no guarantee that a page you are viewing now will exist a day from now or even five minutes from now. If you want to make sure you can view a page again in the future, you can save it on MacBook.

Other pages you encounter are worth sharing. You can easily send links to Web pages to others, or you can even send the contents of the page in an e-mail.

Save or E-mail Web Pages

SAVE WEB PAGES

① Move to a Web page you want to save.

Note: Any receipts or account information you see on a Web page are good candidates for saving.

② From the **File** menu, choose **Save As**.

● The Save sheet appears.

③ Enter a name for the Web page.

④ Choose the location in which you want to save it.

⑤ Choose **Web Archive** on the Format menu.

⑥ Click **Save**.

The page is saved in the location you specified. You can view it again later by double-clicking its icon. It opens in Safari.

Note: A page you save is a copy of what it was at the time you viewed it. To see the current version, you need to move back to it on the Web.

E-MAIL A LINK TO A WEB PAGE

① Move to a Web page you want to share.

② Under the File menu, choose **Mail Link to This Page**.

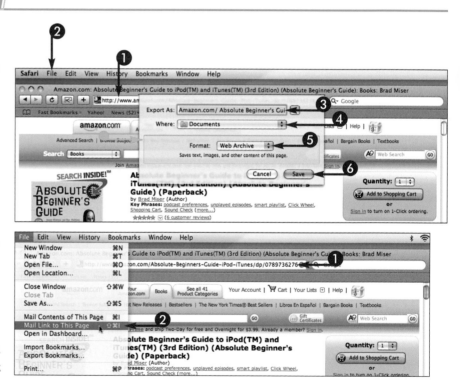

A new e-mail message is created and a link to the page is added to the body of the message.

③ Add recipients.

④ Edit the subject, and add comments.

⑤ Send the message.

When the recipient receives it, he or she can click the link to view the page.

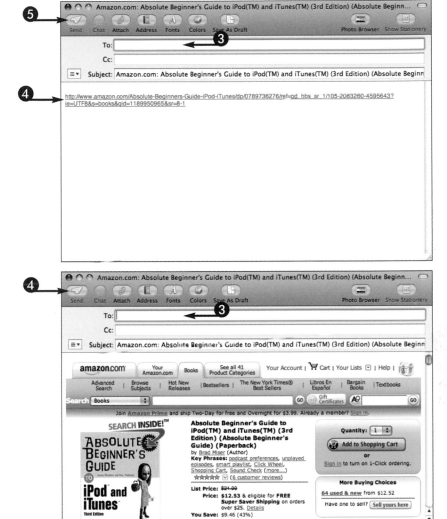

E-MAIL THE CONTENTS OF A WEB PAGE

① Move to a Web page you want to share.

② Choose **Mail Contents of this Page** from the File menu on the Safari toolbar.

A new message is created and the content of the page is pasted into the body.

③ Complete the message by adding recipients, editing the subject, and adding comments.

④ Send the message.

When the recipient receives it, he or she can view the page in the message.

Note: To be able to view a page in an e-mail, the recipient's e-mail application must be capable of displaying HTML messages.

TIPS

How do I tell if I am viewing a page saved on MacBook or one on the Web?

Look at the URL. If it starts with file://, you are viewing a saved Web page. If it starts with http://, you are viewing a live page on the Web.

Should I send a link or contents?

When you are viewing a Web site that does not change frequently or that uses direct URLs to the resource you are viewing, sending a link is better because it reduces the size of the e-mail. However, if you want to make sure your recipients see what you intend them to, send the content instead.

Set Safari Preferences

Safari includes a number of preferences you can set to change the way it looks and works. Earlier, this chapter showed how to set Tab and AutoFill preferences. You set Safari's other preferences similarly.

① Press ⌘+,.

Safari Preferences tools open.

② Click the **General** tab.

③ On the **New windows open with** pop-up menu, choose the page you want to open automatically when you open a new Safari window.

④ Enter the URL for your Home page or click **Set to Current Page** to make the page you are currently viewing your Home page.

⑤ From the remaining fields on the **General** tab, select your preferred settings.

General

Default Web Browser: Safari

New windows open with: Home Page

Home page: http://livepage.apple.com/

Set to Current Page

Remove history items: After one month

Save downloaded files to: Downloads

Remove download list items: Manually

☑ Open "safe" files after downloading
"Safe" files include movies, pictures, sounds, PDF and text documents, and disk images and other archives.

Open links from applications: ⦿ in a new window
○ in a new tab in the current window
This applies to links from Mail, iChat, etc.

⑥ Click the **Appearance** tab.

⑦ To change the standard font used on Web pages, click the top Select button and choose the font you want to use.

Appearance

Standard font: Times 16   Select...

Fixed-width font: Courier 13   Select...

☑ Display images when the page opens

Default Encoding: Western (ISO Latin 1)

8 Click the **Bookmarks** tab.

9 If you want to see links in cards in your Address Book as an option on the Bookmarks Bar, check the upper **Include Address Book** check box.

10 If you want the bookmarks on the Bookmarks Bar to also be available on the Bookmarks menu, check the **Include Bookmarks Bar** check box.

11 To include the Address Book and Bonjour collections in the Bookmarks window, check their respective check boxes.

Bookmarks Bar: ☑ Include Address Book ← **9**
☐ Include Bonjour

Bookmarks Menu: ☑ Include Bookmarks Bar ← **10**
☑ Include Address Book
☑ Include Bonjour

Collections: ☑ Include Address Book ← **11**
☑ Include Bonjour

☐ Synchronize bookmarks with other computers using .Mac (.Mac...)

12 Click the **Security tab**.

13 Use the three **Enable** check boxes to enable plug-ins, Java, and JavaScript. If you disable any of these, many Web sites will not work properly.

14 Check the **Block pop-up windows** check box to prevent Web pages from opening pop-up windows.

15 Close the Preferences window.

Web Content: ☑ Enable plug-ins
13 ☑ Enable Java
☑ Enable JavaScript
14 ☑ Block pop-up windows

Accept Cookies: ○ Always
○ Never
⦿ Only from sites you navigate to
For example, not from advertisers on those sites
(Show Cookies)

☑ Ask before sending a non-secure form to a secure website

TIPS

What are RSS preferences?
RSS is a format designed to deliver information in RSS feeds that change frequently, such as news. You can view RSS pages in Safari; these pages are more efficient to view because you can control how much information you see and you can collect information from different sources on the same page. The RSS preferences enable you to control how Safari works with RSS. For example, you can set Safari to check for updates periodically.

What are Advanced preferences?
Advanced preferences enable you to set universal access features such as minimum font size and enabling Web page navigation with the Tab key. You can also choose a default style sheet and configure a proxy server if you use one.

E-mail

Whether for business, educational, or personal reasons, e-mail is one of the more common forms of communication in today's world. Mac OS X includes the excellent Mail application that you can use to read, send, and organize your e-mail. It even enables you to automate e-mail actions and has a built-in spam tool.

Mail includes many useful features, and it wraps those features in an interface that makes sense and is easy to use. Mail provides all the capabilities that you want in an e-mail application so you can work with e-mail efficiently and effectively.

Explore Mail

Mail icon

Mail's Dock icon enables you to launch the application and also shows you how many new messages you have

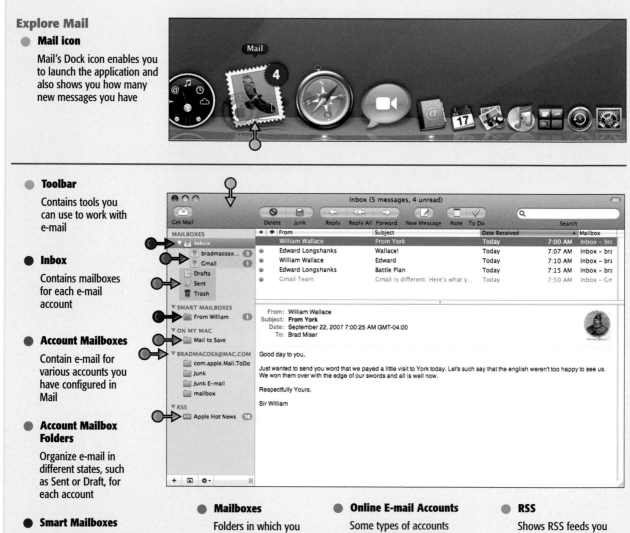

Toolbar

Contains tools you can use to work with e-mail

Inbox

Contains mailboxes for each e-mail account

Account Mailboxes

Contain e-mail for various accounts you have configured in Mail

Account Mailbox Folders

Organize e-mail in different states, such as Sent or Draft, for each account

Smart Mailboxes

Automatically organize e-mail based on criteria you define

Mailboxes

Folders in which you can store and organize e-mail

Online E-mail Accounts

Some types of accounts (such as IMAP) with the folders used by those accounts

RSS

Shows RSS feeds you are managing in Mail

Selected Source

The source of e-mails with which you want to work, such as those you have received in a specific account

Message Pane

Shows the messages in the selected source

Read/Unread

A blue dot indicates a message you have not read

From

The name of the person who sent the message to you

Subject

The subject of the message

Date

The date and time on which you received the message

Sort column

The column highlighted in blue is the one used to sort the message list

Sort direction

The triangle indicates the direction in which the list is sorted

Selected message

To read a message, you select it; the selected message is highlighted in blue

Reading pane

Displays the selected message

Message details

Who the message is from, the subject of the message, when it was sent, and who are the recipients

Sender's image

Shows the image associated with the sender in Address Book

Body

The message's text

Attachments

Shows files attached to the message and enables you to save or view them

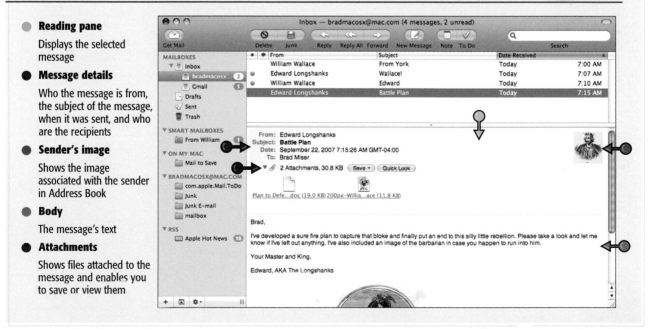

Set Up E-mail Accounts

Before you can work with e-mail, obtain one or more e-mail accounts and configure Mail to access them.

The details of configuring an e-mail account depend on the type of account; for example, configuring a .Mac account is slightly different than configuring one you have received from your Internet service provider (ISP). However, in all cases, you enter the configuration information for an e-mail account in the appropriate fields in Mail.

Set Up E-mail Accounts

① Launch Mail.

② Press ⌘ +,.

Mail Preferences opens.

③ Click the **Accounts** tab.

④ Click the **Add Account** button (+).

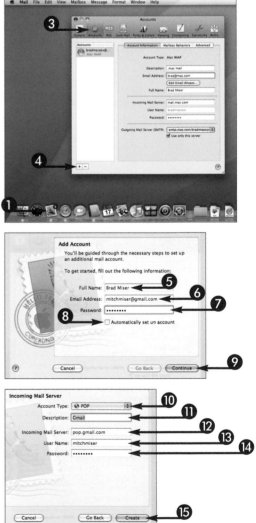

The Add Account sheet appears.

⑤ Enter the full name for the account.

⑥ Enter the e-mail address for the account.

⑦ Enter the password for the account.

⑧ Uncheck the **Automatically set up account** check box.

⑨ Click **Continue**.

⑩ Choose the type of account on the pop-up menu.

⑪ Enter a description of the account in the Description field.

⑫ Enter the incoming mail server's address in the Incoming Mail Server field.

⑬ Enter your user name (usually everything before the "@" in the e-mail address).

⑭ Enter the password for the account.

⑮ Click **Create**.

Mail checks the information and accesses the account.

16 Enter a description for the account.

17 Enter the outgoing mail server address.

18 If you leave **Use only this server** unchecked, you can send mail using another account's outgoing mail server.

19 Enter the user name and password for the outgoing mail server.

20 Click **Create**.

Mail checks the information you entered. The Summary screen appears.

21 Check the **Take account online** check box.

22 Click **Create**.

● The Account appears on the Accounts list and is ready to use.

23 Close the Preferences dialog box.

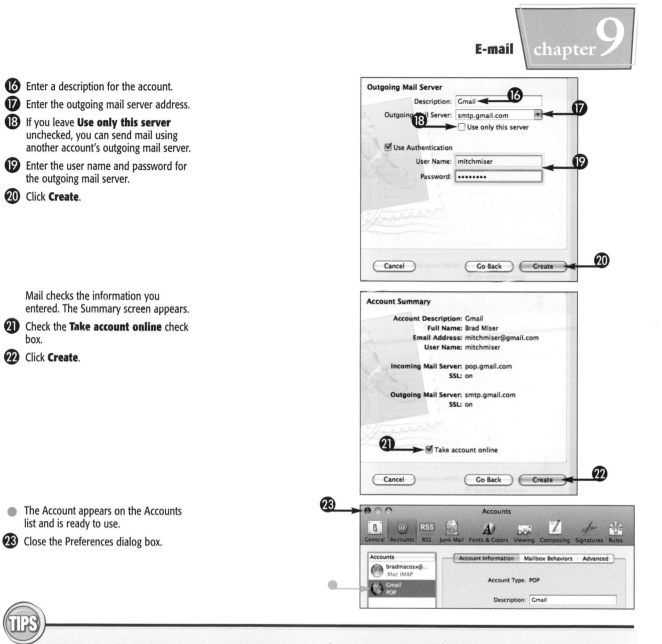

A .Mac e-mail account was already set up when I launched Mail; how did that happen?

When you configure a .Mac account, either during the initial MacBook setup process or on the .Mac pane of the System Preferences application, the .Mac e-mail account is set up in Mail automatically. See Chapter 10 for more information about .Mac.

You mentioned free e-mail accounts; where can I get them?

You can obtain a GMail account at www.google.com. You can also get a free e-mail account at www.yahoo.com. It is a good idea to have at least two e-mail accounts so you can use one to guard against spam (more on that later in this chapter).

Read and Reply to E-mail

One of the reasons to use e-mail is, of course, to read it. Mail makes doing that easy. You can read e-mail in the Reading pane, as described in the following steps, or you can double-click a message to open it in its own window.

You can also easily reply to e-mail you receive to start or continue an e-mail conversation, also called a thread.

Read and Reply to E-mail

READ E-MAIL

1. Select the Inbox or select a specific e-mail account to read e-mail you have received.

2. Select the message you want to read.

   The message you select appears in the Reading pane.

3. Read the message.

Note: *After you have viewed a message in the Reading pane, its blue dot disappears so that you know you have read it. The number of new messages is also reduced by one on the Mail icon and next to each mailbox.*

REPLY TO E-MAIL

1 Read a message.

2 Click the **Reply** button.

● If more than one person is listed in the From or Cc fields, click **Reply All** to send the reply to everyone who received the message.

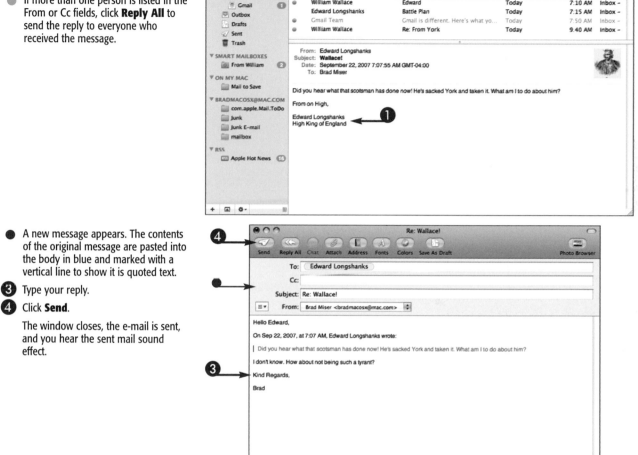

● A new message appears. The contents of the original message are pasted into the body in blue and marked with a vertical line to show it is quoted text.

3 Type your reply.

4 Click **Send**.

The window closes, the e-mail is sent, and you hear the sent mail sound effect.

How do I delete a message I do not want to keep?

Select the message and click the **Delete** button on the toolbar. The message is removed from the Message list and placed in the appropriate Trash folder. How long it remains there depends on the Trash settings for that e-mail account. You can recover a message by opening the Trash folder and moving a deleted message back into the Inbox.

Can I add more recipients to a reply?

Yes, you can add more addresses to a reply e-mail to include others. In fact, all the tools that are available to you when you create a new e-mail message (see the next task) are also available when you reply to messages.

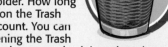

Send E-mail

When you want to communicate with someone, you can use Mail's New Message tool to create and send e-mail. You can send a message to as many people as you want.

People who are the primary recipients should be in the To field. People who are receiving a message for their information only should be in the Cc field. People who should be invisible to other people who receive the message should be included in the Bcc field.

Send E-mail

① Click the **New Message** button on the toolbar.

The New Message window appears.

② Type the name or e-mail address of the first recipient in the To field.

Note: As you type, Mail attempts to match a previously used e-mail address or an address in Address Book to what you type.

③ Press the right arrow button.

④ Enter another e-mail address.

⑤ Click in the **Cc** field or press the **Tab** key to move there.

⑥ Type the subject of message in the Subject field.

⑦ On the From pop-up menu, choose the e-mail address from which you want to send the message.

⑧ Type the message in the body.

Note: You can use the Fonts and Colors buttons to format new messages.

● As you type, Mail checks your spelling. Misspelled words are highlighted in red.

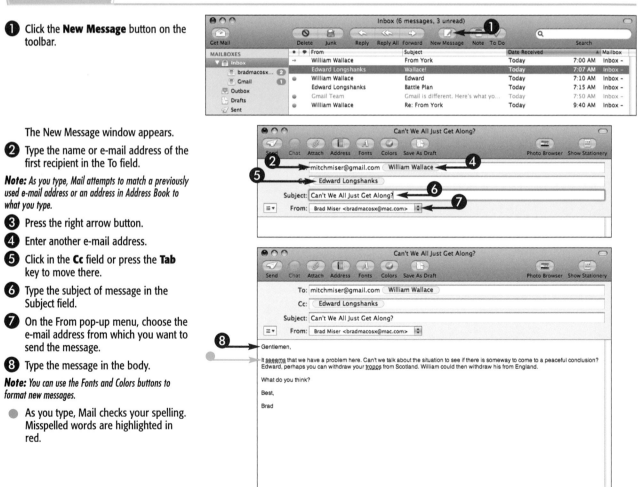

9 To correct a misspelled word, press and hold the **Ctrl** key and click the word.

10 Choose the correct spelling on the list.

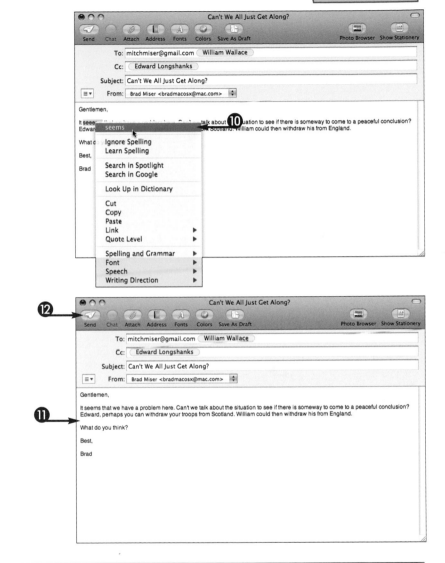

11 Review your message and make sure it is ready to be sent.

Note: *You can save draft versions of messages by clicking the Save As Draft button. You can continue working on it later by selecting the Drafts folder and then opening the message.*

12 Click **Send**.

The window closes, the message is sent, and you hear the sent message sound effect.

Note: *Once you send a message, you cannot retrieve it, so make sure you are comfortable with it before you hit the Send button.*

TIPS

How do I avoid having to type e-mail addresses?

You can store e-mail addresses in Address Book so that you can enter an e-mail address by typing a person's name, which is usually much easier to remember.

From where else can I start a new e-mail message?

When you are using a Mac OS X application, such as Address Book, and see an e-mail address, you can almost always send an e-mail to that address by pressing and holding the **Ctrl** key, clicking the trackpad button, and choosing **Send Email** on the contextual menu.

Work with Files Attached to E-mail

In addition to communicating information, e-mail is a great way to send files to other people and for people to send files to you. Files can be documents, photos, and even applications.

In Mail, some file attachments, particularly photos, can be displayed within an e-mail message. In all cases, you can save attachments to MacBook's hard drive for your use.

1 Select a message containing attachments.

● The Attachments section appears below the To field.

2 Click the expansion triangle to see the attachments to the message.

3 Scroll the message to see the attachments in the body of the message.

● To preview the attachments, click **Quick Look**. The Quick Look viewer appears and you see the contents of the attachments.

● If the attachment can be displayed in the message (most images can be), view it in the body.

4 Click **Save** and press and hold the trackpad button.

5 Choose **Save All** to save all of the attachments or choose a specific attachment to save on it.

The Save sheet appears.

6 Choose the location in which you want to save the attachments (the default location is your Downloads folder).

7 Click **Save**.

The attachments are saved in the location you selected and you can use them just like files you have created.

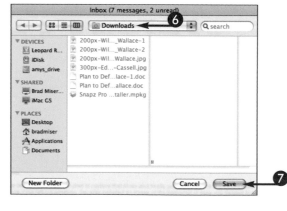

Attach Files to E-mail

You can attach files to e-mail messages you send in order to make those files available to other people. You can attach any file to a message and, assuming the recipient has a compatible application, anyone who receives the message can use the files you attach.

Attach Files to E-mail

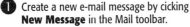

① Create a new e-mail message by cicking **New Message** in the Mail toolbar.

A window appears for you to compose your message in.

② Click **Attach**.

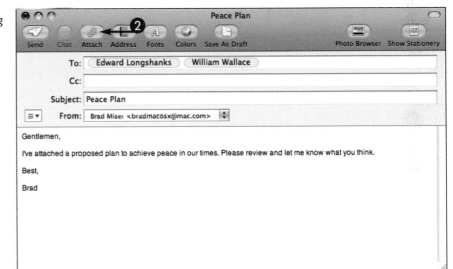

The Attach File sheet appears.

Note: You can also attach files to a message by dragging them from the desktop onto the New Message window.

③ Move to and select the files you want to attach.

④ Click **Choose File**.

The files you selected are attached to the message.

⑤ Complete and send the message.

Organize E-mail

As you use Mail, you are likely to end up with a lot of e-mail messages. Mail provides two great ways to keep your e-mail organized: Mailboxes and Smart Mailboxes. Mailboxes are like folders in the Finder. Smart Mailboxes automatically organize e-mail based on rules you create.

However, one of the best ways to keep your e-mail organized is to delete messages that you do not need, which is probably most of those you receive. The fewer messages you keep, the fewer you have to organize.

ORGANIZE E-MAIL IN MAILBOXES

1 Click the **Add** button (+) in Mail.

2 Select **New Mailbox**.

The New Mailbox drop-down menu appears.

3 On the Location menu, choose **On My Mac**. (This stores e-mail on MacBook rather than on the mail server.)

4 Name the mailbox.

5 Click **OK**.

● The mailbox appears in the On My Mac section of the Mailboxes pane.

6 Drag messages from the Messages list onto the mailbox you created.

The message is moved into the mailbox.

Note: *You can create nested mailboxes by dragging one mailbox into another one.*

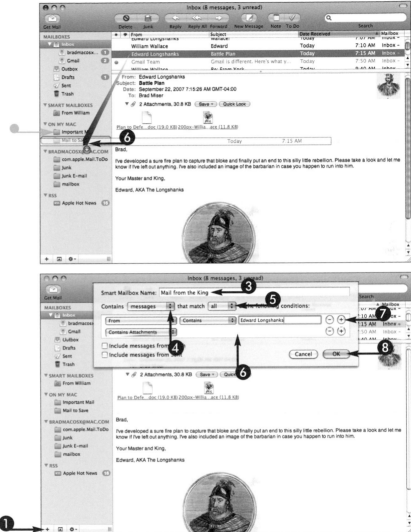

ORGANIZE E-MAIL WITH SMART MAILBOXES

1 Click the **Add** button in Mail.

2 Select **New Smart Mailbox**.

The New Smart Mailbox sheet appears.

3 Name the new smart mailbox.

4 On the Contains menu, choose **Messages**.

5 On the match menu, choose **all**.

Note: *Choose* any *if you want a message to be included if it matches any of the conditions.*

6 Use the rest of the options on the menu to set your preferences for your smart mailbox.

7 To add another condition, click the **Add** button (+).

Note: *To remove a condition, click its* **Remove** *button (−).*

8 Click **OK**.

The mailbox is created and any messages that meet its conditions appear in it.

I have received a message saying that I am over my mail storage quota. What do I do?

E-mail can be stored in two locations. One is on the mail server associated with the e-mail account. Most e-mail accounts have a limit on how much e-mail you can store on the server. When you reach this limit, you can no longer receive or send e-mail with that account. To prevent e-mail server storage overload, store e-mail in mailboxes on MacBook. You should also check account settings to make sure mail is not being stored on the server unintentionally (see "Set Mail Preferences" later in this chapter).

Search
E-mail

As you accumulate messages, you may want to be able to find messages that contain information or attachments you need. You can use Mail's Search tool to quickly find messages of importance.

One of the best ways to be able to find e-mail is to keep it organized well. A little time spent organizing e-mail earlier prevents some of the effort to find it later.

Search E-mail

1 Type the information for which you want to search in the Search bar.

● As you type, Mail presents messages that meet your search in the lower pane.

Note: By default, the messages are sorted by rank, which is Mail's assessment of how relevant the messages are to your search term.

2. To search in all mailboxes, click **All Mailboxes**, or to search in only the selected mailbox, click its button.

3. Click the button to indicate what part of the messages you want to search.

● The results are refined based on the choices you made.

4. To read a found message, select it.

5. To save a search as a Smart Mailbox so you can run it again, click **Save**.

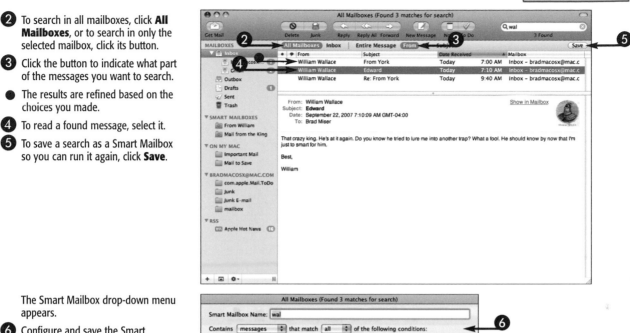

The Smart Mailbox drop-down menu appears.

6. Configure and save the Smart Mailbox.

You can repeat the search at any time by selecting its folder in the Smart Mailboxes section of the Mailbox pane.

TIPS

Do I have to be using Mail to search e-mail?

Mac OX's Spotlight feature enables you to search for information on MacBook no matter where that information is found, including files, folders, and e-mail. If you are sure the information you need is in an e-mail, search in Mail. If not, use Spotlight instead. (To learn how to use Spotlight, see Chapter 4.)

Can I have the same e-mail in more than one mailbox?

An e-mail can exist in only one mailbox on the same location, such as the mailboxes stored on MacBook. (Of course, you can make copies of messages and place the copies in different locations.) Because Smart Mailboxes do not actually contain the messages (a Smart Mailbox makes pointers to the actual e-mail messages), e-mail messages can be included in many Smart Mailboxes at the same time.

One of the perils of e-mail is the dreaded spam. Spam is annoying at best, with messages that stream into your Inbox with advertising in which you have no interest. At the worst, spam contains offensive or dangerous messages that promise all kinds of rewards for just a few simple actions (usually an attempt at identity theft).

Notice that the title of this section is "Avoid Spam," as opposed to "Eliminate Spam" or "Prevent Spam." Unfortunately, spam is part of e-mail and the best you can do is minimize your exposure to it as much as possible.

Avoid Spam

① Press ⌘+,.

The Mail Preferences window appears.

② Click the **Junk Mail** tab.

③ Check the **Enable junk mail filtering** check box.

④ Click **Mark as junk mail, but leave it in my Inbox** if you want Mail to highlight junk e-mail, but not do anything with it.

⑤ Click **Move it to the Junk mailbox** if you want Mail to move spam to the Junk mailbox.

⑥ Click **Perform custom actions** if you want to define what Mail does using a mail rule.

⑦ Check the check boxes to specify e-mails that are exempt from junk mail filtering.

⑧ Close the **Preferences** window.

As you receive e-mail, Mail takes the action you selected when you receive e-mail it identifies as junk.

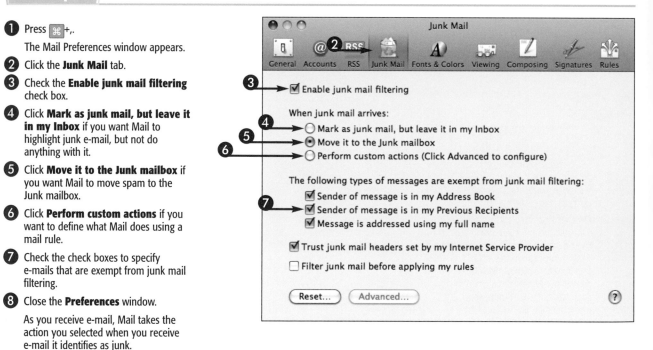

⑨ Review messages that Mail has flagged as junk, such as by selecting the Junk folder.

⑩ If a message is junk, do nothing and the message stays in your Junk Mail.

⑪ If a message is not junk, click **Not Junk**.

Over time, Mail learns from your actions and gets better at identifying junk mail.

⑫ Delete junk messages.

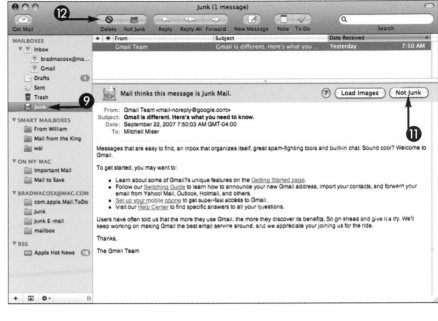

TIPS

I have received an important message saying my account is going to be closed unless I update its information. What should I do?

One of the most effective techniques of spam criminals is to model their spam e-mails so they look just like e-mail from legitimate companies. Examples include eBay, banks, and so on. They usually include some language about your account being out of date or compromised and you need to provide information to correct the situation. These messages are always spam and you should never respond to them. Legitimate companies never ask you to update information via e-mail requests.

How can I tell if a message is legit or spam?
Just by looking at these e-mails, there is no way to tell if they are authentic or not. However, most of these e-mails include a link to take you someplace, usually your account so you can verify some information, which really means they are trying to steal information from you. Point to these links (do not click!) and the URL pops up. You will see that the first part of the URL has nothing to do with the real company, which is a dead giveaway.

Create and Use E-mail Signatures

It is good practice to include a signature at the end of your e-mails to make your communication more personal or to provide important information, such as your phone number. You can even advertise in your signature.

You can configure Mail to make adding signatures easier and faster. You can create many different signatures and easily use the one that is most appropriate for a specific e-mail message you send.

CREATE SIGNATURES

1 Press ⌘+,.

2 Click the **Signatures** tab.

3 Click **All Signatures**.

4 Click the **Add Signature** button (+).

   A new signature is created.

5 Name the signature in the center column and press Return.

6 Edit the signature in the right column.

7 If you use the default font for your messages, check the **Always match my default message font** check box so the signature uses that font too.

8 If you use standard quoting (where your reply is always above the quoted message), check the **Place signature above quoted text** check box.

9 Repeat steps **3** to **6** to create as many signatures as you want to have available.

10 Drag signatures from the center column onto the e-mail accounts with which you want to use them in the left column.

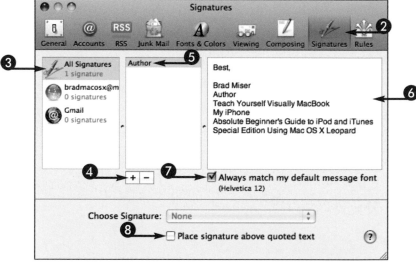

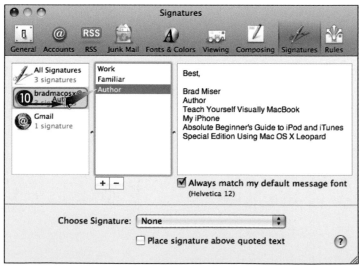

⑪ Select an e-mail account.

⑫ Choose the default signature for the account on the Choose Signature pop-up menu.

Whenever you send an e-mail from the account, the default signature is pasted in automatically.

⑬ Close the **Preferences** window.

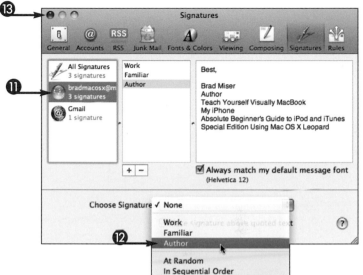

USE SIGNATURES

① Create a new message.

● If you configured a default signature for the e-mail account, it is pasted in the new message.

② To change the signature, choose the signature on the Signature pop-up menu.

Note: If do not select a default signature for an account, you can choose a signature on the menu to add it to a message.

TIPS

What are the other choices on the Choose Signature pop-up menu?
If you choose **At Random** on the Choose Signature pop-up menu, Mail selects a signature randomly each time you create a message. If you choose **In Sequential Order**, Mail selects the first signature on the list for the first message, the next one for the second, and so on.

Can I put images or links in my signature?
Yes. To add an image (for example, a scanned version of your "real" signature) to a signature, drag the image file from the desktop onto the right pane of the Signature tab. You can also add links to a signature by typing the URL in the signature block or copying and pasting it in.

Create E-mail Rules

If you find yourself doing the same tasks with certain kinds of e-mail, you can probably configure Mail to do those tasks for you automatically by configuring rules for each of these tasks.

To determine if you can create a rule, you need to be able to define the conditions under which one or more actions should be taken and the actions you want to happen every time those conditions are met. If the following steps, you learn how to create a rule to automatically file e-mails from specific people in a folder and to alert you they have arrived. You can configure other rules similarly.

Create E-mail Rules

① Press ⌘ +,.

② Click the **Rules** tab.

Note: For a rule to be active, its check box must be checked.

③ Click **Add Rule**.

The New Rule sheet appears.

④ Name the rule.

⑤ Choose **any** on the pop-up menu if only one condition has to be true for the rule to apply or **all** if all of the conditions have to be true for the rule to apply.

⑥ Select the attribute for the first condition on the left pop-up menu, such as **From**.

⑦ Choose the operand for the condition on the center pop-up menu, such as **Contains**.

⑧ Type the condition value in the box.

⑨ Click the **Add Condition** button (+).

⑩ Repeat steps **6** to **8** to configure the new condition.

*Note: To remove a condition, click its **Delete** button.*

⑪ Repeat steps **9** and **10** to add and configure more conditions.

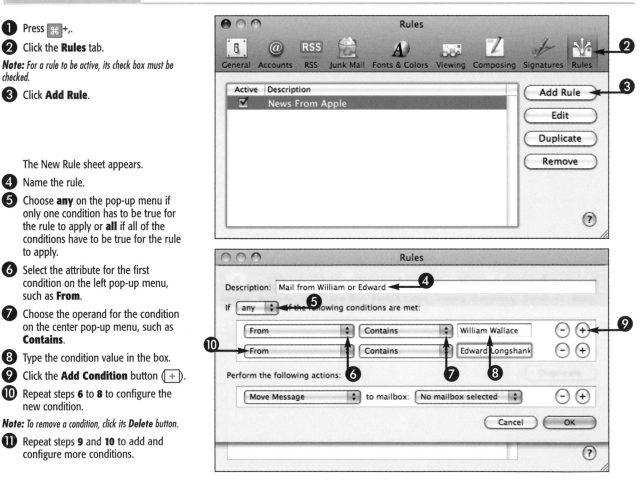

⑫ On the top left Action pop-up menu, choose the action you want to happen when the conditions are met.

⑬ On the right Action pop-up menu, choose the result of the action, such as a location, sound, and so on.

⑭ To add another action, click the **Add Action** button (⊕).

⑮ Repeat steps **12** and **13** to configure the new action.

⑯ Repeat steps **14** and **15** to add and configure more actions.

⑰ Click **OK**.

The rule is created.

⑱ If you want the rule to be applied to the messages currently in your Inbox, click **Apply**; if not, click **Don't Apply**.

The rule is created and appears on the list of rules. When messages are received that meet the rule's conditions, whatever actions it includes are done automatically.

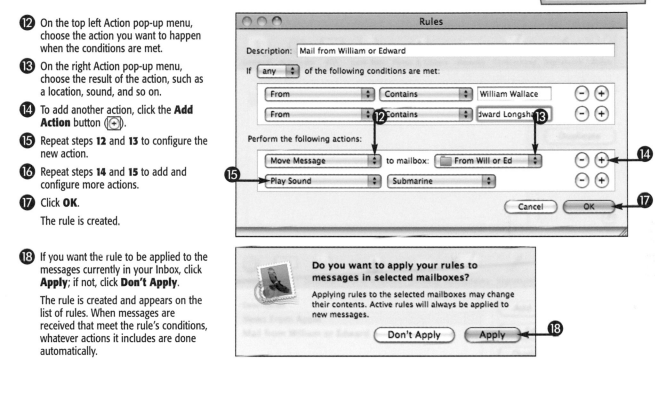

Do you want to apply your rules to messages in selected mailboxes?

Applying rules to the selected mailboxes may change their contents. Active rules will always be applied to new messages.

Don't Apply   Apply ← ⑱

TIPS

What are some examples of useful actions available for rules?
Move Message moves e-mail messages to specific locations, such as mailboxes you have created on MacBook or even the Trash. Forward Message can be useful when you always want to forward messages to another address in specific situations. If you usually reply to a specific person's e-mail, Reply to Message can be useful.

How do I know a rule is working?
To test the actions of a specific rule, select a message to which the rule should apply and choose Apply Rules from the Message menu. If the actions you expect happen, the rule is working. If they do not, something is wrong with the rule and you need to edit it to fix the problem. You should also select a message to which the rule should not apply and do the same thing. If the actions happen, the rule is not configured correctly.

Set Mail Preferences

This chapter has discussed a number of Mail's Preferences tools already, but there are several more than you should explore as you use Mail. The two most important of these are the General and Accounts preferences.

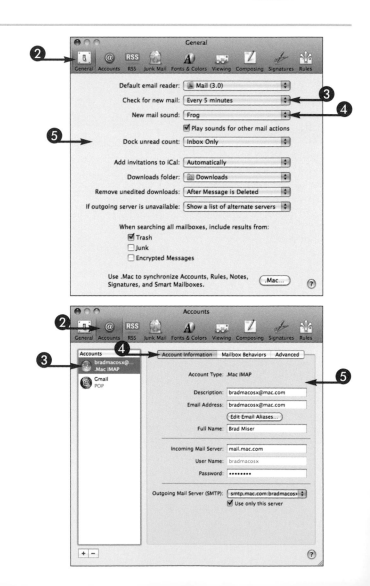

SET GENERAL PREFERENCES

1 Press ⌘+,.

2 Click the **General** tab.

3 On the **Check for new mail** pop-up menu, choose how often you want Mail to check for new messages.

4 On the **New mail sound** pop-up menu, choose the sound you want to hear when you receive new messages.

5 Choose from the remaining options on the General tab to set your Mail preferences.

SET ACCOUNT PREFERENCES

1 Press ⌘+,.

2 Click the **Accounts** tab.

3 Select the account you want to configure.

4 Click the **Account Information** tab.

5 Make any changes to the account's configuration, such as changing the incoming mail server password.

194

⑥ Click the **Mailbox Behaviors** tab.

⑦ Use the check boxes and pop-up menus to configure where messages are stored.

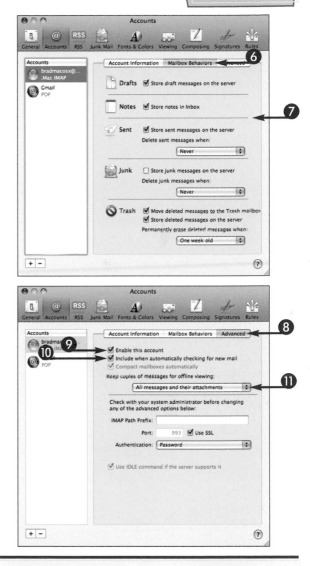

⑧ Click the **Advanced** tab.

⑨ To disable an account, uncheck the **Enable this account** check box.

⑩ To include the account when Mail checks for e-mail, check the **Include when automatically checking for new mail** check box.

⑪ To store all messages on MacBook so you can access them even when you are not connected to the Internet, choose **All messages and their attachments** on the upper pop-up menu.

What are Viewing preferences?
There are a number of options on the Viewing tab. You can set how much detail is shown in the header of messages. You can also configure mail to show the status of chat buddies, have unread messages bolded, disable images stored outside of an HTML message, disable smart addresses (so that e-mail addresses are always shown instead of names), and select the color used to show e-mail threads.

What are Composing preferences?
These impact how Mail works when you create messages. For example, you can choose the format of messages, such as Plain or Rich Text. You can also configure spell-checking and automatically Cc yourself on your messages.

Use
.Mac

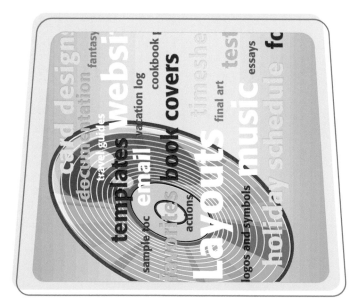

Apple's .Mac services are a perfect companion to MacBook because you literally expand the reach of MacBook to the Internet. There are a variety of .Mac services you can use, including e-mail, Web sites, free software, and, perhaps the most useful of all, an iDisk.

To use .Mac services, you must obtain a .Mac account and then configure MacBook to access that account. Once you do, .Mac services become linked to MacBook so that you can access them from the desktop, Safari, and various applications, such as iPhoto.

Explore .Mac

A .Mac account gives you access to a number of useful services. You can use any or all of these as much as you need. Because your .Mac account is integrated to MacBook, you can consider .Mac to be an extension of your MacBook's desktop to the Internet.

.Mac Account

To use .Mac, you must have a .Mac account. You can obtain an account from the MacBook desktop and Safari. A .Mac account includes, by default, 10GB of storage space on Apple servers, an e-mail account, Web site, and more. You can also purchase a family account that provides several different user accounts under a single .Mac account (for distinct e-mail addresses, Web sites, and so on). At the time of this writing, the cost of an individual .Mac account is about $100 per year while the cost of a family account is about $180 per year. You can also upgrade accounts by adding disk space and e-mail accounts.

iDisk

One of the best features of .Mac is iDisk, which is a virtual disk that you access on Apple servers. Your account includes 10GB of disk space (you can purchase more if you need it) that you can use just like MacBook's hard drive. The iDisk is also where you store the files you use to build your .Mac Web site and where your .Mac e-mail is stored. You can access your iDisk directly from MacBook's desktop and from any other computer you use, including Windows computers.

.Mac E-Mail

Another great feature of .Mac is that you get an e-mail account, with an e-mail address that is *your.Macusername*@mac.com, where *your.Macusername* is the name of your .Mac user account. You can send and receive e-mail from your .Mac account just like you do from other e-mail accounts you may have from an e-mail application such as Mail or directly from the Web.

HomePage

HomePage is the name of the service you can use to create and publish your own Web sites. HomePage makes it easy to create your own presence on the Web because you can build an entire Web site using templates that you complete with your own information. There are many types of pages you can choose from, such as file download pages, photo pages, and résumés. You can even create several different Web sites from one .Mac account.

Synchronization

If you have more than one Mac, such as a MacBook and an iMac, you probably want to be able to access some information from all your machines. Examples include Safari bookmarks and contact information. Using .Mac, you can synchronize Macs so that information changes on one are copied to the others automatically or on your command. This makes it easy to ensure you have access to information you need from any Mac you happen to be using.

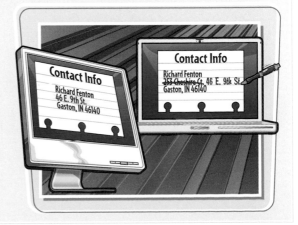

Obtain and Configure a .Mac Account

Because .Mac is integrated into Mac OS X, you can obtain a .Mac account right from MacBook's desktop. When you do, you move to Apple's Web site where you provide the information required to create your account. When that is complete, you configure MacBook to access .Mac, and all its services are ready for you to use.

Obtain and Configure a .Mac Account

① Click **Apple menu** and then **System Preferences.**

The System Preferences application opens.

② Click **View** and then **.Mac** to open the .Mac pane.

③ Click **Learn More**.

Safari opens and moves to the .Mac Web site.

④ Click **Join Now**.

The first page of a three-step form appears.

⑤ Complete each page of the form.

⑥ Scroll down and click **Continue** until you complete all three pages.

Note: *Be thoughtful about what you choose as your member name; in addition to using this to log in to .Mac, it becomes part of your e-mail address and the URL to your Web site.*

The Welcome to .Mac screen that provides information you need to use your .Mac account appears.

7 Move back to the .Mac tab of the System Preferences application by clicking its icon on the Dock.

8 Type your member name.

9 Type your password.

10 Click **Sign In**.

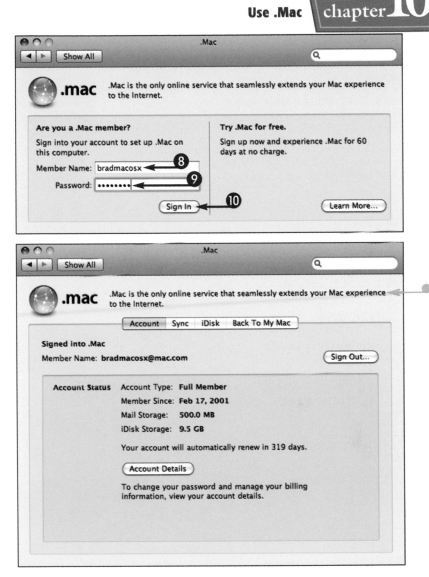

Are you a .Mac member?
Sign into your account to set up .Mac on this computer.

Member Name: bradmacosx — 8

Password: •••••••• — 9

Sign In — 10

Try .Mac for free.
Sign up now and experience .Mac for 60 days at no charge.

Learn More...

● Your account information is configured on MacBook and the .Mac pane updates to show that you have configured .Mac.

.Mac is the only online service that seamlessly extends your Mac experience to the Internet.

Account   Sync   iDisk   Back To My Mac

Signed into .Mac
Member Name: bradmacosx@mac.com   Sign Out...

Account Status   Account Type: **Full Member**
Member Since: **Feb 17, 2001**
Mail Storage: **500.0 MB**
iDisk Storage: **9.5 GB**

Your account will automatically renew in 319 days.

Account Details

To change your password and manage your billing information, view your account details.

 TIPS

Can I try .Mac before I pay for an account?
Apple offers trial .Mac accounts, which enable you to use all .Mac services for two months at no charge. At the end of the trial period, you can upgrade the trial account to a full .Mac account or you can cancel it. After you move to the .Mac Web site, click **Free Trial** instead of Join Now to create a free trial account.

Are .Mac services available outside the U.S.?
You can create and use a .Mac account from many different countries. The rates charged for a .Mac account vary from country to country, but the .Mac services you can access are the same.

iDisk is a volume of disk space on Apple's servers that you can access through your .Mac membership. iDisk is built in to Mac OS X so after you configure MacBook for .Mac, it appears on your desktop just like other hard drives you use.

By default, iDisk has a number of folders on it, such as Public, My Documents, and Sites. You can use these folders or create your own.

Use an iDisk

CONFIGURE IDISK

1. Open the .Mac pane of the System Preferences application and click the **iDisk** tab.

● There is a gauge showing how much of your iDisk space you are currently using.

2. If you want other people to be able to store files in your iDisk's Public folder, select **Read and Write**.

3. To put a password on your Public folder, select the **Password-protect your public folder** check box.

4. Type the password for the folder in the Password field.

5. Confirm the password by typing it again in the Confirm field.

6. Click **OK**.

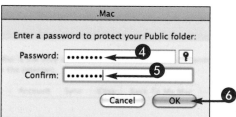

If you only want to access your iDisk over the Internet, skip to step **10**.

⑦ If you want to keep a copy of iDisk on MacBook so you can access it even when you are not connected to the Internet, click **Start**.

⑧ To update your copy of iDisk automatically, click **Automatically**.

⑨ If you want to manually update iDisk, click **Manually**.

⑩ Press ⌘+Q to quit the System Preferences application.

USE IDISK

① Open a Finder window and click the **iDisk** icon.

You can also click **Go**, **iDisk**, and then **MyiDisk**.

● The contents of your iDisk appear.

If you chose to keep a copy of iDisk on MacBook, all its data are copied to MacBook.

Note: If you choose to keep a copy of iDisk on MacBook and select the Manually option, click the Sync button next to the iDisk icon to sync the two versions of iDisk.

TIPS

How do I access my iDisk from a PC?
To use an iDisk with a Windows computer, download and install iDisk Utility for XP; other versions are available for various versions of Windows. After you do this, you can mount your iDisk on the PC by launching the application and typing your .Mac account information; from that point, you can use iDisk from My Computer just like other hard drives. You can get a copy of the iDisk for Windows applications by logging on to your .Mac account. Click the **Member Central** link and then download and install the iDisk Utility for the version of Windows you use.

Can I use iDisk to back up my files?

You can use your iDisk to store any files, including backups. Even better, you can download Apple's Backup application from the .Mac Member Central page and use it to automatically back up files to iDisk. Backing up to iDisk is useful because the files are stored independent of your computer and even your location for maximum protection. Because they are stored online, you can access your backups from any computer that can access your iDisk.

Use .Mac Webmail

You can access your .Mac e-mail in an e-mail application, such as Mail. You can learn how to use Mail to access your .Mac e-mail in Chapter 9.

You can also access it from any computer via the Web. This makes .Mac e-mail very convenient because as long as you are using a computer with Internet access, your .Mac e-mail is not far away.

Use .Mac Webmail

① Open Safari and move to www.apple.com/dotmac/.

② Click **Log In**.

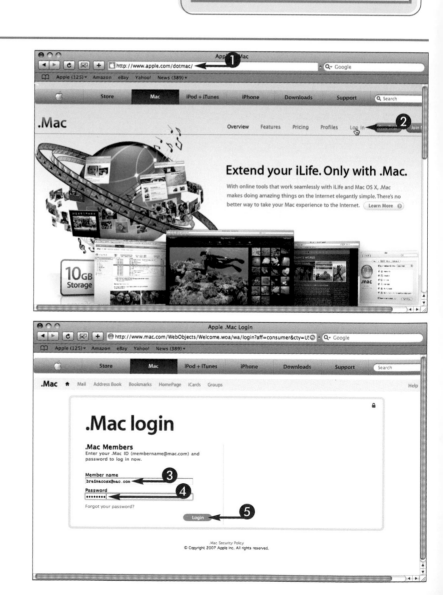

③ Type your .Mac member name if needed.

When you use MacBook, your .Mac member name is remembered for you.

④ Type your password.

⑤ Click **Login**.

Your .Mac home page appears.

6 Click the **Mail** link.

The .Mac Mail page appears.

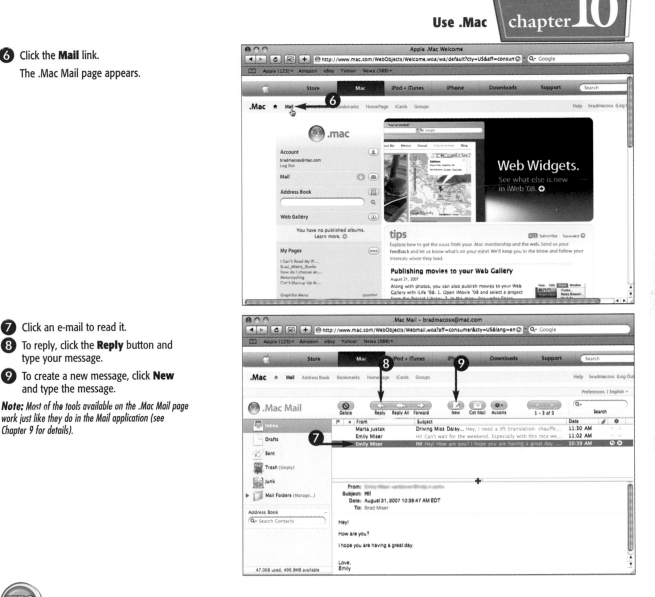

7 Click an e-mail to read it.

8 To reply, click the **Reply** button and type your message.

9 To create a new message, click **New** and type the message.

Note: *Most of the tools available on the .Mac Mail page work just like they do in the Mail application (see Chapter 9 for details).*

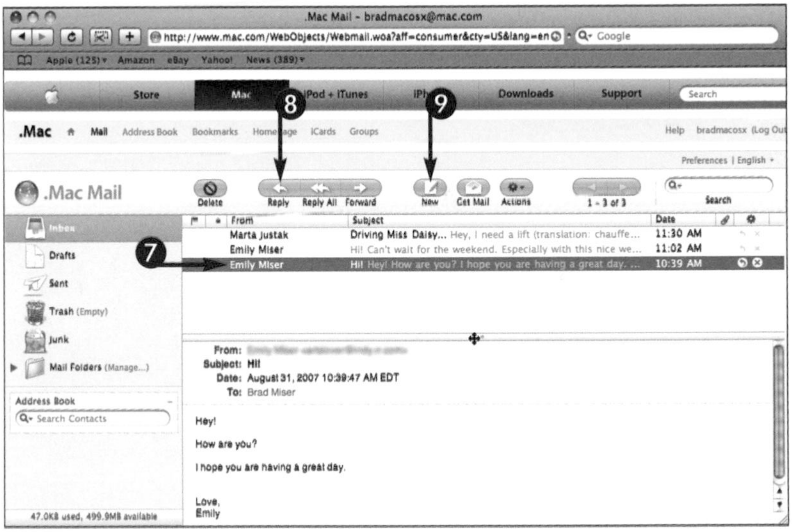

TIPS

How do I access my .Mac e-mail in Mail?

Mail is designed to work with .Mac e-mail accounts. When you configure MacBook to access .Mac services, your .Mac e-mail account is available immediately and can be set up with just a couple of clicks. See Chapter 9 for more information.

Do I have to use Mail or the .Mac Web site to access my .Mac e-mail?

No, you can access .Mac e-mail as you can any other e-mail account. When you sign up for .Mac, information for the servers you need to configure to access .Mac e-mail appears. You can use this information to set up your .Mac e-mail in any e-mail application, such as Entourage on the Mac or Eudora on Windows.

You can use HomePage to create and publish your own Web sites. HomePage is nice because it does most of the work for you. You can build a site by using the page templates HomePage provides and organizing them the way you want. You can also include many individual sites. Each site can have its own group of pages on it.

Publish a .Mac Web Site

ACCESS HOMEPAGE AND PUBLISH A PAGE

1. If you aren't already logged in to your .Mac page, log in.

2. Click the **HomePage** link.

   The HomePage page appears.

3. Scroll down the page until you see all the themes available to you.

4. Click the tab for the kind of page you want to create.

   For example, you can click **File Sharing** to create a Web page you can use to share files.

5. Click the theme you want to use for the page you are creating.

The Edit page for the theme you select appears.

6 Complete the fields on the page.

7 If you add files to the page use the file tools to select the files you want to publish.

8 Click **Preview**.

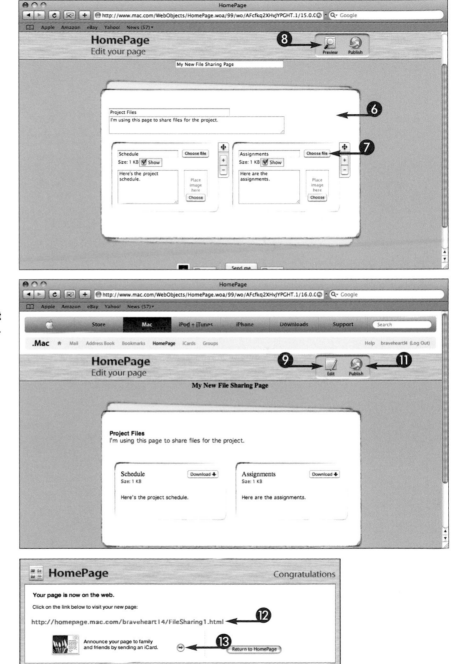

The Web page appears as it will when you publish it.

9 If you want to make changes, click **Edit** and use the Edit page to manage them.

10 Continue previewing and editing the page.

11 Click **Publish** when you are ready to publish the page to the Web.

.Mac creates your page and publishes it, and a notification appears that your page is on the Web.

12 To visit the site, click the URL.

13 To send an iCard announcing the site and providing its URL, click the **Announce** button.

After you build your Web sites, you can publish them by clicking one button. HomePage even helps you send information about the Web sites to people whom you want to visit them.

Publish a .Mac Web Site *(continued)*

CREATE WEB SITES

1 Return to the HomePage page by logging into .Mac (if needed) and clicking the **HomePage** link.

2 Click **Add Site**.

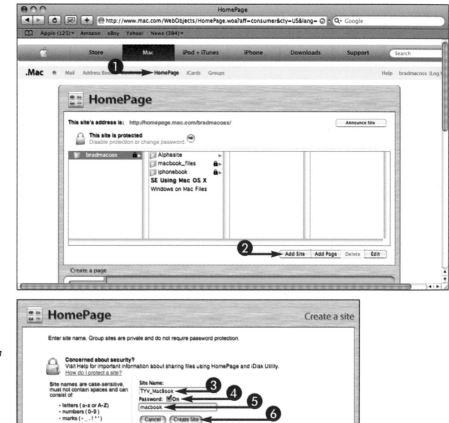

3 Type a name for the site you are creating.

Note: *Pay attention to the naming limitations or you cannot create the site; for example, you cannot include a space in the name.*

4 To require visitors to type a password before they can view it, select the **On** check box.

5 Type the password.

6 Click **Create Site**.

The HomePage pane reappears, and the structure of your Web site is shown in the table.

BUILD AND PUBLISH WEB PAGES

1 Move to the **HomePage** page.

2 Select the site to which you want to add pages.

3 Click **Add Page**.

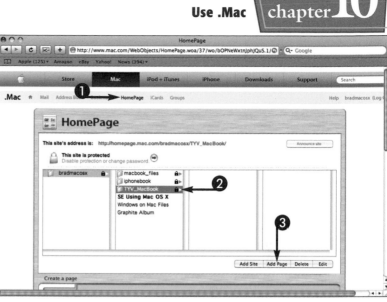

4 Select a theme for the page.

The Edit page for the theme you select appears.

TIPS

Should I use HomePage or iWeb?
iWeb is a Web page creation application that is included as part of the iLife suite. Because iLife is included on MacBooks by default, iWeb is installed on your computer. You can use it instead of HomePage or you can use both of them to build different parts of the site. iWeb is more flexible, but takes a bit more work to use.

Can I publish Web sites built with different Web-publishing applications on .Mac?
Yes. Build the site with the application you want to use. Then drag all the files for the site into the Sites folder on your iDisk. Make sure the index files are included. When you move to your Web site address, you see the Web site you created.

209

Synchronize Bookmarks, Contacts, and Calendars among Multiple Macs

If you have more than one Mac, you can use .Mac to keep a variety of information in sync on each Mac. For example, you can make sure you have the same set of contacts in Address Book on each computer or to ensure all your favorite bookmarks are available when you need them

To get started, you need to configure each computer to be part of the sync process. Then MacBook ensures it is synced automatically or you can perform syncs manually.

① Open the .Mac pane of the System Preferences application and click the **Sync** tab.

② Select the **Synchronize with .Mac** check box.

③ In the pop-up menu that appears, choose how you want syncs to occur.

You can choose **Manually** to sync manually; choose a time, such as **Every Hour**, to sync at those times; or **Automatically** to have syncs performed automatically.

④ Select the check box next to each item you want to include in the sync.

⑤ Click **Sync Now**.

The information you select is copied onto .Mac.

If some of the information already exists, an alert appears.

⑥ On the pop-up menu, choose how you want data to be synced.

You can choose **Merge all data** if you want the data on .Mac to be merged with the information on MacBook.

⑦ Click **Sync**.

The sync process begins.

As changes are made to data, you are prompted about what is going to be done.

⑧ Click the **Sync** button to allow the sync to continue.

This example shows the **Sync Contacts** button.

⑨ Repeat step **8** at each prompt.

The time and date of the last sync appear at the bottom of the Sync tab when the process is complete.

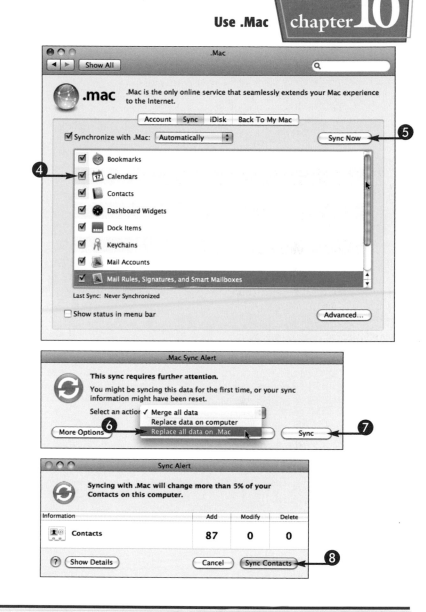

TIPS

Where is synced information stored and can I access it from the Web?

All the information you sync via .Mac is stored on your iDisk. You can access it from the Web by clicking the appropriate links on the .Mac Web page. For example, to access your contact information, click the **Address Book** link.

Can I include documents in syncs?

No. .Mac syncing only works with specific information. However, if you save documents onto your iDisk and set that to Sync Automatically, any documents you save are available on each machine that's configured to access your .Mac account.

CHAPTER 11

Listen to Music and Watch Video with iTunes

Explore iTunes

iTunes enables you to organize and enjoy lots of content right on MacBook or on an iPod or iPhone. With its integration to the iTunes Store, it is also easy to add great stuff to your iTunes Library whenever you want.

Although it is incredibly powerful, iTunes is also designed so that it is easy to use. In fact, the application is so well designed, a number of its interface elements have been used in other applications and even for Mac OS X's Finder application.

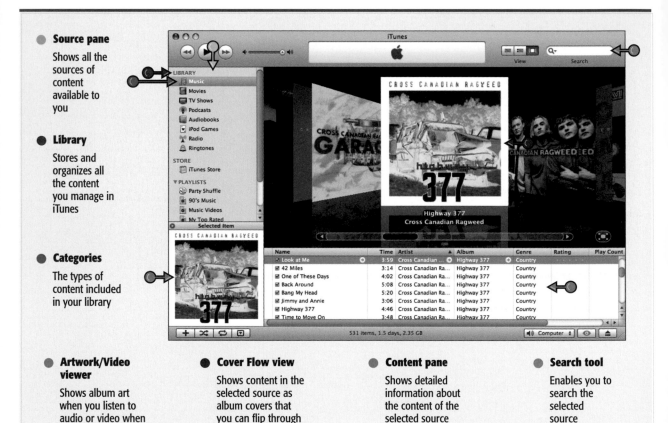

Source pane
Shows all the sources of content available to you

Library
Stores and organizes all the content you manage in iTunes

Categories
The types of content included in your library

Artwork/Video viewer
Shows album art when you listen to audio or video when you play video content

Cover Flow view
Shows content in the selected source as album covers that you can flip through

Content pane
Shows detailed information about the content of the selected source

Search tool
Enables you to search the selected source

● **List view**

Presents content in the selected source in a list

● **Browser**

Enables you to browse the selected source quickly and easily

● **Playback controls**

Use these to control audio and video content

● **Information window**

Displays information about what you are doing

● **View buttons**

Use these to change views

● **Album view**

Shows content in the selected source organized by group

● **Eject**

Click to eject something, such as an iPod or audio CD

● **Show/Hide Browser**

Shows or hides the Browser

● **Show/Hide Artwork/Video Viewer**

Opens or closes the Artwork/ Video Viewer window

● **Repeat**

Causes content in the selected source to repeat

● **Shuffle**

When active, iTunes randomly chooses content in the selected source to play

● **Create playlist**

Creates playlists and smart playlists

Understand the iTunes Library

Before you can enjoy content in iTunes, it has to be available there. The iTunes Library is where you store all of the content, including music, podcasts, movies, and TV shows. Once content is stored in your iTunes Library, you can use iTunes tools to keep that content organized so it is easily accessible to you.

Categories

The content in your Library is organized automatically by categories, including Music, Movies, TV Shows, Podcasts, and so on. Within the Library source, you see an icon for each category. When you select a category, the content it includes is shown in the right part of the iTunes window where you browse and search it. When you find the content you want, you can listen to it, view it, create playlists, or burn it to disc.

Devices

iTunes considers sources of content stored outside of its database it works with as devices. Devices include audio CDs that you can play within iTunes or move into your iTunes Library (called importing content). If you use an iPod or iPhone with iTunes, they also appear in the Devices section when connected to MacBook. Like other sources, you select a device to work with it. For example, to listen to a CD, you select its icon and the songs it contains appear in the right part of the window.

Tracks

Although it is easy to think of tracks as the songs on a CD, iTunes considers everything that you listen to or watch to be a track. So, each episode in a season of a TV series you download from the iTunes Store is a track, as is an audiobook. Tracks are what you see in each row in the Content pane.

Tags

Lots of information is associated with the content in the iTunes Library. This includes artist, track name, track #, album, genre, and rating. Each of these data elements is called a tag. Each tag can be shown in a column in the Content pane, and you can view all of them in the Info window. Tags are important because they are how you identify and organize content. Fortunately, iTunes automatically tags most of the content you will work with, but you can add tags yourself if you need to.

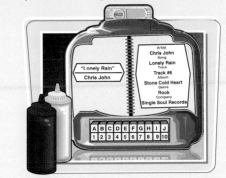

Playlists

One of the best things about iTunes is that you can create custom collections of content you want to listen to or watch. These collections are called playlists. Playlists can include any combination of content organized in any way. There are two kinds of playlists. You manually place content into a playlist, and when you create a smart playlist, you define criteria for content and iTunes automatically places the appropriate content into it. After you have created a playlist, you can listen to it and burn it to disc.

The iTunes Way

Although iTunes enables you to work with lots of different kinds of content (music, audiobooks, movies, and music videos), it uses a consistent process to work with that content. First, select the source of the content you want to work with; this can be a Library category, device, or playlist. Second, browse or search for content you want within the selected source if it is not ready for you immediately. Third, select the specific track you want to use. Fourth, use iTunes controls to play the content. This process is consistent no matter what kind of content you want to use, so once you get the hang of it, you can quickly get to any content you want.

Before you can enjoy audio or video content, you need to select that content. There are two fundamental ways to find content: by browsing or by searching.

Browsing is a good way to find something when you are not quite sure what you want to listen to or watch. Searching is useful when you know exactly what you want, but are not quite sure where it is.

Browse or Search for iTunes Content

BROWSE FOR ITUNES CONTENT

Note: The iTunes window has several views; this section assumes you are using List view.

① Select the source of content you want to browse.

Note: If the Browser does not appear, choose View, Show Browser.

② Browse the list of genres in the **Genre** column.

③ Select the genre you want to browse.

④ Browse the artist list, which shows only those artists with music in the selected genre.

⑤ Select the artist whose music you want to browse.

● All the albums by that artist in the Library are shown in the Album column.

⑥ Select the album you want to browse.

The tracks on that album appear in the Content pane.

⑦ Select the track you want to hear.

⑧ Use the playback controls to play the track.

SEARCH FOR ITUNES CONTENT

① Select the source of content you want to search.

② Type the text or numbers for which you want to search in the Search tool.

● As you type, only content that meets your search appears in the Content pane.

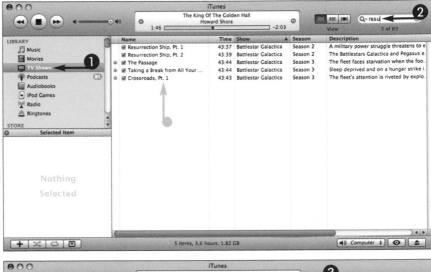

③ Continue typing until the content for which you are searching appears in the Content pane.

④ Select the content you want.

⑤ Use the playback controls to play the content.

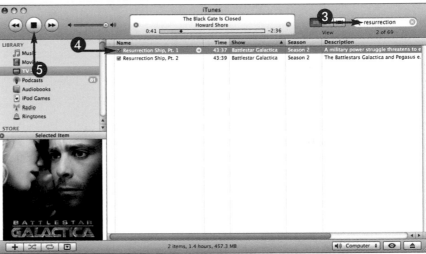

TIPS

I do not see the Genre column in the Browser. Where did it go?

You can use the Browser with or without the Genre column. If it is not shown, choose **iTunes**, **Preferences**. Click the **General** tab. Check the **Show genre when browsing** check box. Click **OK**.

Why does the Browser disappear when I select some sources?

The Browser is not all that useful for some sources, such as an Audio CD, because you can usually see all of the content on the source in the Content pane. When you select such a source, the Browser is hidden. You can show it again by clicking the Show Browser button at the bottom of the iTunes window.

Browse the Library with Cover Flow View

List view is very functional and efficient, but it is not all that pretty and it is not that exciting to browse. Cover Flow view makes browsing for music like flipping through a stack of CDs (only easier). You view content by its cover art, and you can flip through the content available to you until you see something that strikes your fancy.

Browse the Library with Cover Flow View

① Select the source you want to browse.

② Click the **Cover Flow view** button (▥).

③ To change the size of the Browser, drag the resize handle up or down.

④ To move through the content quickly, drag the scroll bar to the left or right.

  As you drag, the covers flip quickly.

● The content in the centermost collection appears on the content list, where you can listen to or watch it.

⑤ To browse in full-screen mode, click the **Full Screen** button.

The Cover Flow browser fills the desktop.

⑥ Browse the content by using the scroll bar or clicking to the left or right of the artwork facing you.

⑦ Control the content with the playback controls.

⑧ To return to the iTunes window, click the **Return** button.

Browse the Library with Group View

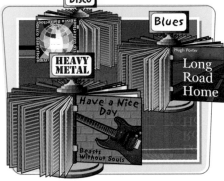

Group view is sort of a combination of the List and Cover Flow views. You can see the Browser and lists as in List view, but the content is organized by collection and you see associated artwork as in Cover Flow view.

Browse the Library with Group View

1 Select the source you want to browse.

2 Click the **Group view** button (⊞).

3 Open the Browser if it is not open already.

The Browser appears at the top of the window.

4 Click the tag by which you want the content to be grouped.

For example, to group it by album, click the **Album** column, or to group it by artist, click the **Artist** column.

The content is rearranged so that it is grouped by the tag you selected.

5 Use the Browser to find the content in which you are interested.

If you have used any device to listen to audio content, you should be able to quickly figure out how to listen to audio content in iTunes. Of course, whereas most audio players give you just basic controls, iTunes really lets you fine-tune the audio experience so you can choose exactly how you want to listen to audio content.

Listen to Audio Content

① Browse or search for the audio content you want to hear.

② Select the first track you want to hear.

③ Click the **Play** button, double-click the track, or press the Spacebar.

The audio content begins to play.

● In the Information window, you see information about it, such as the track name, artist, and a timeline.

● The track currently playing is highlighted and marked with a blue speaker icon (🔊).

④ Click the **Pause** button (⏸ changes to ▶) or press the Spacebar to pause the audio.

⑤ Click the **Previous** button (⏮) to jump back to the previous track.

⑥ Click the **Next** button (⏭) to jump to the next track.

iTunes works as well for video content as it does for audio content. You can watch movies, TV shows, music videos, and video podcasts within the iTunes window or in full-screen mode.

Watch Video Content

1 Browse or search for the video content you want to watch.

2 Select the first video track you want to see.

3 Click the **Play** button (▶) or press the Spacebar.

● The content fills the iTunes window and begins to play.

4 Position the mouse pointer over the video image.

● The video controls appear. You can watch the video in the iTunes window or you can expand it to full screen.

Add Audio CDs to the iTunes Library

You can add many different types of content to the iTunes Library that you have obtained from a number of different sources.

One of the most useful ways to add content to iTunes is to import music from audio CDs you have. Once imported, this music becomes part of your iTunes Library and you can listen to it, add it to playlists, put it on custom CDs you burn, and so on.

Add Audio CDs to the iTunes Library

PREPARE ITUNES TO IMPORT AUDIO CDS

1 Choose **iTunes**, **Preferences**.

The Preferences dialog box appears.

2 Click the **Advanced** tab.

3 Click the **Importing** subtab.

4 From the On CD Insert pop-up menu, choose **Import CD and Eject**.

5 On the Import Using pop-up menu, choose **AAC Encoder**.

6 On the Setting pop-up menu, choose **Higher Quality**.

7 Check the **Automatically retrieve CD track names from Internet** check box.

8 Check the **Create file names with track number** check box.

9 Click **OK**.

iTunes saves your importing preferences.

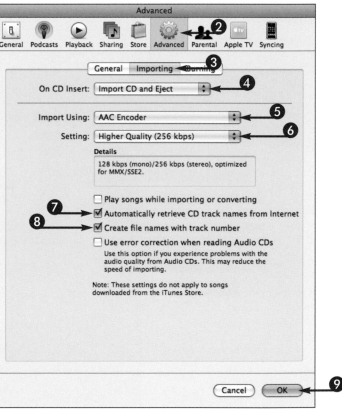

IMPORT AUDIO CDS TO THE ITUNES LIBRARY

1 Insert a CD into the computer.

● iTunes connects to the Internet and identifies the CD you inserted.

The import process starts.

● The song currently being imported is marked with an orange circle (🔄).

● You see information about the import process in the Information window.

● As songs are imported, they are marked with a green circle (✅).

When all the tracks on the disc have been imported, iTunes ejects the disc.

The tracks are now part of the iTunes Library.

How does iTunes recognize an audio CD?

When you insert an audio CD, iTunes connects to the Internet and looks up the CD in online CD databases. When it finds the CD, iTunes adds tags for the album name, artist, and track titles. iTunes remembers CDs so that the next time you insert them, the information iTunes looked up is there automatically. For this to work, MacBook has to be able to connect to the Internet. If it cannot, new CDs show up as unknown with track titles such as Track 1 and Track 2.

iTunes supports many different types of formats when importing music. Should I use something other than AAC?

Although iTunes does support a number of audio formats, AAC (Advanced Audio Coding) is the best option for most people because AAC files provide good sound quality in relatively small file sizes. That is a good thing because you can store more content in your iTunes Library. If you demand the absolute highest audio quality, you can use the Apple Lossless format, which produces significantly larger files with slightly better sound quality. If you have a portable player other than an iPod, you might want to use the MP3 (Motion Picture Expert Group, Audio Layer 3) format, which is supported by all devices.

Explore the iTunes Store

Adding audio CDs to the iTunes Library is easy. Using this process, it is also easy to build your iTunes Library using audio CDs you have on hand. But there is another way.

Apple's iTunes Store provides hundreds of thousands of audio CDs, movies, TV shows, audiobooks, podcasts, and other content that you browse, preview, and then purchase. As soon as you buy content from the iTunes Store, it is downloaded to your iTunes Library and is immediately ready for you to use, including all the important tags. Because access to the iTunes Store is built into iTunes, shopping for audio and video could not be easier.

● **iTunes Store homepage**

Links take you directly to specific content as well as to categories

● **Albums**

Album covers and titles are links to those albums

● **Categories**

Click these links to see the homepages for categories of content

● **Top lists**

There are many kinds of lists in the iTunes Store, such as Top Movies, and Top Albums

● **New Releases**

This area shows content that is new to the Store

● **Page buttons and arrows**

Use the page buttons and arrows to move among pages of content in a specific section

● **Content page**

Displays information about a specific item

● **Buy button**

You can buy an item by clicking its Buy button

● **Related links**

Various links take you to related information

● **Tracks**

The contents of the current item are shown in the bottom of the window

● **Buy buttons**

You can use a track's Buy button to buy only that track

● **Artist links**

Click these to visit the artist's homepage

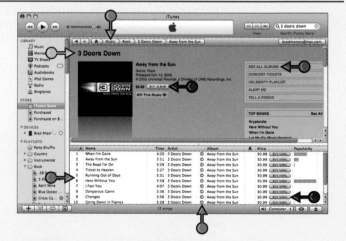

● **Path**

Shows your current location in the Store

Obtain and Log Into an iTunes Store Account

chapter 11

Got iTunes Account?

To be able to purchase content from the iTunes Store, you need to have an iTunes account and be logged into it (you can browse, search, and preview content without being logged into an account).

Like other aspects of the Store, you can get an account from within iTunes.

Obtain and Log Into an iTunes Store Account

iTunes
View
Search iTunes Store
Sign In
LIBRARY
Music
Movies
TV Shows
Podcasts
Audiobooks
iPod Games
Radio
Ringtones
STORE
iTunes Store
Purchased
Purchased on Brad Miser's iP...
DEVICES
Brad Miser's iPhone
PLAYLISTS
Party Shuffle
Country
Instrumental
Rock
.38 Special
3 Doors Down
April Wine
Blue Oyster Cult
Cross Canadian Ragweed
Scrubs New Season
Mothership + The Complete Led Zeppelin
LED ZEPPELIN
Win Tickets
NO PURCHASE NECESSARY. Ends 11/12/07. Rules.
COUNTRY MUSIC'S
CMA
iTunes STORE
Music
Movies
TV Shows
Music Videos
Audiobooks
Podcasts
iPod Games
iTunes Latino
iTunes U NEW
NEW RELEASES
See All
Music
Movies
TV Shows
Rock
Pop
I-Empire
Angels & Airwaves
A Place to Land
Little Big Town
Headlines (Friendsh...
Spice Girls
Ricky Martin... Live ...
Ricky Martin
B.A.R.S. - The Barry ...
Cassidy
To All New Arrivals (...
Faithless
Serve2 (Fighting Hu...
Various Artists
From Where You Are...
Lifehouse
TOP MOVIES
Ratatouille
Kids & Family
Oh, the Places You'll Go!
Just Added
FREE
CHERI DENNIS
Computer

1. Click **iTunes Store** on the Source list.

   iTunes connects to the iTunes Store and you see the Home page.

2. Click Sign In.

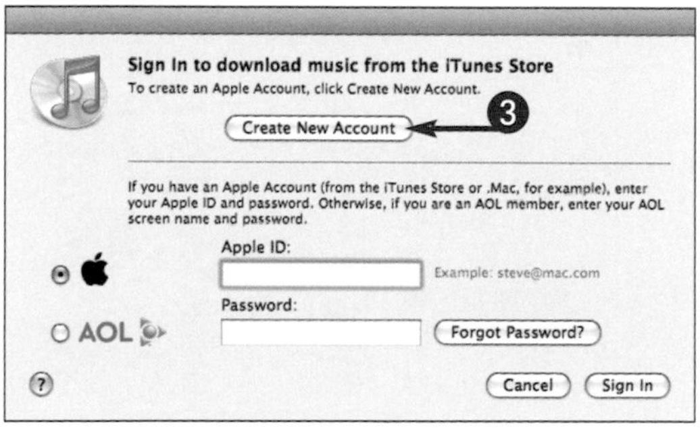

Sign In to download music from the iTunes Store
To create an Apple Account, click Create New Account.
Create New Account
If you have an Apple Account (from the iTunes Store or .Mac, for example), enter your Apple ID and password. Otherwise, if you are an AOL member, enter your AOL screen name and password.
Apple ID:
Example: steve@mac.com
Password:
AOL
Forgot Password?
Cancel
Sign In

   The Sign In dialog box appears.

3. Click **Create New Account**.

   The Welcome to iTunes Store screen appears.

4. Follow the on-screen instructions to create your account.

   When you are done, you will have an Apple ID and password. This enables you to log into your account on the iTunes Store.

Buy Music, TV, Movies, and More from the iTunes Store

The iTunes Store has lots of great content that you can easily preview, purchase, and download to MacBook, where it is added to your iTunes Library automatically. When you are interested in content, you can preview 30 seconds of it to decide if you want it or not.

Buy Music, TV, Movies, and More from the iTunes Store

CONFIGURE YOUR SHOPPING PREFERENCE

1 Press ⌘+,.

The iTunes Preferences dialog box appears.

2 Click the **Store** tab.

3 Click the **Buy using a Shopping Cart** radio button.

4 Check the **Automatically download prepurchased content** check box if you intend to buy content before it is released and want them to be downloaded automatically.

5 Check the **Automatically create playlists when buying song collections**.

When you buy collections, playlists for those collections are created automatically.

6 If you have a slow Internet connection, check the **Load complete preview before playing** check box.

7 Click **OK**.

You are ready to shop.

BROWSE THE ITUNES STORE

1 Click the **iTunes Store** link on the Source list.

The iTunes Store home page fills the right part of the window.

2 Click the **Browse** link.

The Store Browser appears.

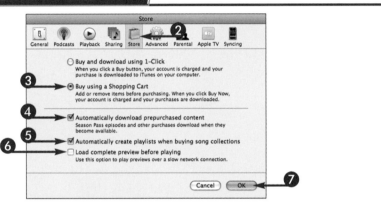

❸ Click a category.

❹ Select a genre.

❺ Select a subgenre.

❻ Select an artist.

❼ Select an album.

● The contents of the selected album appear in the bottom of the window.

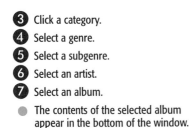

SEARCH THE ITUNES STORE

❶ Click the **iTunes Store** link on the Source list.

The iTunes Store home page fills the right part of the window.

❷ Type information for which you want to search.

As you type, iTunes attempts to match what you are typing.

❸ If a match is found, select it to perform the search.

❹ Press the **Return** key.

● The results of your search appear.

❺ Review the results of the search.

continued

There are two ways to shop in the iTunes Store. Using the 1-Click method, you can purchase content with a single click. Using the Shopping Cart method, you place content in a shopping cart; when you are ready to buy, you go to your shopping cart and check out of the store.

Buy Music, TV, Movies, and More from the iTunes Store *(continued)*

PREVIEW ITUNES STORE CONTENT

1 Select the item you want to preview.

2 Click the **Play** button (▶) or press the Spacebar.

A 30-second preview plays.

BUY AND DOWNLOAD CONTENT FROM THE ITUNES STORE

1 Preview the content you want.

Note: If you see Buy buttons instead of Add buttons, you are using the 1-Click method; as soon as you click a Buy button, you immediately buy and download that content.

2 Click **Add Album** to add the album to your shopping cart.

3 Click **Add Song** to add an individual song.

4 Click **Shopping Cart** on the Source list.

● Your Shopping Cart appears in the right part of the window and you see the content you have placed there.

5 To buy individual tracks, click their Buy buttons.

6 To buy all of the content in the shopping cart, click the **Buy Now** button.

The Sign In dialog box appears.

7 Enter your Apple ID or AOL password and click **Buy**.

The content you selected is purchased and downloaded to your iTunes Library.

8 Click **Purchased** on the iTunes Source list.

● Content you have downloaded from the iTunes Store is shown ready to use.

TIPS

What are the restrictions on content I purchase from the iTunes Store?

iTunes Plus content is not restricted by any limitations, so you can have and use it on as many computers as you want, and burn it to as many discs as you want. Other iTunes Store content is digitally protected, which still is not very limiting. For this kind of content, you can use it from up to five computers at the same time, and you can burn unique playlists to disc up to seven times.

iTunes Plus
No Restrictions

iTunes
No more than 5
computers at once.
Burn to disc no more
than 7 times.

How do I authorize a computer to play protected content?

When you attempt to play content for which a computer is not authorized, you see the Authorization dialog box. This is similar to the iTunes Store Sign In dialog box except that the Apple ID shown is the one under which the content was purchased. Enter the password for that account and click **Authorize**. You see how many computers are currently authorized to play that content and you can play it (the computer on which you purchased the content is authorized automatically)

Subscribe to Podcasts

Podcasts are episodic audio or video programs that you can listen to or watch. Many podcasts are like radio shows, and in fact, many *are* radio shows. Most radio shows offer podcast versions that you can download to MacBook and copy to an iPod. Podcasts go way beyond just radio shows, however. You can find podcasts on many different topics.

You can subscribe to many different podcasts in the iTunes Store. Once you have subscribed, episodes are downloaded for you automatically so that they are available for you to listen to or watch, which you do in the same way as other content in the Library.

Subscribe to Podcasts

① Click **iTunes Store**.

The iTunes Store fills the Content pane.

② Click **Podcasts**.

The Podcasts home page appears.

③ Click the **Browse** link.

The Browser opens.

④ Click a category.

⑤ Click a subcategory.

⑥ Select a podcast.

⑦ Click the **Play** button, or just double-click the podcast (▶ changes to ■).

The podcast plays.

Note: Because most podcasts are free, the entire episode plays instead of just a preview.

⑧ When you find a podcast that you want to listen to regularly, click its **Subscribe** button.

⑨ Click **Subscribe** in the confirmation prompt.

⑩ Continue to subscribe to other podcasts until you have subscribed to all those of interest to you.

LISTEN TO PODCASTS

1 Click the **Podcasts** source in the Source list.

● You see all the podcasts to which you have subscribed.

2 Select and play an episode of a podcast just like other content.

Note: Podcasts you have not listened to are marked with a blue dot (●).

3 If an episode you want to listen to has not been downloaded yet, click its **Get** button.

4 Click **Get All** to get all the episodes in a podcast.

CONFIGURE PODCAST SETTINGS

1 Click the **Podcasts** source in the Source list.

2 Click **Settings**.

The Podcasts tab of the iTunes Preferences dialog box appears.

3 On the **Check for new episodes** pop-up menu, choose how often iTunes looks for new episodes.

4 On the **When new episodes are available** pop-up menu, choose what you want iTunes to do.

5 On the **Keep** pop-up menu, choose how you want iTunes to manage your podcasts.

6 Click **OK**.

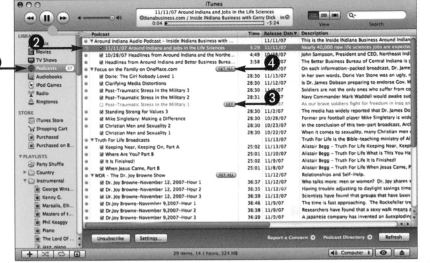
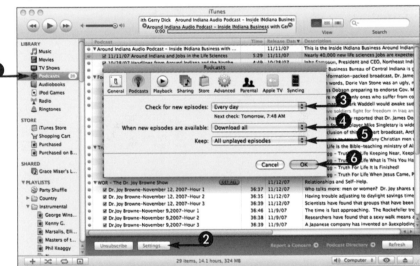

 TIPS

What if a podcast I want to subscribe to is not available in the iTunes Store?

For various reasons, some podcasts are not available in the iTunes Store. Some Web sites provide a URL to a podcast subscription; copy this, choose **Advanced**, **Subscribe to Podcast**, paste the URL in the dialog box, and click **OK**. Others provide podcasts as MP3 files that you download and add to the iTunes Library; you work with these just like tracks from a CD instead of a podcast.

A radio show I listen to has a podcast application; what does it do?

When shows offer podcasts as MP3 files for which you have to pay a fee to access, they often provide an application that downloads the files automatically. After you install and configure such an application, the show's MP3 files are downloaded to the location you specify. Add them to the iTunes Library by dragging them there or by choosing **File**, then **Add to Library**.

Create a Standard Playlist

Playlists enable you to create your own custom content collections (music, video, and so on) that you can then play, burn to disc, move to an iPod or iPhone, and so on. You can create as many playlists as you want, and playlists are completely customizable; you can include as many tracks as you want in the order you want them. You can even include the same track in a playlist multiple times for those tracks you have just got to hear over and over again.

A standard playlist is one in which you manually place and organize songs. Smart playlists are discussed in the next section.

Create a Standard Playlist

1 Click the **Create Playlist** button (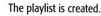).

A new playlist is created.

2 Name the new playlist and press Return.

The playlist is created.

3 Select the playlist on the Source list.

● The content pane is empty because you have not added any songs to the playlist yet.

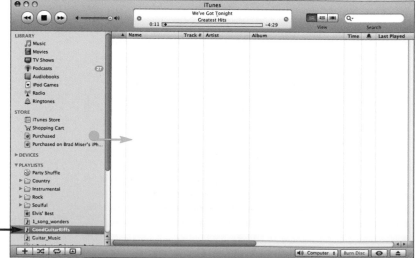

④ Select the category of content you want to add.

⑤ Browse or search for content you want to add to the playlist.

⑥ Drag tracks from the Content pane onto the playlist you created.

Note: When you double-click a playlist, it opens in a separate window.

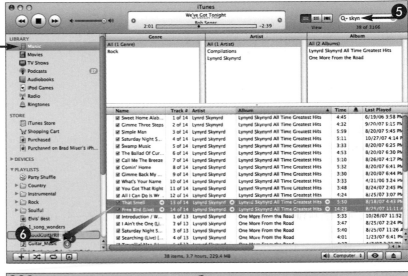

⑦ Select the playlist.

Its contents appear in the Content pane.

⑧ Drag tracks up and down the playlist until they are in the order in which you want them to play.

The playlist is complete.

TIPS

Can I sort the contents of a playlist?

You can sort a playlist that you create by clicking the column heading by which you want to sort the playlist just like any other source. However, when you sort a playlist you have organized manually so the tracks play in a specific order, that order is lost. You have to manually place the tracks back in the order you want if sorting by one of the column headings does not create the order you want.

How can I create a playlist for an album I just downloaded from the iTunes Store?

Select all the tracks on the album. Choose **File**, **New Playlist from Selection**. A new playlist containing all the tracks you selected is created. If they are all from the same album, the name of the playlist is the name of the album.

Create a Smart Playlist

Standard playlists are great because you can easily create custom content collections, but you need to do some work to create and fill them. Why not let iTunes do the work for you? That is where a smart playlist comes in.

Instead of placing content into a playlist manually, you define the criteria for content and iTunes grabs the appropriate content from the Library and places it into the smart playlist for you automatically.

Create a Smart Playlist

1. Select **File** in iTunes' menu, then **New Smart Playlist**.

   The Smart Playlist dialog box appears.

2. Select the first tag on which you want the smart playlist to be based in the Tag menu.

3. Select the operand you want to use on the Operand menu.

4. Type the condition you want to match in the Condition box.

5. To add another condition to the smart playlist, click the **Add Condition** button (⬍).

   A new, empty condition appears.

6. Select a second tag.

7. Select an operand.

8. Type a condition you want to match in the Condition box.

9. Select **all** on the pop-up menu at the top of the dialog box if all the conditions must be met for a track to be included in the smart playlist.

   Select **any** if only one of them must be met.

Smart Playlist

☑ Match the following rule:

| Genre | ⬍ | is | ⬍ | Rock | ⊖ ⊕ |

☐ Limit to [25] [items ⬍] selected by [random ⬍]
☐ Match only checked items
☑ Live updating

(Cancel) (OK)

Smart Playlist

☑ Match [all ⬍] if the following rules:

Genre	⬍	is	⬍	Rock	⊖ ⊕
Play Count	⬍	is greater than	⬍	10	⊖ ⊕
Year	⬍	is in the range	⬍	1965	to	2005	⊖ ⊕

☐ Limit to [25] [items ⬍] selected by [random ⬍]
☐ Match only checked items
☑ Live updating

(Cancel) (OK)

10 If you want to limit the playlist, check the **Limit to** check box.

11 Select the parameter by which you want to limit the playlist in the first menu.

12 Type the data appropriate for the limit you selected in the **Limit to** box.

13 Select how you want iTunes to choose the songs it includes based on the limit in the **selected by** menu.

14 To include only tracks whose check box in the Content pane is checked, check the **Match only checked items** check box.

15 If you want iTunes to update its contents over time, check the **Live updating** check box.

16 Click **OK**.

The smart playlist is added to the Source list and is ready for you to edit.

17 Type the playlist's name and press Return.

The playlist is complete.

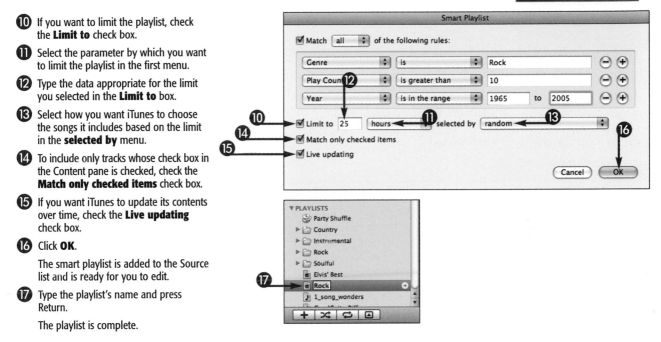

How do I change the contents of a smart playlist?

If a smart playlist has live updating enabled, the contents of the playlist change over time as new content is added, content is removed, or existing content changes so it meets the playlist's criteria. If you want to change the contents of a smart playlist, you have to change the criteria for the list. To do so, select it, press and hold the Ctrl key, and choose **Edit Smart Playlist**. Use the resulting Smart Playlist dialog box to make changes to the conditions, which will change the content.

Can I drag the contents of a smart playlist onto another playlist to move it there?

The smart playlist does not actually contain the content you see or even pointers to that content, so you cannot move tracks from a smart playlist to another playlist. Likewise, you cannot delete tracks from a smart playlist; you must change the list's criteria so the content no longer meets them or delete the content from the Library (only do this if you are sure you do not want it).

iTunes enables you to burn content from the iTunes Library onto CD or DVD. An Audio CD is the standard audio CD format that plays in any CD player. An MP3 CD stores MP3 versions of content on a CD; this enables you to get more content on one disc, but requires a player capable of playing MP3 tracks. A Data CD or DVD makes a copy of content on a CD or DVD in the data format; this format can be used only in a computer.

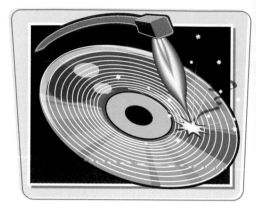

Burn a CD or DVD

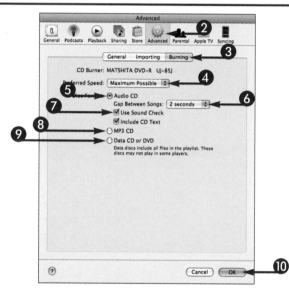

SELECT THE TYPE OF DISC TO BURN

① Press ⌘+,.

The iTunes Preferences dialog box opens.

② Click the **Advanced** tab.

③ Click the **Burning** subtab.

④ On the Preferred Speed pop-up menu, choose **Maximum Possible**.

Note: *If you experience errors when burning discs, reduce the preferred speed.*

⑤ To burn an Audio CD, click the **Audio CD** radio button.

⑥ On the **Gap Between Songs** pop-up menu, choose the amount of silence you want to be between the tracks on the disc.

⑦ To adjust each track's relative volume level, check the **Use Sound Check** check box.

⑧ To create an MP3 CD, click the **MP3 CD** radio button and skip to step **11**.

⑨ To create a Data CD or DVD, click the **Data CD or DVD** radio button.

Note: *If MacBook can burn only CDs, you only have the option to burn a data CD.*

⑩ Click **OK**.

The Preferences dialog box closes and your settings are saved.

CREATE A PLAYLIST FOR THE DISC

① With a playlist selected, check the Source Information.

If you want the content to fit onto one disc, the amount of content has to be equal to or less than the disc's capacity.

Note: *If you do not mind the content being placed on more than one disc, you can ignore this because iTunes automatically handles placing the content on multiple discs.*

BURN THE DISC

① Select the playlist that you want to burn to disc.

② Click **Burn Disc**.

③ Insert a blank CD (Audio CD, MP3 CD, or Data CD) or DVD (Data DVD).

MacBook checks the playlist.

④ If you are prompted that the content will not fit on one disc, click the Audio CDs button.

iTunes starts burning the disc.

Note: When the playlist requires multiple discs, MacBook ejects each disc as it is filled up; insert the next disc to continue the burn process.

When the process is complete, you see the disc in the **Devices** section of the Source list.

 TIPS

How can I back up my iTunes Library?

You should use Time Machine to back up MacBook (see Chapter 19). You should also back up your iTunes Library on discs so that you can protect the content you have stored there, especially content you have purchased from the iTunes Store (you can download this content only once). Choose **File**, then **Back Up to Disc** and follow the on-screen instructions to back up the Library. You can choose to back up only purchased content or the entire library.

When I try to burn an MP3 CD, I see a message stating that some of the content cannot be converted to MP3. Why not?

iTunes cannot convert some kinds of content to the MP3 format to be able to burn that content to an MP3 disc. The most notable of this is protected content you have purchased from the iTunes Store. If you attempt to burn a playlist containing this kind of content to an MP3 disc, the protected content is skipped and you see a warning message. You can either accept the content being left out of the disc or choose a different disc format.

Create Photo Books and Other Projects with iPhoto

What iTunes does for audio and video content, iPhoto does for images. Even better, you use iPhoto to work with photos you create, whereas in iTunes you most often use content other people create. As a photo manager, you can use iPhoto to build and organize your photo library and edit your photos to make improvements or apply interesting effects. You can also create slide shows, calendars, greeting cards, Web pages, and photo books. You can easily have photos and your projects printed professionally by Apple. You can also quickly and easily e-mail photos.

Explore iPhoto

iPhoto is a powerful and easy-to-use application that enables you to do lots of cool things. From storing and organizing photos to publishing your photos to the Web to creating professional quality photo books, iPhoto does it all for you.

If you read Chapter 11, you might think that iPhoto looks and works a lot like iTunes. If you think that, you're right. The two applications use similar interfaces and concepts, so once you learn how to use one of them, using the other comes quickly and easily.

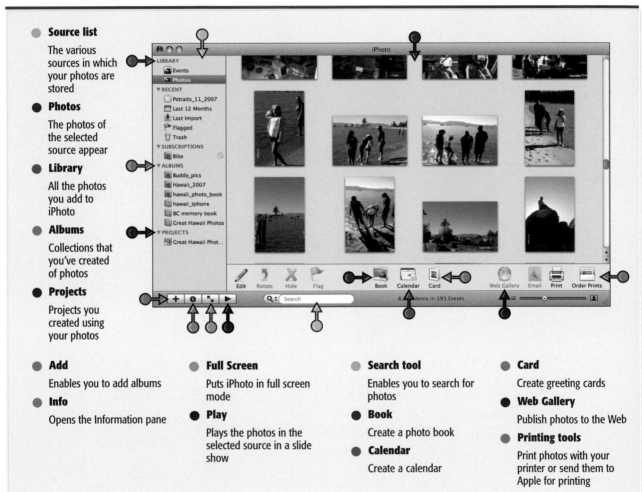

- **Source list**

  The various sources in which your photos are stored

- **Photos**

  The photos of the selected source appear

- **Library**

  All the photos you add to iPhoto

- **Albums**

  Collections that you've created of photos

- **Projects**

  Projects you created using your photos

- **Add**

  Enables you to add albums

- **Info**

  Opens the Information pane

- **Full Screen**

  Puts iPhoto in full screen mode

- **Play**

  Plays the photos in the selected source in a slide show

- **Search tool**

  Enables you to search for photos

- **Book**

  Create a photo book

- **Calendar**

  Create a calendar

- **Card**

  Create greeting cards

- **Web Gallery**

  Publish photos to the Web

- **Printing tools**

  Print photos with your printer or send them to Apple for printing

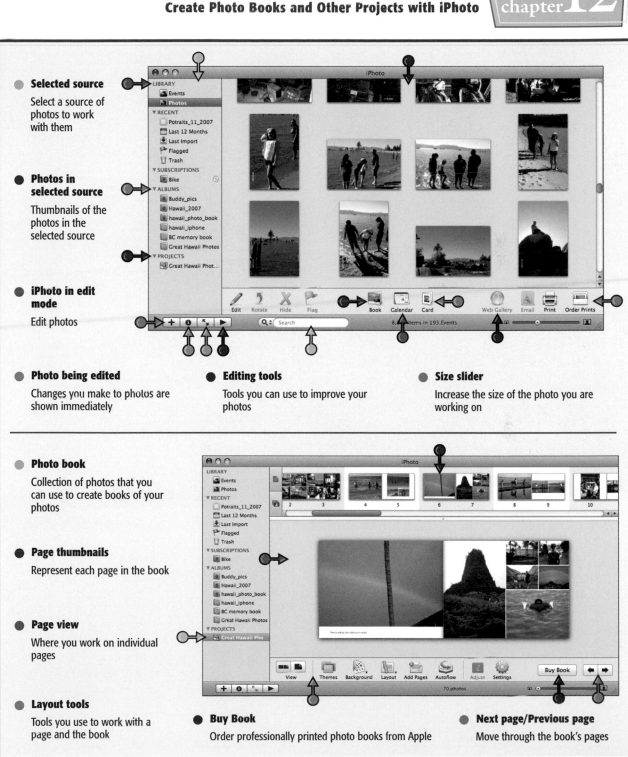

Selected source

Select a source of photos to work with them

Photos in selected source

Thumbnails of the photos in the selected source

iPhoto in edit mode

Edit photos

Photo being edited

Changes you make to photos are shown immediately

Editing tools

Tools you can use to improve your photos

Size slider

Increase the size of the photo you are working on

Photo book

Collection of photos that you can use to create books of your photos

Page thumbnails

Represent each page in the book

Page view

Where you work on individual pages

Layout tools

Tools you use to work with a page and the book

Buy Book

Order professionally printed photo books from Apple

Next page/Previous page

Move through the book's pages

Import Photos from a Digital Camera

Before you can create a photo book in iPhoto, you have to have photos with which to work. The most common way to add photos to your iPhoto Library is to import them from a digital camera. Once imported, the photos are added to your iPhoto Library at which point you can edit them, create photo books, and do all the other amazing things iPhoto empowers you to do.

1 Connect your digital camera to one of MacBook's USB ports.

2 Turn the camera on.

iPhoto launches and mounts the camera.

● The camera is selected as the import source in the Devices section of the iPhoto Source list.

3 Type a name in the **Event Name** field for the collection of photos you are importing.

4 Type a description of the photos in the **Description** field.

● To have iPhoto automatically create events based on the dates of the photos, select the **Autosplit events after importing** check box.

● If you have already imported some of the photos on the camera, select the **Hide photos already imported** check box.

5 Click **Import All**.

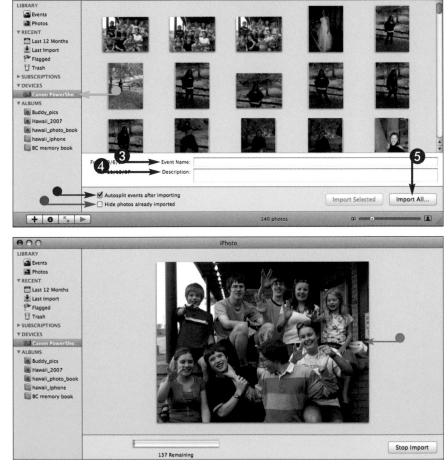

● As each photo is imported, you see a preview in the iPhoto window.

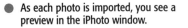

6 When the import is complete, click **Delete Originals** to delete the photos from the camera, or click **Keep Originals**.

The import process completes.

Delete Originals

140 photos were successfully imported. Would you like to delete their originals on the camera?

6 → Delete Originals   Keep Originals

● The Last Import source is selected automatically and you see the photos you imported.

7 Disconnect the camera.

8 Select the title of an event.

The event name becomes editable.

9 Type the event name.

10 Press Return.

The event name you typed is saved.

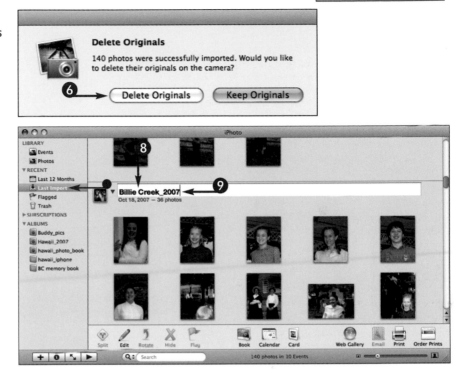

Billie Creek_2007
Oct 18, 2007 — 36 photos

TIPS

How do I import photos taken on an iPhone?

When you connect an iPhone on which you captured photos to MacBook, it opens in iPhoto just like a digital camera does. The same steps you followed to import photos from the camera are used to import photos from the iPhone.

How can I import photos from other sources?

Choose **File**, then **Import to Library**. Use the resulting dialog box to move to and select the images you want to import. Then click **Import**. The image files are imported into the iPhoto Library where they can be used just like photos you import from a camera.

Browse and Search the iPhoto Library

One of the first steps for most of the projects you do in iPhoto is to find and select the photos with which you want to work. There are a couple of ways to do this. You can browse for photos and you can search for photos by various information associated with those photos. After you find some photos, select them to work with them.

Finding photos through either method is easier when photos are properly labeled, which you learn about in the next section.

Browse and Search the iPhoto Library

BROWSE FOR PHOTOS

1 With iPhoto open, browse photos by clicking **Events** in the Source list.

2 To browse photos individually, click **Photos**.

3 To browse by one of the recent collections, select a collection.

● You can click **Last Import** to browse the photos from your most recent import.

4 Click and drag the Display Size slider to make the thumbnails larger or smaller.

5 Click and drag the vertical scroll bar down to see the more recent photos

● As you drag, the month and year of the photos currently shown in the window appears.

SEARCH FOR PHOTOS

1 Click the source you want to search.

The photos in the selected source appear.

2 On the pop-up menu in the Search tool (🔍), choose the tag by which you want to search.

In this example, **Keyword** is selected.

The tool appropriate to the tag you select appears.

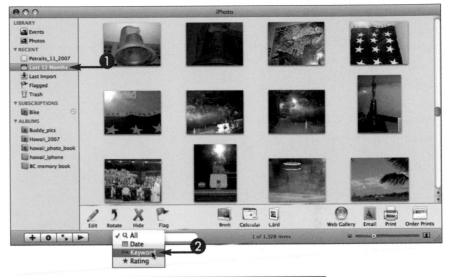

3 Select the values in the Search tool for which you want to search.

Note: *If you click* **All** *on the Search pop-up menu, type the text or numbers for which you want to search in the Search box.*

Only photos that meet your search criteria are shown.

What is an event?
iPhoto uses the concept of an event to group photos together. The application assumes that any photos captured within a specific amount of time (within one week, within one day, within the same 8-hour period, or within the same 2-hour period, depending on the preference set on the Events tab) are part of the same event. By default, iPhoto automatically organizes photos into events based on the timeframe selected. This is also called autosplitting.

How do I browse an event?
When you browse events, you see a thumbnail for each event, which can include multiple photos. When you point to an event, the number of photos it contains and the associated date are shown. Drag within an event's thumbnail to browse the other photos it contains. Double-click an event to browse all of its photos in the Event Browser window.

Label Photos

As you accumulate large numbers of photos in iPhoto, it is important to label those photos so that you can more easily find and identify photos.

There are two primary ways to label photos. You can associate combinations of keywords with images so that you can easily find images by searching for keywords. Another way to label photos is by typing a title, description, and rating.

CONFIGURE KEYWORDS

1 Click **Window**, and then click **Show Keywords**.

● The Keywords window, showing all the keywords currently available, appears.

2 Click **Edit Keywords**.

The Edit Keywords dialog box appears.

3 Click the **Add Keyword** button (+).

A new, untitled keyword appears.

4 Type the keyword you want to create.

5 Press the Tab key to navigate to the Shortcut column.

6 Press the key that you want to use for the shortcut.

By default, this is the first letter of the keyword.

7 Press Return.

8 Click **OK**.

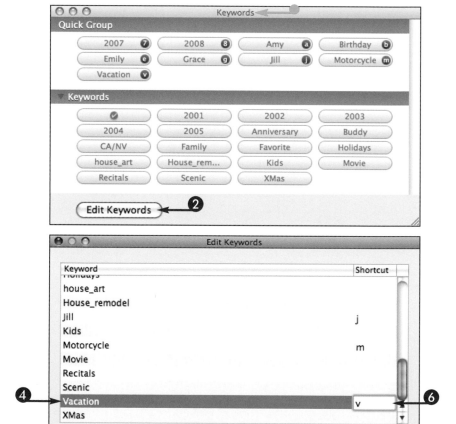

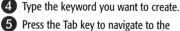

ASSOCIATE KEYWORDS WITH PHOTOS

① Browse or search for the photos with which you want to associate keywords.

② Select the photos with which you want to associate keywords.

③ Press ⌘+K to open the Keywords window.

Keywords to which shortcuts are assigned appear at the top of the window; remaining keywords appear on the bottom.

④ Click the first keyword that you want to associate with the selected photos.

The keyword becomes highlighted to show it is associated with the photos.

● The check mark keyword is a generic marker that you can use to temporarily mark photos for a specific project.

RATE AND DESCRIBE PHOTOS

① Select a photo.

② Click the Info button (ⓘ).

The Information pane appears.

③ Type a title for the photo by clicking on its default name.

④ Rate the photo by clicking the dot corresponding to the number of stars you want to give the photo.

⑤ Type notes about the photo in the description area.

TIPS

What labels does iPhoto assign to photos automatically?

iPhoto enters a title for each photo you import, which is the filename for the photo file; you can change this to be any text you want. It also adds the date and time on which the photo was captured; you should usually leave this information alone unless there was a problem with the camera's date function when you took a photo. iPhoto also captures information about the kind of image, its resolution, and file size.

Typing all this information takes a long time; do I really need to do it?

When it comes time to do a project, the value of making photos easier to find becomes apparent when you need them. At the least, associate keywords with photos you import because even a single keyword helps you find photos. Applying several keywords enables you to locate specific photos even more quickly. It's a good idea to label photos as soon as you import them. Unlabeled photos make creating projects harder than it needs to be.

Edit Photos

One of the great things about working with digital photos is that you can easily edit photos to make them better. Before you jump into a project, such as creating a photo book, take some time to edit the photos you are going to use to make them the best they can be. This makes the end project much better.

Using iPhoto's Edit tools, you can rotate, crop, straighten, enhance, remove red-eye, and retouch. You can also apply effects and adjust specific aspects of photos. Each of these tools has specific functions that you can use to make improvements in your photos. The more common editing tasks of rotating and cropping and removing red-eye are covered here.

Edit Photos

ROTATE AND CROP PHOTOS

1. Select the photos you want to edit.

   This example shows photos grouped as Events collections.

2. Click **Edit**.

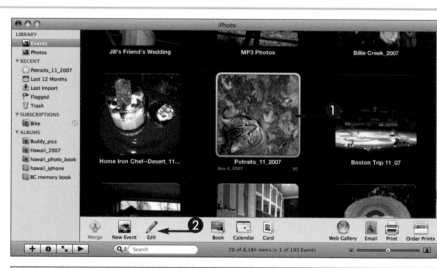

iPhoto switches to Edit mode.

- Thumbnails of each photo you selected appear at the top.

- The currently selected photo appears in the center part of the window.

- The Edit tools appear at the bottom.

3. To rotate the photo in the counterclockwise direction, click the **Rotate** button (🔄).

Note: *You can Option+click the Rotate button to rotate the photo clockwise.*

4. To crop the photo, click the **Crop** button (🔲).

   The Crop tools appear.

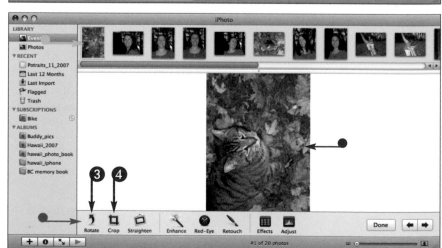

5 Select the Constrain check box.

6 From the pop-up menu choose the proportion you want to maintain.

7 Click and drag the edges of the selection box until just the part of the photo you want to keep is in the box.

8 Click **Apply**.

The photo is cropped and the Crop tools close.

9 Click **Done** to save your changes and return to the browsing window.

REMOVE RED-EYE

1 In the Edit view, click and drag the Size slider to the right to zoom in on the photo.

2 Use the Scroll bars to move the eyes to the center of the screen.

3 Click the **Red-Eye** button ().

The Red-Eye tool appears.

4 Click the eye from which you want to remove red.

● Red is replaced by black.

5 Repeat step **4** until all the red-eyes are fixed.

6 Click **Done** to save your changes and return to the browsing window.

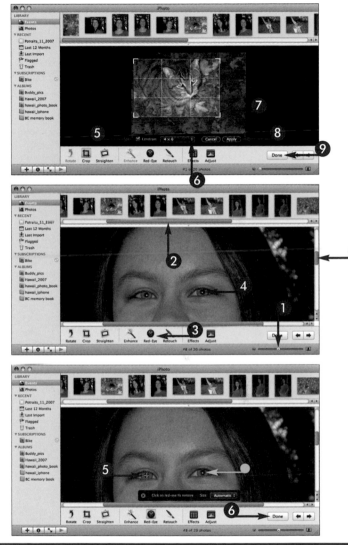

What do the other editing tools do?

The Straighten tool aligns the subject of a photo with a grid; this is typically used to improve a distorted photo. The Enhance tool improves the color balance and other characteristics of a photo. Retouch enables you to remove scratches and other imperfections. The Effects tool opens a palette of effects you can apply to photos. The Adjust tool opens a palette of tools that enable you to make very detailed changes, such as tint, sharpness, and so on.

Should I really edit photos before I collect them for a project?

In some cases, it makes sense to organize the photos you plan to use for a project before editing them, in which case you do the steps in the next section before you do those in this one. This way, you do not spend time editing photos you are not going to use anyway. And, sometimes the project in which you are going to use photos impacts how you edit them.

Organize a Photo Book's Photos in an Album

A required step in most projects, such as creating a photo book, is to collect the photos you plan to use in a photo album. You use the album to gather and organize the photos from which you create the project.

There are two kinds of photo albums. For a standard photo album, you manually place photos into the album. For a smart album, you define criteria for the photos to be included and iPhoto automatically finds the photos to match and places them in the album. The following steps show you how to create a standard photo album.

Organize a Photo Book's Photos in an Album

① Click **File**, and then **New Album**.

   The New Album sheet appears.

② Type a name for the album you are creating.

③ If you have already selected some photos to be included in the new album, select the **Use selected items in new album** check box.

④ Click **Create**.

   The album is created and is selected on the Source list.

⑤ Drag photos from the browse window onto the photo album you created.

⑥ Release the trackpad button when the album is highlighted.

   The photos are placed into the album.

⑦ Select the album on the Source list.

All the photos in the album appear in the Browse window.

⑧ Click and drag the photos around the album until they are in the order you want them.

Photos are ordered from left to right and top to bottom.

You can remove a photo from the album by selecting it and pressing Delete.

The deleted photo is removed from the album but remains in the Library so you can use it again later.

 TIPS

What happens when I edit a photo in an album?

When you add a photo to an album, you actually are just adding a pointer to that photo instead of making a copy of it. Any changes you make to a photo in an album, such as cropping or rotating, are made on the photo everywhere it appears, including the Library, other albums, and so on. So, be careful if you use the same photos in multiple projects because changing it in one location changes it in every location.

What if I want to have multiple versions of the same photo?

Select the photo, click **Photos** and then click **Duplicate**. A copy of the photo is made so that there are two versions of the same photo. The copies are independent so you can make different changes to each version and use them in different projects.

Create a Photo Book

Once you've created a photo album in iPhoto, you can create a photo book of it. You can choose from a variety of layouts, with each having a different printing price. After you create the book, you lay out each page.

 Select an album.

Click the Book button.

The Book sheet appears.

 Click the **Book Type** pop-up menu.

Choose the type of book you want to create.

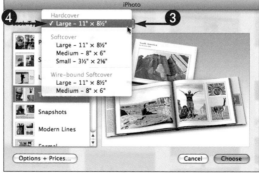

5 Click a layout from the list shown on the left pane of the sheet.

● A preview of the layout you select appears in the right pane.

To see how much the type of book you want will cost to print, click the **Options + Prices** button to open a Web page that shows current pricing.

6 Click **Choose**.

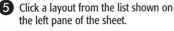

● The photo book is created in the Projects section.

● The photo book window appears.

● At the top of the window, you see previews of the photos you selected.

● In the center of the window, you see the page preview that you use to build each page.

● At the bottom of the window, you see the book tools.

You're ready to lay out the book's pages.

 TIPS

Do I have to have a book printed by Apple?
You can print photo books yourself, and I recommend that you usually print a draft version that you check before you order a copy from Apple. Except for resolution problems, Apple doesn't check a book when it is printed; what you get is what you get back. Print a draft copy or a PDF to check the book before you print it. You can also take the PDF version to a local printing store to have it printed.

How much does printing a book cost?
At press time, 8.5-x-11-inch hardcover books were $29.99 for 20 pages (double-sided) or 10 pages (single-sided). Additional pages cost $.99 for a double-sided page (100 pages maximum) or $1.49 for single-sided (50 pages maximum). Check Apple's Web site for current prices for all options.

Lay Out a Photo Book

The process of laying out a photo book is definitely the most time-consuming part of the process. It is also the most important one. For each page in the book, you choose the photos that appear on the page, the page's theme, and other aspects of its design.

USE AUTOFLOW TO LAY OUT PAGES

1 Select the book on the Source list.

● You see the book's cover with a title.

2 Click the **Autoflow** button.

iPhoto places the photos in the album on various pages in the book starting with the first photo in the album placed on the book's cover.

You can manually adjust the autoflow layout as needed.

Note: *When a photo is marked with an exclamation point, it means that the photo's resolution is too low to print properly at its current size.*

ADJUST EACH PAGE'S LAYOUT MANUALLY

1 Select the cover thumbnail.

Note: *If you see photos instead of pages at the top of the window, click the **Show Pages** button, which is the top button to the left of the thumbnails.*

The cover along with its text appears in the center pane of the window.

2 Click the cover page photo.

The size and placement tools appear.

3 Click and drag the slider to increase or decrease the size of the photo.

4 Click the Hand icon (⬚).

5 Drag the photo to position the part that is visible in the frame.

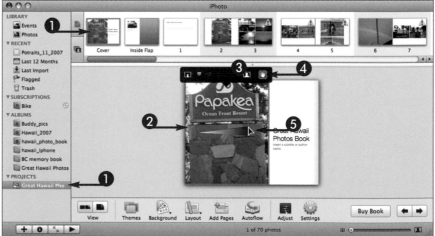

⑥ Click the book's title to edit it.

⑦ Click other text on the cover and edit it.

⑧ Click the thumbnail of the next page.

The page appears in the editing area.

⑨ Drag the Size slider as needed.

⑩ Use the scroll bars to change location on the page.

⑪ Adjust the size and position of any photos on the page by dragging the edge of the photos.

⑫ Edit any text on the page.

⑬ Click the **Next** button (➡).

continued

Lay Out a Photo Book (continued)

Fortunately, you can use the Autoflow tool to get started and then make manual adjustments from there as needed.

Lay Out a Photo Book (continued)

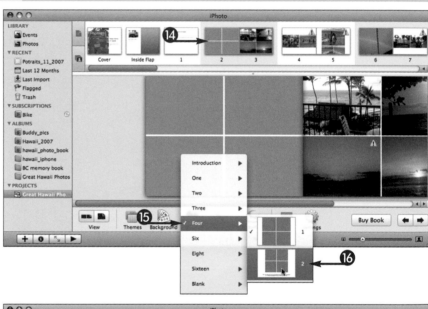

⓮ Select the first photo page in the book.

⓯ To change the layout of the page, open the Layout pop-up menu.

⓰ Choose the page's layout.

Placeholders appear for each photo on the page.

⓱ To add a photo from those available in the book, click the **Show Photos** button ().

The photos you added to the book are shown.

⓲ Scroll through the photos to find one you want to add to the page.

⓳ Drag the photo onto the open position.

The photo is added to the page.

⓴ Move photos between pages by dragging them from one page to another.

If a photo exists in the previous location, the photos swap places.

㉑ Complete any text on the page.

㉒ Remove a photo from a page by dragging it from the page back onto the photo browser, or click it and press Delete.

㉓ When you finish with pages being displayed, click the **Next** button (➡).

㉔ Continue moving through the pages in the book until you lay out all of them.

The book is ready for an editing pass.

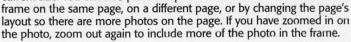

TIPS

How do I fix photos that are marked with an exclamation point icon?

When a photo's resolution is too low to print with the best quality at its current size, it is flagged with an exclamation point icon. This means that the photo is sized too large for its resolution. If you have cropped the photo, uncrop it to restore more of the original photo so that its resolution is sufficient at its current size. You can also place the photo in a smaller frame on the same page, on a different page, or by changing the page's layout so there are more photos on the page. If you have zoomed in on the photo, zoom out again to include more of the photo in the frame.

What if I need to edit a photo in a book?

Double-click a photo on a book page and it opens in the Edit window. After you edit the photo, click **Done**. You return to the photo in the book.

Editing passes are necessary to find those problems that you may have missed when you layed out the book. It is better to discover problems when you can fix them rather than after you spend money on printing the book.

1 Select the photo book.

2 Set the preview size so you can see all of the pages in the window.

3 Look for photo problems or layout issues.

4 Click the **Next** button (➡).

The next set of pages appears.

5 Zoom in on pages with text so that you can read the text easily.

6 If you find a text problem, fix it.

Note: iPhoto has a spell checker that underlines misspellings and suggests corrections.

⑦ To apply a background to a page, click the Background button.

⑧ Select a background from the pop-up menu.

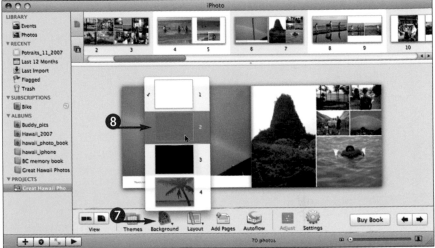

⑨ When you get to the end of the book, note how many pages there are to determine how much the book costs.

⑩ If you want to remove pages, move to the page you want to remove and click **Edit** and then **Remove Page**.

⑪ To add pages, click **Add Pages**.

Note: If you are using a double-sided book, you must add and delete pages two at a time.

 TIPS

Can I change a book's design after I lay it out?

Using the Themes menu, you can choose a different design for a book you have layed out. When you choose a new design, the pages are redone according to the new design. This can cause problems with some of the pages, especially if the pages have text on them. Make sure you do some additional editing passes with the new design to make sure they are acceptable with the new design.

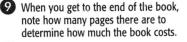

What does the Adjust button do?

When you select a photo and click the Adjust button, the Adjust palette appears. The Adjust palette has tools that enable you to apply effects and adjust many aspects of the photo, such as brightness, color temperature, and so on. These are the same tools available in the Editing window.

Configure a Photo Book's Settings

Each book has a set of configuration options that you can adjust. These include fonts, whether you want the Apple logo included on the book, and so on.

① Select the photo book.

② Click **Settings**.

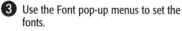

The Settings sheet appears.

③ Use the Font pop-up menus to set the fonts.

④ If you don't want an Apple logo included on the book when it is printed, deselect the **Include Apple logo** check box.

⑤ Select the **Automatically enter photo information** check box to have photo information such as titles added automatically.

⑥ Select the **Double-sided pages** check box to use double-sided pages.

⑦ Click **OK**.

Any changes you make are reflected in the book.

Cover Title:	Helvetica Neue	Light	38
Cover Subtitle:	Helvetica Neue	Regular	18
Flap Title:	Helvetica Neue	Light	20
Flap Body:	Helvetica Neue	Regular	12
Back Title:	Helvetica Neue	Light	20
Back Subtitle:	Helvetica Neue	Regular	12
Headings:	Helvetica Neue	Light	32
Paragraphs:	Helvetica Neue	Regular	15
Page Text:	Helvetica Neue	Regular	13

☑ Include Apple logo
☑ Automatically enter photo information
☑ Double-sided pages

Restore Defaults   Cancel   OK

You can print photo books yourself or have Apple print them for you.

Apple prints photo books using high-quality printers, binds the books for you, and ships them to the location of your choice. However, you should know how to print books yourself, especially for proofing a book before you send it to Apple for printing.

Print a Photo Book

PRINT PHOTO BOOKS YOURSELF

1 Select the photo book you want to print.

2 Click **File**, and then click **Print**.

The Print dialog box appears.

3 Click the **Preview** button.

A preview of your book appears in the Preview application.

4 Review the book in Preview.

5 If you want to make changes, go back into iPhoto and make the changes.

6 When you finish, click **Print**.

The book prints using your selected printer.

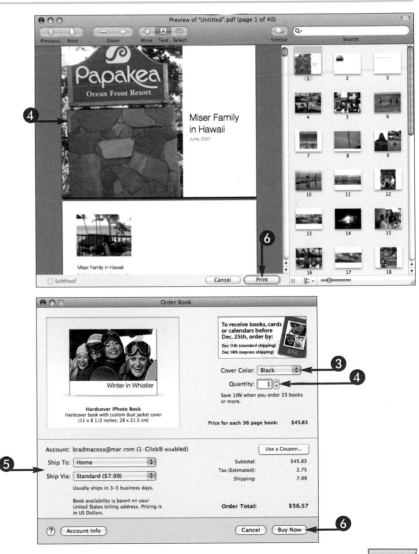

HAVE APPLE PRINT PHOTO BOOKS

1 Select the photo book you want to print.

2 Click **Buy Book**.

The Order Book dialog box appears.

3 Select the color of the cover.

4 Select how many copies of the book you want.

5 Select where and how to ship your book.

6 Click **Buy Now**.

Your order is complete.

Note: You need an Apple ID to order books. This is the same account you use to order from the online Apple Store and the iTunes Store.

CHAPTER 13

Chat

Text chatting is a favorite way to communicate for many people. It is not as intrusive as a phone call, but more immediate than e-mail; and text chatting is easy to use. With iChat, you can text chat with other people using a variety of accounts.

iChat also enables you to audio and video chat just as easily as you can text chat. Because MacBooks include a built-in iSight camera and microphone, you do not need any additional hardware to have true audio- and videoconferences. You can even communicate with more than one person at the same time.

Like the other "i" applications, iChat is both powerful and easy to use. Its interface is simple and elegant, but packs all the features you need to have great text, audio, and video chats.

After you have done some quick configuration of iChat, you can use it to communicate with people all over the world in any format you choose. It can even help when you have problems because you can also use iChat to share your MacBook's desktop.

Text chat window

Text conversations appear in their own window

Who you are texting with

At the top of the window, you see who you are texting with

What the other person is saying to you

On the left side of the window, you see the other person involved in the conversation

What you have said

On the right side of the window, you see your contributions to the conversation

Text box

When you want to add to the conversation, enter text in the text box

Emoticon menu

You can add emoticons to a conversation by selecting them on the menu

Audio Chat window

When you audio chat with people, you see a visual representation of the sounds you hear

How many people are involved

At the top of the window, you see how many people are participating

Each person participating

Participants in the conversation have their own sound bar so you can see when they speak

Your volume level

The bottom bar represents how loud your speech is

Add button

Use this button to add more people to the conversation

Mute button

Click this button to mute your sound

Volume slider

Use this to set the volume level of a conversation

Video chat window

Shows each of the people you are videoconferencing with

Participant windows

Each participant gets his or her own window for the chat

Your window

During a video chat, you see yourself as the other participants see you

Effects

You can use the Effects tools to distort the video images in different ways

Add

You can add up to three other people in a videoconference

Mute

Use the Mute button to block sound from your end

Full-screen

When you click this, the videoconference fills the desktop

Shared screen

You can use iChat to view and control another person's computer

Your computer

When you are sharing a desktop, you see a preview of your desktop; click it to move back to your computer

Shared documents

When someone shares a screen with you, you can work with documents and commands just as if you were seated in front of the other computer

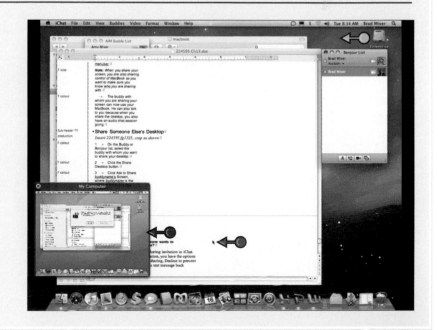

Configure an iChat Account

Before you start chatting, you need to do some basic configuration of iChat, such as setting up the chat accounts you are going to use, and setting volume levels for the microphone. iChat's Setup Assistant guides you each step of the way.

Configure an iChat Account

① Launch iChat by clicking its icon on the Dock or by double-clicking its icon in the Applications folder.

The first time you launch iChat, the Setup Assistant runs.

② Read the information in the first screen.

③ Click **Continue**.

④ From the Account Type pop-up menu, choose the type of account you want to use to chat.

Note: You can use a .Mac, America Online Instant Messenger (AIM), Jabber, or Google Talk account with iChat.

⑤ Enter a member, screen, or user name for your account.

⑥ Enter the password for your account.

Note: If you do not have a chat account, click the **Get an iChat Account** button and follow the on-screen instructions.

⑦ Click **Continue**.

If you use a .Mac account, you see the Encrypted iChat screen.

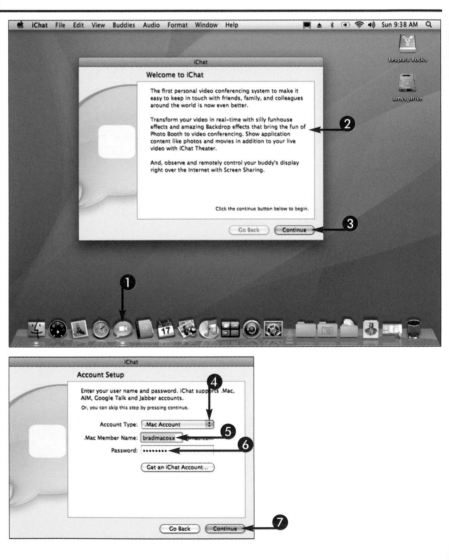

8 If you want your chats with other .Mac users to be encrypted for better security, check the **Enable iChat encryption** check box.

9 Click **Continue**.

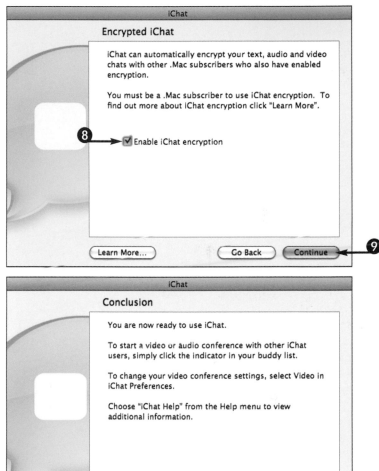

iChat

Encrypted iChat

iChat can automatically encrypt your text, audio and video chats with other .Mac subscribers who also have enabled encryption.

You must be a .Mac subscriber to use iChat encryption. To find out more about iChat encryption click "Learn More".

8 ☑ Enable iChat encryption

(Learn More...)   (Go Back) (Continue) **9**

10 Click **Done**.

iChat opens, you see your buddy lists, and you are ready to start chatting.

iChat

Conclusion

You are now ready to use iChat.

To start a video or audio conference with other iChat users, simply click the indicator in your buddy list.

To change your video conference settings, select Video in iChat Preferences.

Choose "iChat Help" from the Help menu to view additional information.

Click Done to start using iChat.

(Go Back) (Done) **10**

TIPS

Do I have to use the Assistant to configure iChat?

You can configure all aspects of iChat using its Preferences dialog box (press ⌘+,). For example, you can use the Accounts pane to configure your chat accounts, and using the Messages pane, you can configure the format of text chats.

What kind of Internet connection do I need to audio and video chat?

Audio and video chats require broadband Internet connections. As long as you can connect via a Wi-Fi, DSL, cable, or T1 connection, you can chat with audio and video. Be prepared to be amazed at the quality of both audio and video chatting.

Chat with Text

Text chatting is a great way to have almost real-time conversations with other people while not consuming all of your and their attention throughout the conversation. Text messaging is a great way to communicate short messages in the format of a conversation.

iChat enables you to text message other people (called buddies) easily and quickly.

Chat with Text

ADD A BUDDY

1️⃣ Launch iChat.

2️⃣ Expand the list of Buddies and the Offline list.

If the person with whom you want to chat is not on either list, continue with the following steps.

Note: *A buddy that appears on the Offline list is unavailable for chatting.*

3️⃣ At the bottom of the AIM Buddy List, click the **Add** button (➕).

4️⃣ Choose **Add Buddy**.

The Add Buddy sheet appears.

5️⃣ Choose the type of account on the Account Name pop-up menu.

6️⃣ Enter the person's e-mail address in the Account Name field.

7️⃣ On the Add to Group pop-up menu, choose **Buddies**.

8️⃣ Enter the buddy's name in the appropriate name fields.

9️⃣ Click the **Show Address Book** button.

The sheet expands to show a mini Address Book.

🔟 If the person is in your Address Book, select his or her card to associate the buddy with the address card.

⓫ Click **Add**.

The person is added to your buddy list.

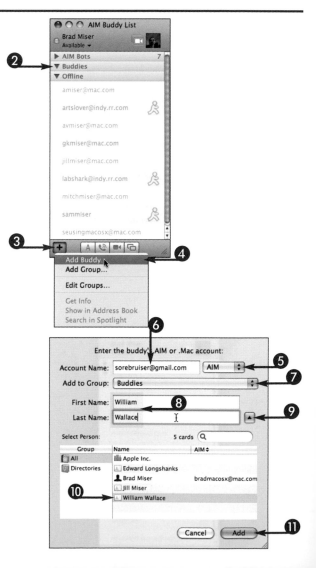

START A TEXT CHAT

1 Launch iChat.

2 Select the buddy with whom you want to chat.

3 Click the **Text chat** button (A).

A new text chat window appears.

4 Type your message.

5 Press Return.

Your message is sent and is added to the message log at the top of the window next to your icon.

● You see the person's response in the message window next to his or her icon.

6 Read the reply.

7 Type your response.

8 To add an emoticon to it, choose one on the pop-up menu.

9 Press Return.

Your response is sent and added to the conversation log.

Note: Text chatting is supposed to be fast and simple. So, expect to see misspellings and shorthand in chats.

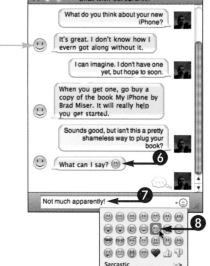

TIPS

What happens when someone starts a chat with me?
When someone wants to chat with you, a new message window appears in iChat and you see the message sent to you. Click the message; the window expands to show the response box. To decline the chat, click the **Decline** button. To block all attempts to chat, click the **Block** button. To accept the chat, type your response and click **Accept**. Chat just like when you start a chat session.

What is the Bonjour List?
You can use iChat and Mac OS X's Bonjour networking function to text, audio, and video chat on your local network. When people on your local network sign in to chat, they appear on your Bonjour List. You can chat with them just like chatting over the Internet, except the conversation never leaves the local network.

Chat with Audio

Text chatting is great, but being able to talk to someone can be even better. Of course, you can always use the phone, but that can be expensive. Using an iChat audio chat, you can have conversations with one or more people at the same time at no cost to you.

Before you start talking, take a couple of moments to set up your MacBook's microphone. Then you can talk at will.

Chat with Audio

CHECK THE MICROPHONE

1. Press ⌘+,.

   The iChat Preferences dialog box opens.

2. Click the **Audio/Video** tab.

3. Choose **Internal microphone** on the Microphone pop-up menu.

4. Speak normally.

5. As you speak, the level indicator just above the pop-up menu measures the relative input volume.

6. Open the System Preferences application and click the Sound icon.

7. Click the **Input** tab.

8. Drag the Input volume slider to the right to increase the level of sound input.

9. If you are in a noisy environment, check the **Use ambient noise reduction** check box.

10. Quit the System Preferences application and close the iChat Preferences window.

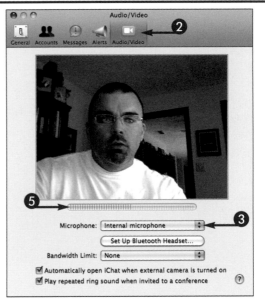

AUDIO CHAT

1 On the buddy or Bonjour list, select the buddy with whom you want to chat.

Note: If the Audio Chat button does not become active when you select a buddy, the buddy is not capable of audio chatting with you.

2 Click the **Audio Chat** button (📞).

● The Audio Chat window opens.

3 Speak to the person and listen as you would on a telephone.

4 To change the volume, drag the slider.

5 To mute your side of the conversation, click the **Mute** button (🎤); click it again to unmute it.

6 To add another person to the chat, click the **Add** button (+) and choose the buddy you want to add to the conversation.

● Once the second person accepts, all three are able to hear each other.

7 Keep adding people and chatting.

8 When you are done, close the chat window.

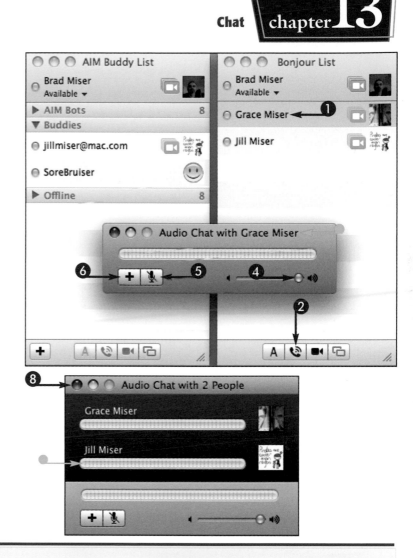

What if I do not want to chat in any form?

To prevent any chat requests from popping up, you need to quit iChat. If you want to show your status to others, open the Status pop-up menu that is just below your name at the top of the buddy and Bonjour list windows. Choose the status you want them to see on their buddy lists. Choose **Offline** if you do not want to chat. To chat again, choose **Available** on the menu. No matter what status you choose, you see windows pop up when someone tries to chat with you. You can just ignore those windows or decline the chats if you do not want to chat.

Are audio chats basically free phone calls?

Yes. If you already have an account that supports audio and video chats, there is no additional charge for the chats. In effect, you can make free phone calls and have free videoconferences with anyone with whom you can chat, no matter where the person is located in the world.

With the rise of iChat, iSight cameras, and broadband Internet connections, video conferencing has become simple and easy to do. With MacBook and an Internet connection, you can see people while you talk to them. This is the next best thing to being there in person.

Chat with Video

CHECK THE CAMERA

1 Click the camera icon at the top of the Buddy or Bonjour lists.

The My Built-in iSight window opens.

2 Move MacBook or yourself until the image is what you want others to see.

Note: Click the **Preferences** button to open the Audio/Video pane of the iChat Preferences dialog box.

3 Resize the window by dragging its resize handle.

4 When you are satisfied with the view, close the window.

BEGIN A VIDEO CHAT

1 On the buddy or Bonjour list, select the buddy with whom you want to chat.

2 Click the **Video Chat** button (■).

● The video chat window opens. When the person accepts your chat invitation, you see his or her image in the window.

❸ Talk to and see the other person.

● The inset preview window shows you what the other person is seeing in his or her chat window.

❹ Drag the preview window so it is where you want it to be on the screen.

❺ To apply special effects to the image, click the **Effects** button.

❻ To mute your end of the conversation, click the **Mute** button (🎙); click it again to unmute it.

❼ To make the window fill the desktop, click the **Fill Screen** button (🔳).

❽ To add another person to the conversation, click the **Add** button (➕).

● When the person accepts, a third video window appears and you see the second person.

❾ You can talk to and see the other people and they can see and talk to each other.

❿ When you are done, close the window.

TIPS

How many people can I have in a video or audio conference at the same time?
You can have up to four participants (including yourself) in a single videoconference. You can have up to ten people in an audio conference at the same time.

Is iChat compatible with other kinds of videoconference systems?
No. To use iChat for videoconferences, all participants must be using iChat.

Share MacBook's Desktop

With iChat, you can share your desktop with other Macs so that the people with whom you are chatting can see what is happening on your screen. This is useful for many things, such as doing online presentations, collaborating on a document, and so on.

But it can also be very useful when you need to get help from people. You can share your desktop with them and they can watch to see exactly how and where you are getting into trouble, which is usually most of the remote troubleshooting battle (more on getting help with problems in Chapter 19). They can also take control of MacBook to help you fix problems.

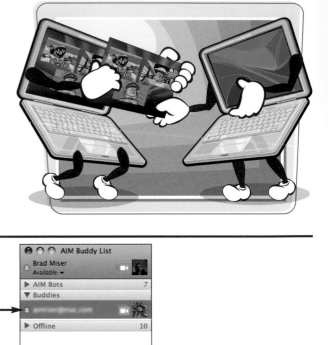

Share MacBook's Desktop

SHARE YOUR DESKTOP

① On the Buddy or Bonjour list, select the buddy with whom you want to share your desktop.

② Click the **Share Desktop** button (⊡).

③ Click **Share My Screen with** buddyname, where *buddyname* is the name of the buddy you selected.

● When the buddy accepts your invitation, the Sharing status indicator appears at the top of the iChat menu on the toolbar.

The buddy with whom you are sharing your screen can now use your MacBook.

SHARE SOMEONE ELSE'S DESKTOP

1 On the Buddy or Bonjour list, select the buddy with whom you want to share your desktop.

2 Click the **Share Desktop** button ().

3 Click **Ask to Share *buddyname*'s Screen**, where *buddyname* is the name of the buddy you selected.

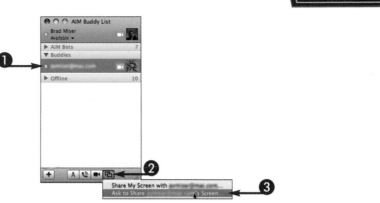

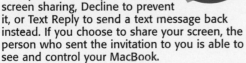

iChat sends a share request to the buddy. When he or she accepts, you see two windows on the screen.

● One window is the buddy's desktop, which is the larger window by default.

● The other window is a preview of your desktop, which is labeled with My Computer.

Note: You can move the preview window around the screen if it blocks the part of the shared desktop that you want to see.

4 You can work with the buddy's computer just as if you were sitting in front of it.

5 To move back to your desktop, click in the My Computer window.

The two windows flip-flop so your desktop is now the larger window.

6 When you are done sharing, click the **Close** button on the My Computer window.

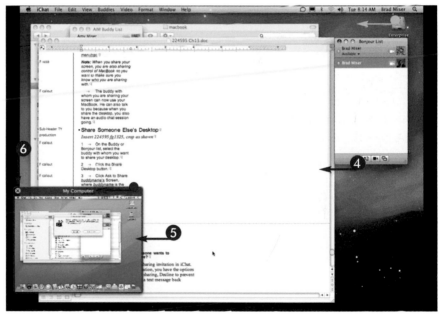

TIPS

What happens when someone wants to share his or her screen with me?
You receive a screen sharing invitation in iChat. When you click the invitation, you have the options to Accept to start screen sharing, Decline to prevent it, or Text Reply to send a text message back instead. If you choose to share your screen, the person who sent the invitation to you is able to see and control your MacBook.

What if I just want to show something to someone without letting him or her have control?
You can use the iChat Theater to present documents to people. Choose **File, Share a File With iChat Theater**. Move to and select the file you want to share. Click **Share**, then choose the buddy to whom you want to present the document. That person sees two windows. One contains the document you are sharing, and the other shows you. You can move through the document, such as a slideshow, and the buddy sees it in the document window.

Manage Contacts

You can use Mac OS X's Address Book application to store and manage all of your contact information, including physical addresses, phone numbers, e-mail addresses, important dates, and notes. As you build your contacts in Address Book, you can easily synchronize its information with iPods, iPhones, cell phones, PDAs, .Mac, and even with other computers, so your contacts are always available when and where you need them.

Address Book is both powerful and easy to use. You can quickly build your contact information and then use that information in many ways.

Open Address Book by clicking its Dock icon, which is a book with the @ symbol on its cover, or double-clicking its icon in the Applications folder.

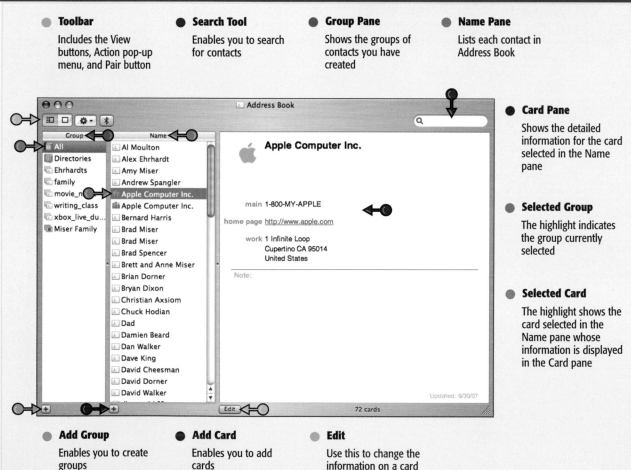

● **Toolbar**

Includes the View buttons, Action pop-up menu, and Pair button

● **Search Tool**

Enables you to search for contacts

● **Group Pane**

Shows the groups of contacts you have created

● **Name Pane**

Lists each contact in Address Book

● **Card Pane**

Shows the detailed information for the card selected in the Name pane

● **Selected Group**

The highlight indicates the group currently selected

● **Selected Card**

The highlight shows the card selected in the Name pane whose information is displayed in the Card pane

● **Add Group**

Enables you to create groups

● **Add Card**

Enables you to add cards

● **Edit**

Use this to change the information on a card

Understand Address Book

Before you jump into Address Book, check out a few important concepts to help you master your contacts quickly and easily.

Cards

Each contact is represented by a card. Like Rolodex cards of old, Address Book cards contain contact information. Unlike physical cards, Address Book cards are virtual (vCards), making them flexible because you can store a variety of information on each card; and you can store different information for various contacts.

Contact Information

Each card in Address Book can hold an unlimited number of physical addresses, phone numbers, e-mail addresses, dates, notes, and URL addresses. Because vCards are flexible, you do not have to include each kind of information for every contact; you include only the information that is appropriate for a contact. Address Book displays only fields that have data in them so your cards are not cluttered up with lots of empty spaces.

Groups

Groups are collections of cards. They are useful because you can do something once with a group and the action affects all the cards in that group. For example, you can create a group containing family members whom you regularly e-mail. Then, you can address a message to the one group instead of addressing each person individually.

Smart Groups

Smart groups are also collections of cards, but unlike regular groups, you do not have to manually add each card to the group. Instead, you define criteria for the cards you want to be included in the smart group, and Address Book automatically adds the appropriate cards. Suppose you want a group for everyone with the same last name; you can simply create a smart group with that criterion, and Address Book adds all the people with that last name to the group automatically.

Address Book Actions

In addition to using information stored on cards indirectly — for example, looking at a phone number to dial it — you can use some data to perform an action by right-clicking the information and choosing an action. Some of the most useful actions are sending e-mails, visiting Web sites, and dialing a cell phone.

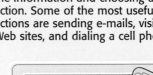

Before you can work with contacts, you need to create a card for each contact you want to manage. One way to do this is to manually create a card and add contact information to it.

1 Click the **Add Card** button (+).

A new, empty card appears in the Card pane.

2 Type the contact's first name in the First field, which is highlighted.

3 Press Tab.

4 Type the contact's last name in the Last field.

5 Press Tab.

6 Enter the contact's company in the Company field.

Note: *If the card is for a company, check the Company check box and enter the company name; first and last name information is optional for companies.*

7 Press Tab.

8 Click the pop-up menu (⬍) next to the first field (**work** by default).

9 Select the type of contact information you want to enter.

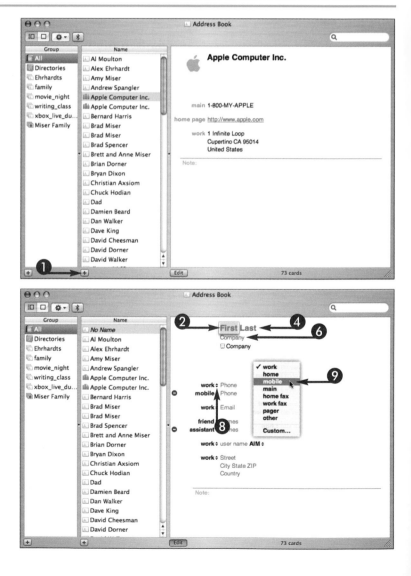

⑩ Type the selected information in the field, such as a phone number or e-mail address.

Note: *When you select a data type, Address Book automatically creates a field of the right format, such as for phone numbers, when you select mobile.*

⑪ Repeat steps **7** to **9** to enter information into each field you want filled.

⑫ To remove a field from the card, click the **Delete** button (⊖).

⑬ To add another field of the same type to a card, click the **Add** button (⊕).

⑭ To add an image to the card, drag it from the desktop and drop it onto the Image Well.

A dialog box that enables you to resize the image pops up automatically.

⑮ Drag the slider to resize the image.

⑯ Click **Set**.

⑰ Click **Edit**.

The card is created and only fields containing information are shown.

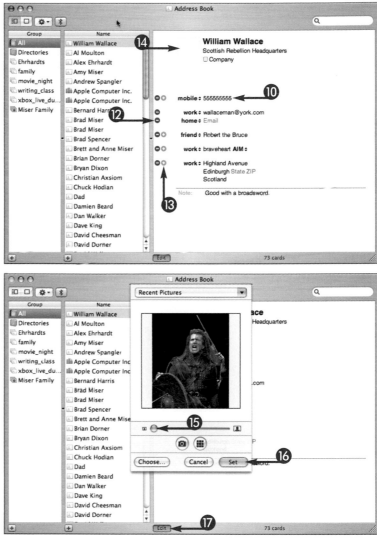

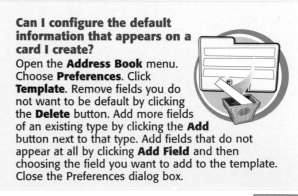

What if the information I want to enter is not available on the pop-up menu?
Open the pop-up menu and choose **Custom**. Type the label for the field you want to add and click **OK**. You return to the card and the custom label appears on the card. Enter the information for that field. The custom field is added to the card.

Can I configure the default information that appears on a card I create?
Open the **Address Book** menu. Choose **Preferences**. Click **Template**. Remove fields you do not want to be default by clicking the **Delete** button. Add more fields of an existing type by clicking the **Add** button next to that type. Add fields that do not appear at all by clicking **Add Field** and then choosing the field you want to add to the template. Close the Preferences dialog box.

Work with vCards

Many applications use vCards to store contact information, including contact managers and e-mail. You can add cards to Address Book easily by using vCards other people send to you; once you have added these cards, you can use them just like those you create directly in Address Book. You can also create a vCard for yourself to send to others so they can add your information to their contact manager just as easily.

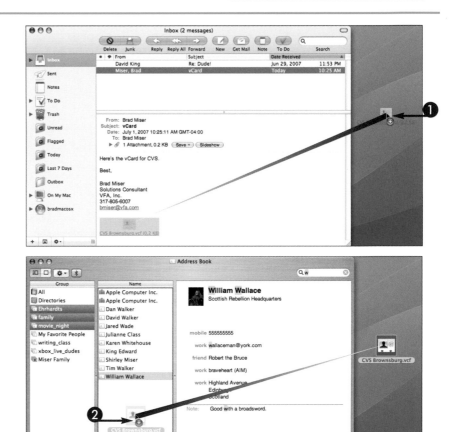

Work with vCards

ADD CONTACTS WITH VCARDS

1 Drag the vCard file onto your desktop.

Note: One of the most common ways to receive vCards is through e-mail as attachments. Simply drag the vCard from the e-mail onto your desktop. vCard files have .vcf as their file name extension.

2 Drag the vCard file from the desktop onto the Name pane of the Address Book window.

A dialog box appears confirming that you are adding a new card.

3 Click **OK**.

● The vCard is added to Address Book and you can work with it just like cards you create within Address Book.

CREATE VCARDS FROM ADDRESS BOOK CARDS

1 Search or browse for the cards for which you want to create vCards.

Note: To quickly find your card, open the Card menu and choose Go to My Card. Your card, which is marked with a silhouette icon, appears in the Card pane.

2 Drag the card from Address Book onto your desktop.

Note: The file name of the vCard is the name of the contact.

The vCard is created, and you can provide it to other people. They can then add its contact information to their contact manager.

Can I use a vCard from Microsoft Outlook or some other contact manager?

vCards are a standard file format which almost all applications that deal with contact information use. You should be able to add a vCard to Address Book regardless of the program used to create that vCard. One caveat is that not all information stored in all applications can be moved into Address Book via vCards, but you get the most important information.

How can I add contact information to Address Book from e-mails when a vCard is not attached?

When you receive an e-mail in Mail, you can add the sender's name and e-mail address to Address Book. Position the pointer over the address shown next to "From," and when the address becomes highlighted, click the mouse button to open the action menu. Choose **Add to Address Book**. A new card is created with as much information as Address Book can extract, usually first and last name along with an e-mail address.

Find Contact Information

The whole point of having contact information is being able to find and use the information you need. Address Book makes it simple to quickly find information you are interested in.

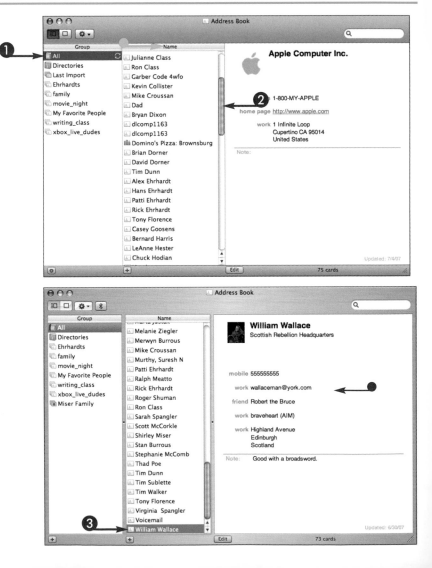

BROWSE FOR A CONTACT

1 Select the group that you want to browse; to browse all of your contacts, click **All**.

● All the cards in the selected group appear in the Name pane.

2 Use the scroll bar to browse up and down the list of names.

3 Select the name for the contact information you want to use.

● The card containing contact information appears in the Card pane.

SEARCH FOR A CONTACT

1 Select the group that you want to search; to search all of your contacts, click **All**.

● All the cards in the selected group appear in the Name pane.

2 Type search text in the Search box.

Note: *Address Book searches all the fields at the same time so you do not need to define what you are searching for, such as a name instead of an address.*

As you type, Address Book starts searching all the fields in the cards.

3 Continue typing in the Search box until the card you want appears in the Name pane.

4 Select the card.

● The card containing contact information appears in the Card pane.

5 Clear the Search box by clicking the **Stop Search** button (⊗).

All the cards in the selected group appear again.

TIPS

Can I search for contact information by phone number or e-mail address?

When you search in Address Book, it searches all the fields on all your cards simultaneously. If it finds a match in any of these fields, a card is included in the search results shown in the Name pane. For example, if you enter text or numbers, it searches name fields, e-mail addresses, and other fields to look for matches.

Can I search or browse in multiple groups at the same time?

You can browse the cards in multiple groups at the same time by pressing and holding the Command key (⌘) while you select each group you want to browse. The Name pane shows the cards in each group. You can search only in one group at a time; usually, it makes more sense to search all of your contacts at the same time.

Create an
Address Group

A group is useful because it enables you to store many address cards within it. When you want to send an e-mail to the group, you can do so easily and quickly by using the group instead of addressing each person individually.

Create an Address Group

1 Click the **Add Group** button (+).

● A new group appears in the Group pane with its name ready to be edited.

2 Type the name of the group.

3 Press Return.

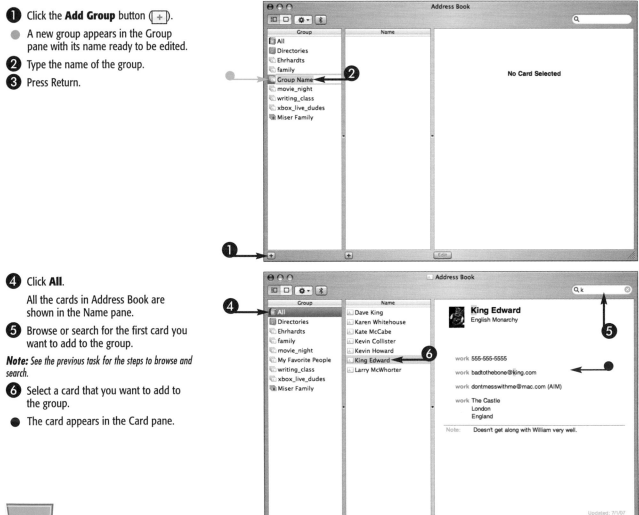

4 Click **All**.

All the cards in Address Book are shown in the Name pane.

5 Browse or search for the first card you want to add to the group.

Note: *See the previous task for the steps to browse and search.*

6 Select a card that you want to add to the group.

● The card appears in the Card pane.

7 Drag the card from the Name pane and drop it onto the group to which you want to add it.

Note: When you drag a card over a group, a green circle containing a plus sign appears below the card's icon ( ). When the group into which you want to place the card is highlighted, release the mouse button.

8 Select the group to which you added cards.

● The cards included in the group are shown in the Name pane.

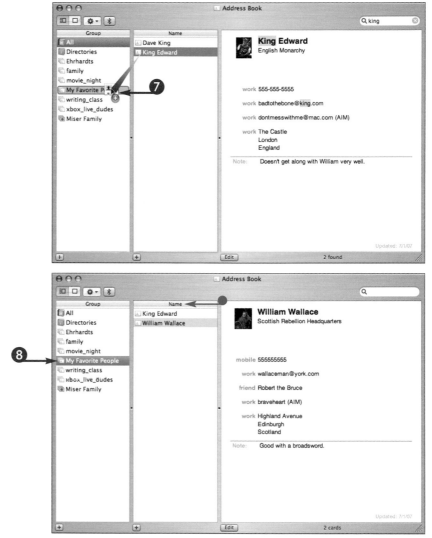

How do I create a smart group?
Open the File menu and choose **New Smart Group**. Type the name of the group. Use the pop-up menus and other controls to configure the first criterion, such as "Name includes Smith." Click the **Add** button to create more criteria until you have defined all you want to use. Choose **all** if you require that all the criteria be met or **any** if you want only one criterion to be required. Click **OK**. The smart group is created and all the cards that meet the criteria you defined are added to it automatically.

Use Address Cards and Groups

After you have added all that great contact information, Address Book will help you use your contacts in many ways. Check out the following tricks Address Book can do for you.

ADDRESS E-MAIL

1. Find the card for the person you want to e-mail.

2. Right-click the e-mail address to which you want to send a message.

3. Choose **Send Email**.

   Your default e-mail application opens and a new message to the address you chose is created.

VISIT WEB SITES

1. Find a card with a home page or other Web page URL on it.

2. Click the URL you want to visit.

   Your default Web application takes you to the URL you clicked.

MAP A PHYSICAL ADDRESS

1. Find the card containing the address you want.
2. Right-click the address you want to see on a map.
3. Choose **Map Of**.

   Your default Web application takes you to a Google map showing the address you clicked.

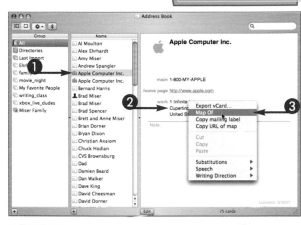

PRINT AN ENVELOPE OR MAILING LABEL

1. Find the card containing the address for which you want a mailing label.
2. Right-click the address you want to place on an envelope or label.
3. Choose **Copy mailing label**.

4. Open the application you use to print envelopes or labels.

   This example uses a widget called EasyEnvelopes by Ambrosia Software.

5. If the address is not inserted automatically, choose **Edit,** then **Paste** or ⌘ + V to insert the address.

   Once the address is in the application, use its printing tool to print the envelope or label.

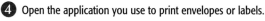

TIPS

How do I know what actions are available for a card or a group?

Each type of information on an address card has a different set of actions available for it. To see what actions are available for specific information on a card, simply right-click that information. To see what actions are available for a card or group, right-click the card or group. On the resulting pop-up menu, you see all of the actions available.

Can I share my Address Book with other people?

You can easily share your Address Book with people who also have a .Mac account. Open the **Address Book** menu and choose **Preferences**. Click the Sharing tab. Check the **Share your Address Book** check box. Click the **Add** button, which is a plus sign, and select the other .Mac users with whom you want to share your Address Book. Click **OK**. If you want those people to be able to change your Address Book, check the **Allow Editing** check box.

Change or Delete Address Cards or Groups

Over time, you want to be able to update your Address Book by adding new information, changing existing information, or removing information you no longer need. Fortunately, with Address Book, all these tasks are simple.

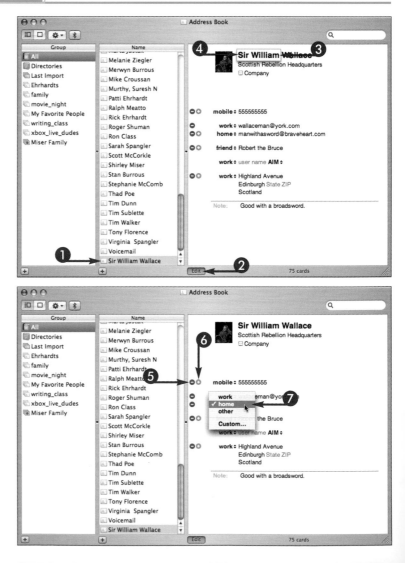

Change or Delete Address Cards or Groups

CHANGE ADDRESS CARDS

1 Search or browse for the address card you want to change.

2 Click the **Edit** button.

Existing fields become editable and the Delete (⊖) and Add (⊕) buttons appear.

3 Click the information you want to change.

4 Make needed changes to that information.

5 To delete information from the card, click (⊖).

The field clears; after you save your changes, that field no longer appears on the card.

6 To add information to the card, click (⊕) next to the type of information you want to add.

7 Choose a label for the new field on the pop-up menu.

8 Type information into the new field.

9 After you have made all the changes to the card, click **Edit**.

The changes you made to the card are saved.

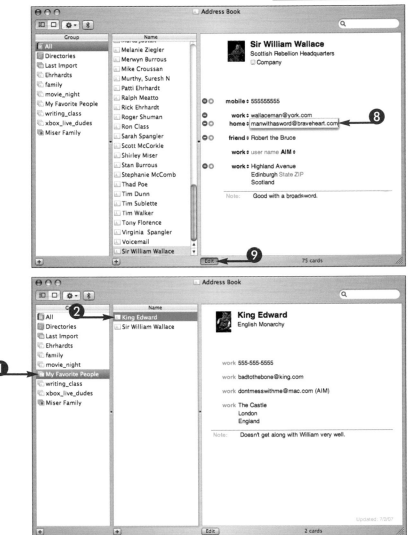

CHANGE ADDRESS GROUPS

1 Select the group you want to change.

2 To remove a card from the group, select the card you want to remove.

3 Press **Delete**.

The card is removed from the group, but remains in Address Book.

TIPS

How do I delete a card I do not need any more?
Select the card you want to remove and press **Delete**. Click **Delete** in the confirmation sheet. The card is removed from Address Book.

How do I delete a group I do not need?
Select the group you want to delete and press **Delete**. Click **Delete** in the confirmation sheet. The group is removed from Address Book; however, the cards in that group remain.

CHAPTER

15

Manage Calendars

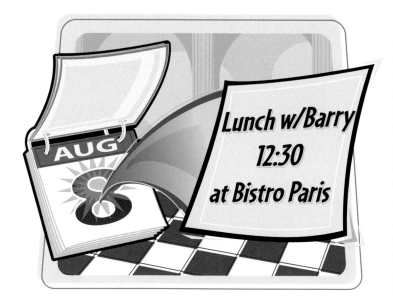

Lunch w/Barry
12:30
at Bistro Paris

MacBook can help you manage your time more effectively with the iCal application.

Using iCal, you can create and manage your own calendars that include To Do items and events (to which you can easily invite other people). If you have a .Mac account, you can publish your calendars to the Web so that other people can view them. Of course, you can subscribe to other people's published calendars in iCal as well.

iCal is Mac OS X's full-featured calendar application. As you can guess, you can use it to record To Do items and events; however, iCal goes beyond these basics.

One of the best things about iCal is that you can publish your calendars on the Web so that other people can view them. By subscribing to other people's calendars, you can see what they are up to, which makes coordinating events among a group of people much easier.

● **Back and Forward buttons**

Click these to move back or ahead in the calendar

● **View selection buttons**

Use these to determine how you view the calendar, such as by day, week, or month

● **Search tool**

Enables you to search events and To Do items

● **Personal calendars**

The calendars you create and manage

● **Subscribed calendars**

Calendars other people have created to which you have subscribed; when a calendar's check box is checked, you see it in the iCal window

● **Mini-Month pane**

Mini-view of month; current date is shown in dark blue and the date in focus is shown in lighter blue

● **Events**

Colored bars represent events; the color matches the calendar's color on which those events are stored

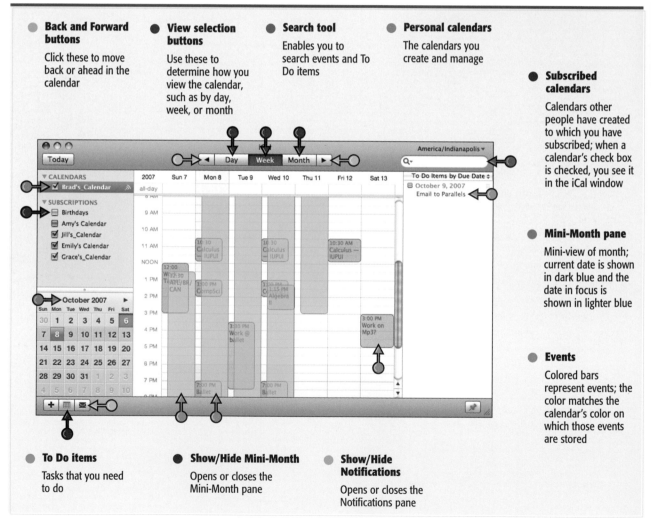

● **To Do items**

Tasks that you need to do

● **Show/Hide Mini-Month**

Opens or closes the Mini-Month pane

● **Show/Hide Notifications**

Opens or closes the Notifications pane

In iCal, you store events and To Do items on a calendar. You can have as many calendars as you want. For example, you might want one calendar for work information and another for family events. A calendar whose check box is checked appears in iCal. When you uncheck its check box, the calendar is hidden.

Add a Calendar

① Launch iCal by clicking its icon on the Dock.

The iCal window opens and you see two default calendars, labeled Home and Work, on the Calendars list.

② Click the **Add** button (`+` changes to `▣`).

A new calendar appears on the list, and its name is highlighted so you know it is ready to edit.

③ Type the name of the calendar and press Return to save it.

④ Select the new calendar.

⑤ On the iCal toolbar menu, choose **File**, then **Get Info**.

The calendar's Info sheet appears.

⑥ Enter a description of the calendar in the Description field.

⑦ If you want alarms on the calendar to be ignored, check the **Ignore alarms** check box.

⑧ Choose the color you want to associate with the calendar on the Color pop-up menu.

⑨ Click **OK**.

The sheet closes and the new calendar is ready to use.

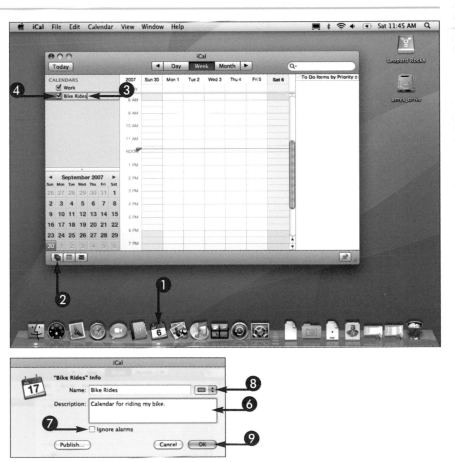

A calendar without events is not that useful; you can create events on a calendar and then configure them in many ways, such as the time, date, alarms, and so on. If you want other people to attend an event, you can easily invite them to it.

Add an Event to a Calendar

1 Select the calendar to which you want to add an event.

2 Move the calendar view so the date on which the event starts is shown.

3 When viewing by month or day, drag over the time period for the event; drag across days if the event extends beyond one day.

4 Release the trackpad button.

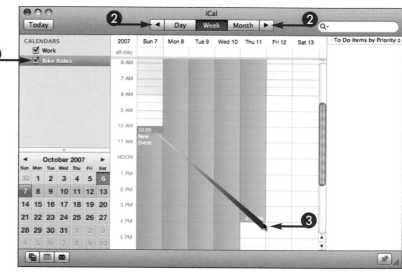

The new event is created and its name is highlighted.

5 Type the name of the event.

6 Press Return to save it.

7 Double-click the event.

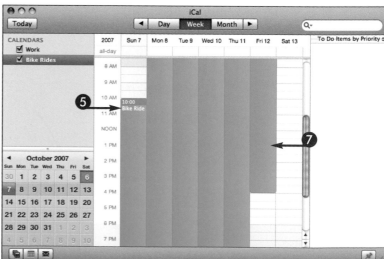

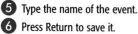

The Info window appears.

8 Click **Edit**.

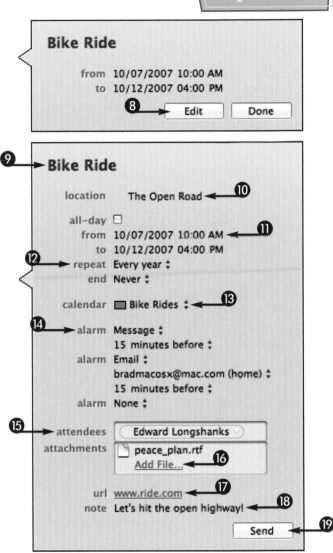

Bike Ride

from 10/07/2007 10:00 AM
to 10/12/2007 04:00 PM

8 ──▶ Edit   Done

The window moves into edit mode.

9 Edit the name if needed.

10 Enter a location for the event.

11 Change the event's dates and times using the date and time tools.

12 If the event repeats, choose the frequency of the event on the repeat pop-up menu.

13 To change the calendar with which the event is associated, choose a different calendar on the calendar pop-up menu.

14 To set alarms for the event, choose the kind of alarm on the alarm pop-up menu and then configure it.

15 To send an invitation to other people, click **Add Attendees** before entering the e-mail addresses for each invitee.

16 To store a file on the event, click **Add File** and select the file you want to attach.

17 To include a URL with the event, enter it in the url field.

18 Enter notes for the event in the note field.

19 Click **Send** if you included attendees or **Done** if you have not.

The event is saved on the calendar, and invitations are sent to other invitees.

Note: To delete an event, select it and press Delete.

9 ──▶ **Bike Ride**

location   The Open Road ◀── **10**

all-day ☐

from 10/07/2007 10:00 AM ◀── **11**
to 10/12/2007 04:00 PM

12 ──▶ repeat Every year ⬍
end Never ⬍

calendar ▪ Bike Rides ⬍ ◀── **13**

14 ──▶ alarm Message ⬍
15 minutes before ⬍
alarm Email ⬍
bradmacosx@mac.com (home) ⬍
15 minutes before ⬍
alarm None ⬍

15 ──▶ attendees (Edward Longshanks ⌄)
attachments ▯ peace_plan.rtf
Add File... ◀── **16**

url www.ride.com ◀── **17**
note Let's hit the open highway! ◀── **18**

Send ──▶ **19**

Is there an easy to way to see the current date?
iCal displays the current month and date in its icon on the Dock.

When I invite someone to an event, what does that person receive?
Each invitee receives an e-mail containing information about the event with a calendar item as an attachment. If the invitees also use iCal or another compatible calendar application, they can double-click the attachment to add the event to their own calendar.

Add a To Do Item to a Calendar

If you have a good memory for the things you have to do, you might not need iCal to help you. However, being able to capture To Do items can be helpful in ensuring that you actually get them done; and, sometimes, it feels nice to be able to check something off a list, even if you do remember to do it.

CREATE A TO DO ITEM

① Select the calendar with which you want the To Do item to be associated.

② On the iCal toolbar menu, choose **File**, then **New To Do**.

A new untitled To Do item appears on the To Do list.

Note: *If you do not see the To Do list, choose View, Show To Do List.*

③ Type the name of the To Do item, such as a description of what you need to do.

④ Press Return.

The new name is saved.

⑤ Double-click the To Do item.

The Info window appears.

6 Edit the name if needed.

7 Use the **priority** pop-up menu to assign a priority to the item.

8 To assign a due date to the item, check the **due date** check box and set the due date.

9 To set alarms for the item, choose the kind of alarm on the alarm pop-up menu and then configure it.

10 To change the calendar with which the item is associated, choose a different calendar on the calendar pop-up menu.

11 To include a URL with the item, enter it in the url field.

12 Enter notes for the event in the note field.

13 Click **Done**.

The item is saved on the To Do list.

MANAGE TO DO ITEMS

● As events become due, their completion check box changes to an exclamation point.

1 After you have completed a task, check its check box.

2 To sort the list of tasks, choose how you want them sorted on the pop-up menu at the top of the list.

When I open Mail, I see To Do items also. Are these related to the items in iCal?
Mail and iCal share To Do items. If you have a .Mac account, any To Do items you create in one application show up in the other one as well. Likewise, if you mark an item as complete in iCal, it gets marked as complete in Mail too. To work with To Do items in Mail, choose **Mailbox**, then **Go To**, and finally select **To Do**. If you add items in Mail, they appear under a section labeled your .Mac e-mail address.

How can I set iCal to remove older completed items so the list is not cluttered with them?
Open the iCal Preferences dialog box and click the **Advanced** pane. Check the **Hide To Do items days after they have been completed** check box and enter the number of days that should pass before a completed item is removed from the list. When that number of days passes since an item was marked as completed, it is removed from the list.

Publish Calendars

If you have a .Mac account, you can easily publish your calendars to the Web. Other people can then view your calendar in a Web browser or subscribe to them so they can see them in iCal (see the next section for the details of subscribing to calendars).

Publish Calendars

① Select the calendar you want to publish.

② Choose **Calendar** on the iCal toolbar menu, then **Publish**.

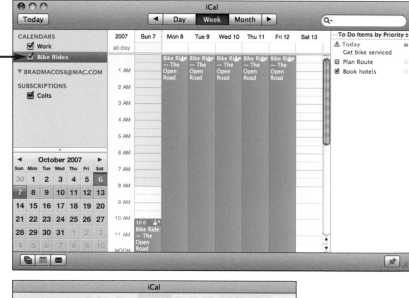

The Publish calendar sheet appears.

③ Enter the name of the published version of the calendar in the **Publish calendar as** field.

④ On the **Publish on** pop-up menu, choose **.Mac**.

⑤ If you want changes you make to be published automatically, check the **Publish changes automatically** check box.

⑥ If you want both titles and notes to be included, check the **Publish titles and notes** check box.

⑦ If you want to publish the To Do items associated with the calendar, check the **Publish To Do items** check box.

⑧ If you want alarms to be included, check the **Publish alarms** check box.

⑨ If you want attachments to be available on the published version, check the **Publish attachments** check box.

⑩ Click **Publish**.

iCal publishes the calendar. When the process is complete, you see the Calendar Published dialog box.

⑪ To send the URL and subscription invitation to someone, click **Send Mail**.

An e-mail message is created with the information about the published calendar.

⑫ To see how the calendar appears on the Web, click **Visit Page**.

● Your Web browser opens and you see the Web version of your calendar.

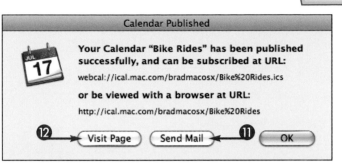

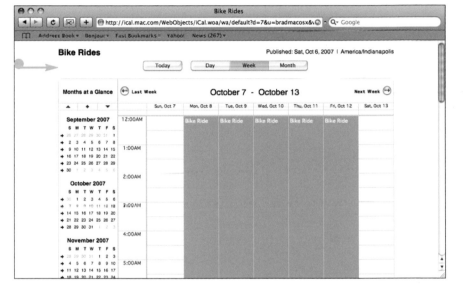

TIPS

Do I really have to have a .Mac account to publish my calendar?

If you do not have a .Mac account, you can publish your calendars to a WebDAV server. If you do not know if you have access to one of these, you can check with your system administrator if you use MacBook for work or with your ISP if you use MacBook at home. To be able to publish calendars to these servers, you need to know the URL for the server and have a user name and password.

I like to have a hard copy of my calendar at times. Can iCal help?

Choose **File** on the iCal toolbar menu, then **Print**. In the resulting Print dialog box, you can choose many output options. For example, you can print a weekly view or monthly view, choose a time range to include, set the paper size, and so on.

Subscribe to Calendars

Other people who use iCal can publish their calendars as easily as you can publish yours. When someone sends his or her calendar information to you, you can subscribe to the calendar or visit it on the Web.

When you subscribe to a calendar, it is added as a calendar to iCal where you can use iCal's tools to work with it. When you visit a calendar on the Web, you view it through Safari.

SUBSCRIBE TO A PUBLISHED CALENDAR IN ICAL

① Open an e-mail containing calendar information.

② Click the link starting with **webcal://ical.mac.com**.

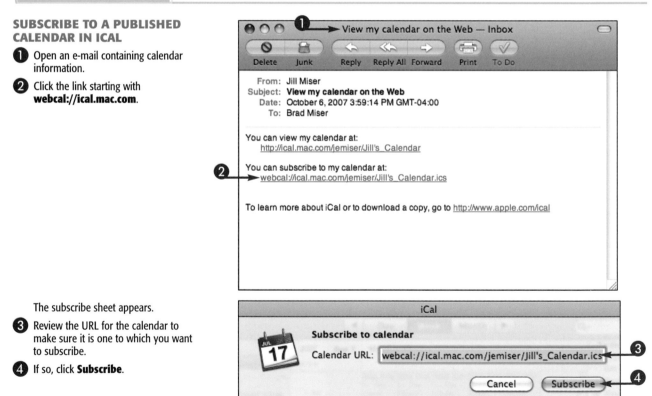

The subscribe sheet appears.

③ Review the URL for the calendar to make sure it is one to which you want to subscribe.

④ If so, click **Subscribe**.

304

iCal downloads the calendar information and you see the calendar's Info sheet.

5 If you want to change the name of the calendar, edit the name in the **Name** field.

6 Use the **Color** pop-up menu to associate a color with the calendar.

7 Enter a description of the calendar in the **Description** field.

8 If you do not want alarms, attachments, or To Do items removed, uncheck the respective **Remove** check boxes.

9 On the **Auto-refresh** pop-up menu, choose how often you want the calendar's information updated.

10 Click **OK**.

The calendar is added to iCal in the Subscriptions sections and you see its events.

VISIT A PUBLISHED CALENDAR ON THE WEB

1 Open an e-mail containing calendar information.

2 Click the link starting with **http://ical.mac.com**.

Safari opens the calendar on the Web.

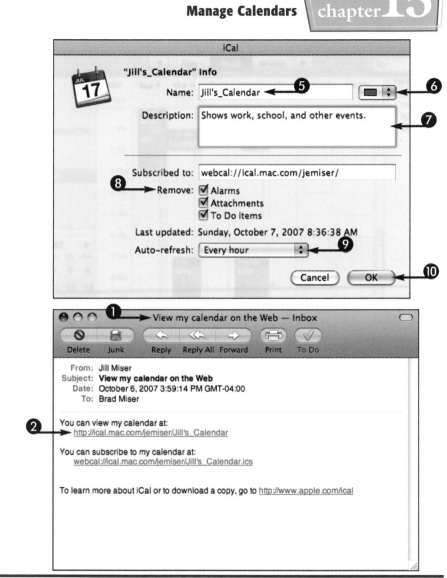

TIPS

Can I add events to a calendar to which I am subscribed?
Calendars published to iCal are read-only, meaning that you can view them, but you cannot change them.

Do organizations share their calendars?
Many organizations, such as professional sports teams, publish calendars to which you can subscribe in iCal. To find these, choose **Calendar** then **Find Shared Calendars**. You go to the iCal Library Web site on which you can find and subscribe to many different kinds of calendars.

Configure iCal Preferences

You can further tailor how iCal works by changing its preferences. For example, you can determine whether weeks are five or seven days long and when days start.

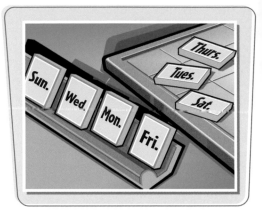

CONFIGURE GENERAL ICAL PREFERENCES

1 Press ⌘+,.

The iCal Preferences dialog box opens.

2 Click the **General** tab.

3 On the **Days per week** pop-up menu, choose 5 if you want weeks to be shown as the five workdays, or 7 if you want to see all seven days.

4 On the **Start week on** pop-up menu, choose the first day of the week.

5 Choose from the **Day** pop-up menus to define when days start and end.

6 Choose from the **Show** pop-up menu to determine how many hours iCal shows at once.

7 If you want the timeline to be shown in the Month view, check the **Show time in month view** check box.

8 If you want a default alarm for all events, check the **Add a default alarm to all new events and invitations** check box.

General

General   Accounts   Advanced

Days per week: 7 — **3**

Start week on: Sunday — **4**

Day starts at: 8:00 AM

5 → Day ends at: 6:00 PM

6 → Show: 12 hours at a time

7 → ☑ Show time in month view

☐ Show Birthdays calendar

8 → ☐ Add a default alarm to all new events and invitations

15 minutes before the start time

☐ Synchronize my calendars with other computers using .Mac

Your .Mac account information is not correct or you did not turn on synchronization in the .Mac Preference Pane.

.Mac...

CONFIGURE ADVANCED ICAL PREFERENCES

1. Press ⌘+,.

   The iCal Preferences dialog box opens.

2. Click the **Advanced** tab.

3. If you want to be able to manage events in different time zones, check the **Turn on time zone support** check box.

4. To manage how and when To Do items display on your calendars, select or deselect this section's checkboxes.

5. To disable all iCal alarms, check the **Turn off all alarms** check box.

6. To disable alarms only when iCal is closed, check the **Turn off all alarms only when iCal is not open** check box.

7. If you want Mail to automatically retrieve event invitations you receive, check the last check box.

8. Close the Preferences dialog box.

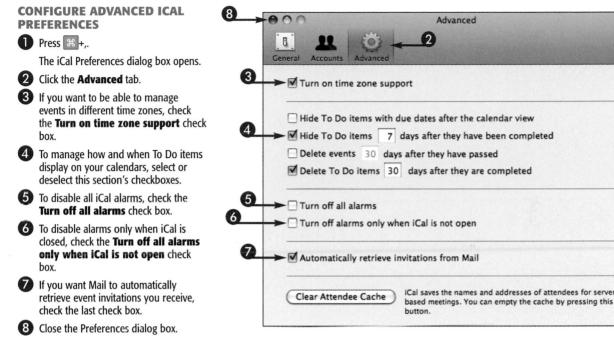

What is the Birthdays calendar?

One of the attributes you can collect for people in Address Book is **birthday**. If you enable the Birthdays calendar to be displayed, iCal creates events for each birthday captured in Address Book and presents them to you on the Birthdays calendar.

How does time zone support work?

When you enable time zone support, iCal can help you manage the often confusing situation when you are managing events across multiple time zones. When you create an event, you can associate it with a specific time zone. When viewing your calendars, you can set the current iCal time zone using the Time Zone pop-up menu located in the upper right corner of the iCal window. When you set this, all events are shifted according to the relationship between their specific time zones and iCal's so that you see all events according to the current time zone. To see an event in a specific time zone (such as when you travel there), choose that time zone on the pop-up menu.

CHAPTER

16

Print on Paper or Electronically

You will want to share the great things you create with MacBook with the world. One of the best ways to do that is to print your creations; with today's printers, you can get very high-quality documents at a relatively low cost. You can also print any document in the Portable Document Format (PDF) which is ideal for sharing documents electronically via e-mail or by posting on a Web site. There are many different kinds of printers available and several different ways to connect those printers to MacBook.

Understand Printers

Although we live in an electronic world, printing is still an important part of using a MacBook. There are a number of concepts you need to understand as you build a printing system for your MacBook and the network it is on.

Inkjet Printers

Inkjet printers create text and graphics by spraying droplets of ink on paper in various combinations. Inkjet printers produce high-quality output, especially when the output is matched to the right kind of paper. These printers are very inexpensive and many of them offer additional features such as scanning and faxing. Inkjet printers are less expensive than laser printers initially, but consume large amounts of ink that is relatively expensive; you can expect to pay a significant portion of the purchase price of the printer each time you replace one or more ink cartridges. Still, for many people, inkjet printers make a lot of sense.

Laser Printers

Laser printers use a laser, mirrors, and an imaging drum to transfer toner onto paper. Laser printers produce very high-quality output and are fast relative to inkjet printers. Although more expensive initially than inkjets, the cost per page of a laser printer can actually be significantly less than that of an inkjet printer. Like inkjet printers, most laser printers print in color. Because they were previously very expensive and printed mostly in black and white, laser printers were primarily used in businesses and other organizations. However, with some careful shopping, you can often get a color laser printer for not much more than an inkjet.

Printer Connections

No matter what kind of printer you use, MacBook needs to be able to communicate with it to send documents to print. There are three basic ways to connect MacBook to a printer; each model of printer can support one or all of these types of connections. Some printers use USB to communicate. Networkable printers have an Ethernet port that you can use to connect MacBook directly to the printer, or more likely, to connect the printer to your network. The third, and most convenient, way to connect is wirelessly. Some printers support wireless connections directly; however, with Mac OS X's printer sharing and a wireless network, you can connect to any printer wirelessly.

Printer Sharing

If you have more than one computer, you can share the same printer with all the computers over a local network (wired, wireless, or both). The shared printer can be connected directly to a Mac via USB or Ethernet, or it can be connected to an AirPort Base Station (this is the best option because it does not depend on the Mac running for the printer to be available on the network).

PDF

Adobe invented the Portable Document Format (PDF) as a means to share and print documents that do not depend on the specific applications or fonts installed on a computer. The PDF is the standard format for electronic documents no matter how they are distributed. That is good news for Mac users because support for PDF documents is built into Mac OS X. You can read any PDF document using the Preview application, but more importantly for this chapter, you can also print any document in the PDF format so that you can easily share it with others via e-mail or over the Web.

Install and Configure a USB Printer

Connecting a USB printer directly to MacBook is simple and all inkjet printers, and some laser printers, support USB connections. After you have connected the printer to MacBook, you need to configure MacBook to use it.

Install and Configure a USB Printer

① Connect the printer to a power source and turn it on.

② Connect MacBook to the printer using a USB cable.

③ Open the System Preferences application.

④ Click the Print & Fax icon.

The Print & Fax pane appears.

⑤ Click the Add Printer button (+).

The Printer Selection window appears.

⑥ Select the printer with USB shown in the Kind column.

⑦ If you want to give the printer a name, edit the name shown in the Name field.

⑧ Describe the location of the printer in the Location field.

⑨ If the correct printer is shown on the **Print Using** pop-up menu, Mac OS X has found a driver for the printer.

⑩ Click **Add**.

The Printer Selection window closes.

● You return to the System Preferences application and see the printer you added.

⑪ If you want the printer to be MacBook's default, choose it on the **Default Printer** pop-up menu.

⑫ Choose the default paper size on the **Default Paper Size in Page Setup** pop-up menu.

⑬ Quit the System Preferences application.

⑭ Open any document and choose **Print** under the **File** menu.

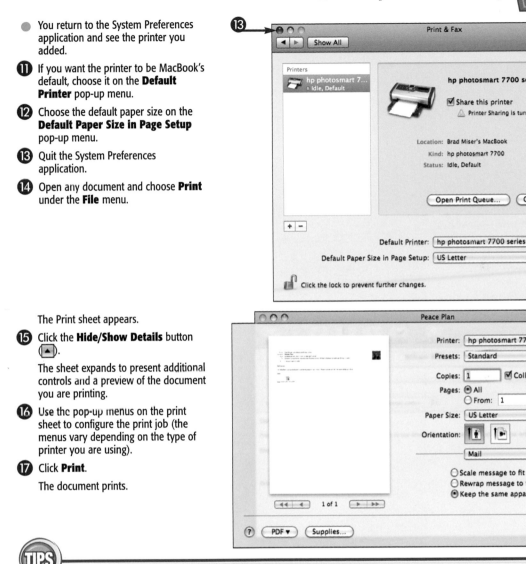

The Print sheet appears.

⑮ Click the **Hide/Show Details** button (▲).

The sheet expands to present additional controls and a preview of the document you are printing.

⑯ Use the pop-up menus on the print sheet to configure the print job (the menus vary depending on the type of printer you are using).

⑰ Click **Print**.

The document prints.

TIPS

Can I use any printer with MacBook?

First, the printer must support a connection technology that MacBook supports; this is not much of a limitation because MacBook can use USB or Ethernet connections. Second, it must have Mac-compatible drivers. Most printers do have Mac drivers available and almost all of these are built into Mac OS X.

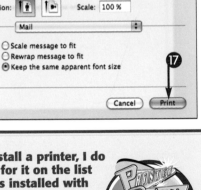

When I try to install a printer, I do not see a driver for it on the list of printer drivers installed with Mac OS X. What now?

Go to the manufacturer's Web site, look for the Support page, and then look for the Downloads section; there you can search for a Mac driver for the printer. When you find it, you can download and install it. Then, add the printer again; this time, you will be able to select the appropriate driver.

Install and Configure a Networked Printer

Many printers, especially laser printers, are designed to be connected to a network so that any computer that can connect to that network can use the printer. One way to connect a printer to a network is through Ethernet. This provides fast and trouble-free connections. The only downside is that the printer has to be within cable range of a hub (or a computer on the network, as described in the next chapter).

Install and Configure a Networked Printer

① Connect the printer to a power source and turn it on.

② Connect the printer to a hub (such as an Airport Extreme Base Station) using an Ethernet cable.

③ Connect MacBook to the same network using an Ethernet cable or an AirPort connection.

④ Open the System Preferences application.

⑤ Open the **Print & Fax** pane.

⑥ Click the **Add Printer** button (➕).

The Printer Selection window appears.

⑦ Select the printer to which you want to connect; the kind is **Bonjour**, indicating it is a network resource.

⑧ If you want to give the printer a name, edit the name shown in the **Name** field.

⑨ Describe the location of the printer in the **Location** field.

● If the correct printer is shown on the **Print Using** pop-up menu, Mac OS X has found a driver for the printer.

⑩ Click **Add**.

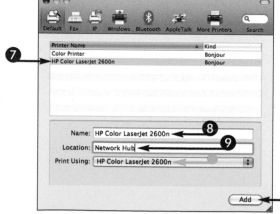

The Printer Selection window closes and you return to the System Preferences application.

● You see the printer you added in the **Printers** pane.

⓫ If you want the printer to be MacBook's default, choose it on the **Default Printer** pop-up menu.

⓬ Choose the default paper size on the **Default Paper Size in Page Setup** pop-up menu.

⓭ Quit the System Preferences application.

⓮ Open any document and choose **Print** under the **File** menu.

The Print sheet appears.

⓯ Click the **Hide/Show Details** button (▲).

The sheet expands to present additional controls and a preview of the document you are printing.

⓰ Use the pop-up menus on the print sheet to configure the print job (the menus vary depending on the type of printer you are using).

⓱ Click **Print**.

The document prints.

TIPS

What is Bonjour?

Bonjour is Mac OS X's network discovery technology. When a device can use Bonjour, it broadcasts its identity on the network. When you connect to that network to search for a device, such as a printer, Bonjour devices are discovered automatically and you do not have to search for them or deal with their network addresses. You simply select the device you want to access and connect to it.

So, what is the best printer for me?

If you do not print very often or you mostly print pictures, an inkjet printer might be your best option, especially if you get one with additional capabilities, such as scanning. However, if you print a lot or print mostly text documents, a laser printer saves you money over the long run. For the ultimate in printing, get a color laser printer, which is not as expensive as it sounds (search on eBay and you can often find reconditioned printers for less than $100).

Share a Printer

Using Mac OS X, you can share any printer connected to MacBook with other computers over a network. This is most useful when you have a USB printer or other printer that is not capable of being added to a network on its own. You simply configure the printer on a Mac and turn on printer sharing. Other computers can then access the printer you share.

Share a Printer

CONFIGURE MACBOOK TO SHARE A PRINTER

1 Connect the printer to MacBook.

Note: *You can share a networkable printer as well, but if a printer is networkable, it is better to connect it to the network and access it there.*

2 Open the Print & Fax pane of the System Preferences application.

3 Select the printer you want to share.

4 Click the **Share this printer** check box.

5 Click **Sharing**.

The Sharing pane opens.

6 Check the **Printer Sharing** check box.

Printer Sharing starts.

7 Check the check boxes next to the printers you want to share.

8 Quit the System Preferences application.

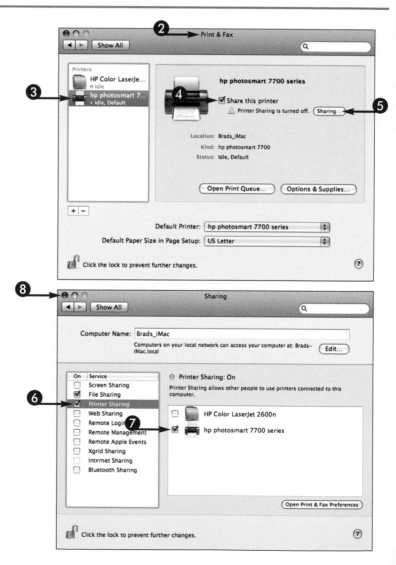

ACCESS A SHARED PRINTER

1 Open the **Print & Fax** pane of the System Preferences application.

2 Click .

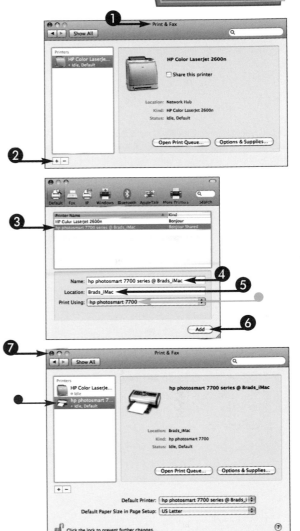

The Printer Selection window appears.

3 Select the printer to which you want to connect.

Note: Its name includes @ macname, where macname is the name of the Mac sharing it. Its kind is Bonjour Shared, which also indicates that a Mac is sharing it.

4 If you want to give the printer a name, edit the name shown in the **Name** field.

5 Describe the location of the printer in the **Location** field.

● If the correct printer is shown on the **Print Using** pop-up menu, Mac OS X has found a driver for the printer.

6 Click **Add**.

The Printer Selection window closes and you return to the System Preferences application.

● You see the printer you added.

7 Quit the System Preferences application.

8 Print to the printer.

Is it better to put a printer on a network than to share it?

Yes, because when you share a printer on a Mac with a network, the Mac has to be running for the printer to be available to the network. When a printer is connected directly to the network, it is available all the time that the network is available. But sharing comes in handy when you do not have the means to connect a printer to a network directly.

How come I see the same printer several times in the Printer Selection window?

In the Printer Selection window, you see each instance of a printer that MacBook can access. So, if a printer is connected to a network that MacBook is on and another Mac is also sharing that printer, you see the printer twice. In this case, select the printer on the network instead of the one being shared so that you can access it whenever the network is available.

Connect to a Printer Wirelessly

Because you will be moving MacBook around, you want to be able to print wirelessly from wherever you are. If you have created an AirPort network using an AirPort Extreme Base Station, you can connect a USB printer to it so that any computer that can access the network can print to that printer.

Every computer that prints to a Base Station-connected printer has to have the printer's software driver installed on it before it can use that printer. If the correct driver is not installed on MacBook, download and install it before configuring the Base Station to share a printer.

Connect to a Printer Wirelessly

CONFIGURE AN AIRPORT EXTREME BASE STATION TO SHARE A PRINTER

1 Connect the printer to the USB port on the AirPort Extreme Base Station.

2 Open the AirPort Utility application, located within the Utilities folder in the Applications folder.

3 Select the Base Station to which the printer is connected.

4 Click **Manual Setup**.

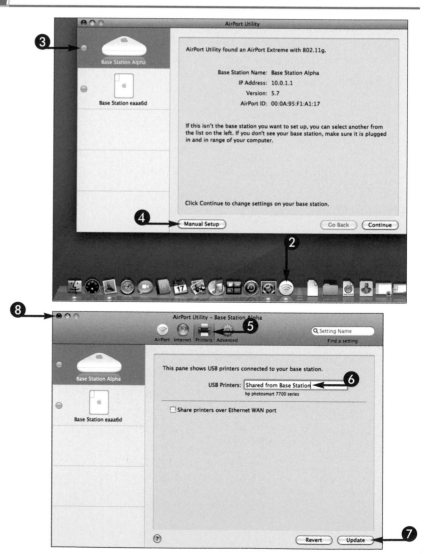

The Manual Configuration window appears.

5 Click the **Printers** tab.

6 Enter a name for the printer in the **USB Printers** box.

7 Click **Update**.

The AirPort Utility updates the Base Station and restarts it.

8 Quit the AirPort Utility.

The printer is accessible wirelessly via AirPort and on a wired network connected to the Base Station.

CONNECT TO A PRINTER BEING SHARED BY AN AIRPORT BASE STATION

① Open the **Print & Fax** pane of the System Preferences application.

② Click +.

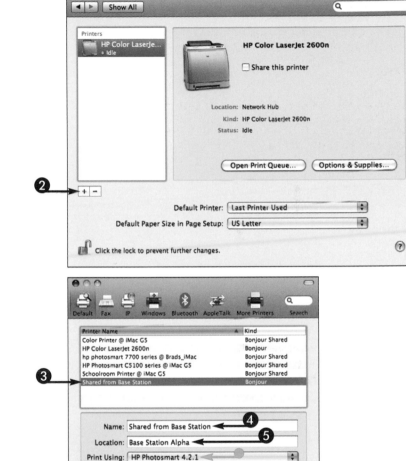

The Printer Selection window appears.

③ Select the printer to which you want to connect; the kind is Bonjour, which indicates it is a network resource.

④ If you want to give the printer a name, edit the name shown in the Name field.

⑤ Describe the location of the printer in the Location field.

● If the correct printer is shown on the **Print Using** pop-up menu, Mac OS X has found a driver for the printer.

⑥ Click **Add**.

The printer is added to the **Printers** pane in System Preferences. You can now print to it.

TIPS

Can I share a printer connected to a computer over an AirPort network, or do I have to have an AirPort Base Station?

You can share a printer connected directly to a Mac using USB over an AirPort network as long as that Mac is connected to the AirPort network. This works just like sharing a printer connected to a Base Station except that the Mac always has to be running for the printer to be available.

Can I print wirelessly to an Ethernet printer by connecting it to a Base Station using an Ethernet cable?

Yes. If a printer is networkable via Ethernet, just connect it to one of the Base Station's Ethernet ports or to a hub on the network. It is added to the network as a network resource. You can print to the printer because an AirPort Station connects the wired and wireless networks together.

Print to PDF

The Portable Document Format is a great way to distribute documents you create to other people. That is because PDF files appear correctly on any computer regardless of the fonts or other formatting options installed on it, and people cannot easily change PDF documents you create.

Support for creating PDF documents is built into Mac OS X so that you can create a PDF of any file you work with.

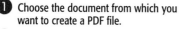
Print to PDF

① Choose the document from which you want to create a PDF file.

② Choose **Print** from the document's **File** menu.

The Print dialog box appears.

③ Open the **PDF** menu.

④ Choose **Save as PDF**.

The Save dialog box appears.

⑤ Enter a name for the PDF file you are creating.

⑥ Choose the location in which you want to save the PDF file.

⑦ Enter a title for the PDF.

⑧ Enter the author name.

⑨ If you want to enter an additional subject, do so in the Subject field.

⑩ Create keywords (used during Spotlight and other searches) in the Keywords field.

⑪ If you want to require passwords for the PDF to be used, click **Security Options**.

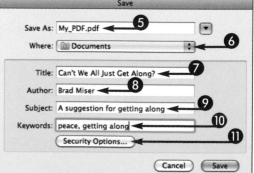

The PDF Security Options dialog box appears.

⑫ If you want people to have to enter a password to open the PDF, check **Require password to open document** check box.

⑬ If you want a password to be required for someone to copy content from the document, check the **Require password to copy text, images and other content** check box.

Note: *If you check these check boxes, you must enter a password in the Password and Verify fields.*

⑭ If you want a password to be required for the document to be printed, check the **Require password to print document** check.

Note: *If you created an open password, you must use the same password for printing.*

⑮ Click **OK**.

The dialog box closes and you return to the Save dialog box.

⑯ Click **Save**.

The PDF file is created.

⑰ Open the PDF file.

⑱ If the PDF file is password protected, enter the password at the prompt and press Return.

The document appears and is ready to print.

PDF Security Options

⑫ ☑ Require password to open document

    Password: ••••••••

    Verify: ••••••••

⑬ ☑ Require password to copy text, images and other content

⑭ ☑ Require password to print document

    Password: ••••••••

    Verify: ••••••••

(?)   (Cancel) (OK)◀ ⑮

Save

Save As: My_PDF.pdf

Where: 📁 Documents

Title: Can't We All Just Get Along?

Author: Brad Miser

Subject: A suggestion for getting along

Keywords: peace, getting along

(Security Options...)

(Cancel) (Save)◀ ⑯

TIPS

What applications can open a PDF document?

By default, PDF documents open in Mac OS X's Preview application, which provides the basic set of tools you need to view and print them. A number of other applications can open PDF files as well, most notably Adobe's free Acrobat Reader application, available at www.adobe.com. Acrobat Reader offers more features for viewing and working with PDF documents, so if you view lots of PDFs, try it to see if it works better for you than Preview.

What if I want to configure or change a PDF document?

One of the benefits of PDF documents is that they are hard to change. If you want to change a PDF or to create more sophisticated PDFs with features such as tables of contents, hyperlinks, combinations of PDF documents in different formats, and so on, you need to get Adobe Acrobat. This is also available on Adobe's Web site at www.adobe.com.

CHAPTER 17

Travel with a MacBook

One of the great things about a MacBook is that you can take it with you wherever you go. Using MacBook away from your regular location is not all that different either. You still can make the most of MacBook's capabilities to do what you want to do, no matter where you are located. There are a few things to know when you take MacBook on the road. The most important is to be able to connect to the Internet. Following closely is managing MacBook's power so you can work as long as possible. Security tools can help protect your data. Finally, when you get back, you need to synch up any files you have changed while traveling.

Connect to the Internet while Traveling

When you are on the move, there is no reason to be disconnected from the Internet. In most public places, businesses, hotels, restaurants, and other locations, Internet access is readily available through either a wireless or wired network connection.

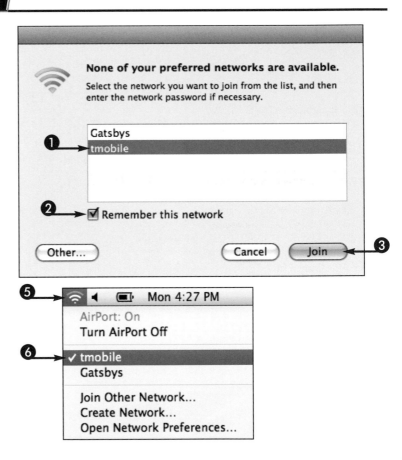

Connect to the Internet while Traveling

CONNECT TO A WIRELESS NETWORK

Note: When MacBook wakes up, it scans the area for available wireless networks and presents a list of available networks to you.

1 Select the network you want to join.

2 If you will be returning to the location and want to access the network again, check the **Remember this network** check box.

3 Click **Join**.

4 If the network is secured, enter the network password and click **OK** at the prompt.

MacBook joins the network.

5 Open the AirPort menu ().

6 Verify that you have connected to the network and that the signal strength is good.

You are ready to access the Internet over the network.

CONNECT TO A WIRED NETWORK

 Connect an Ethernet cable to the network and to MacBook.

2 Open the System Preferences application.

3 Click the **Network** icon.

The Network pane appears.

4 Check the Ethernet connection to ensure its status is Connected.

You are ready to access the Internet over the network.

OBTAIN AND LOG INTO AN INTERNET ACCOUNT

 Open Safari and try to go to any Web page.

If the page appears, you do not need an account to connect to the Internet and can skip the rest of these steps because you are already connected to the Internet.

If the page does not appear, you have to connect to an Internet provider's login screen to access an Internet account.

2 Click the Connect link.

Connect to the Internet while Traveling (continued)

Connecting to the Internet in a different location is a two-step process. First, establish the connection to the network. Second, register MacBook to access the Internet over that network. The second step is required most of the time, especially when you are charged a fee to access the Internet.

Connect to the Internet while Traveling (continued)

③ If you already have an account with the provider, enter your username and password.

④ Click the login button.

You should see a message confirming that you have Internet access and can skip the rest of these steps.

Note: *When you connect from a hotel, you usually see a page that enables you to charge the Internet access to your room.*

⑤ To obtain an account, click the link to sign up.

⑥ Follow the onscreen instructions to create an account.

Note: *You can usually choose from a variety of accounts, such as one day, monthly, and so on. Each has specific costs.*

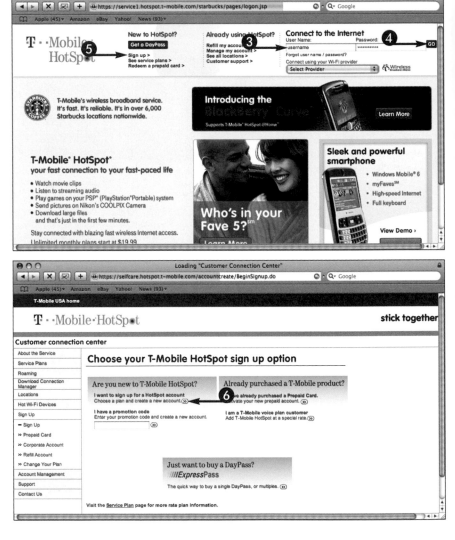

7 Log into the account you created.

8 Click the login button.

● You should see a page confirming that you are connected.

Use your Internet applications, such as Safari, Mail, iChat, and so on.

What about a wireless broadband card for Internet access?

To be able to use AirPort to connect to a network, MacBook has to be in range of that network and you have to have an account with the service provider. This is fine if you visit places connected to a network on which you have an account. However, if you travel a lot, consider obtaining a wireless broadband connection card. With these cards, you can connect to the Internet at high speeds anywhere within the network's coverage area via a cell network like that used for cell phones. National networks provide pretty broad coverage areas so you can usually get a connection when you need it. This can also be a less-expensive option because you can use the same account no matter where you are and all access is included in one monthly fee. Most of the large cell phone companies offer this service.

Manage MacBook's Power

MacBook needs power to operate, just like any other electronic device. Because it has an internal battery, you do not need to be connected to an outlet for MacBook to run. One of the most important tasks as you travel with MacBook is to manage its power so that you do not run out of juice at an inconvenient time.

There are a number of things you can do to manage MacBook's power. First, configure MacBook to use as little power as possible. Second, monitor MacBook's power status. Third, build a MacBook power toolkit.

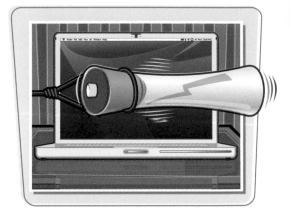

Manage MacBook's Power

CONFIGURE MACBOOK TO MINIMIZE POWER USE

1 Use the **Energy Saver** pane of the System Preferences application to configure MacBook so it uses a minimum amount of power while running on battery.

Note: See "Save Energy" in Chapter 6 for the details.

MONITOR MACBOOK'S BATTERY POWER

1 Look at the **Battery** icon in the menu bar.

As battery power is used, the filled part of the icon decreases to give you a relative idea of how much battery power remains.

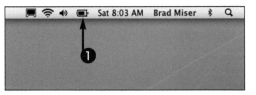

② To get more detailed information, open the **Battery** menu.

● The amount of operating time you have left is shown at the top of the menu.

③ Click **Show**.

④ Choose how you want battery information to appear.

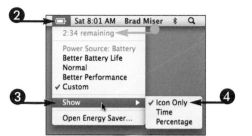

BUILD A MACBOOK POWER TOOLKIT

① When you travel with MacBook, bring its power adapter with you so you are able to recharge when you can.

② Purchase an additional battery so that when MacBook's battery gets low, you can swap it out for a fresh one.

③ If you travel on long plane flights frequently, purchase an Apple MagSafe Airline Adapter. This enables you to connect MacBook to the power outlets provided in some airplanes.

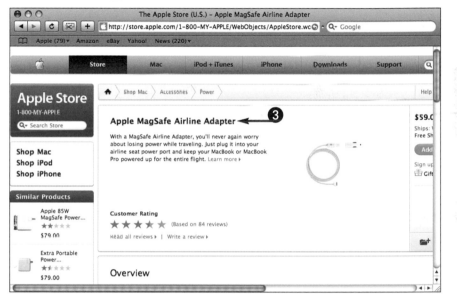

How else can I extend my working time on the road?
Put MacBook to sleep when you are not using it. When it is sleeping, MacBook uses very little power. If you have an iPod, use it to listen to music or watch video instead of iTunes on MacBook. Using iTunes uses significant amounts of power because it requires lots of hard disk activity. In general, the more disk activity required to run an application, the faster MacBook runs out of power, so be aware of the applications you use; keep only those applications you are actively using open to prevent unnecessary disk activity. Also, turn off AirPort and Bluetooth to save the power they consume.

How do I swap out MacBook's battery?
Save your work and put MacBook to sleep (or wait until it sleeps automatically because of low battery power) and close the lid. Turn MacBook upside down and rotate the battery lock to the Unlocked position so the battery pops up. Remove the battery and replace it with another one. Press the battery in and rotate the lock to the Locked position. If you do this relatively quickly, MacBook remains in Sleep mode and you can wake it up again. If you wait too long, you have to restart MacBook.

Protect MacBook's Data with FileVault

With MacBook, you run the risk of someone either accessing it or stealing it. In either situation, data stored on MacBook can be compromised. Mac OS X's FileVault feature encrypts your data so that it cannot be used without a password. Even if someone does get into your MacBook, he or she cannot access its data without the password.

Protect MacBook's Data with FileVault

1 Open the System Preferences application.

2 Click the **Security** icon.

3 Click the **FileVault** tab.

4 Click **Set Master Password**.

The Set Master Password button becomes the Change button to show you that a master password is set.

5 Click **Turn On FileVault**.

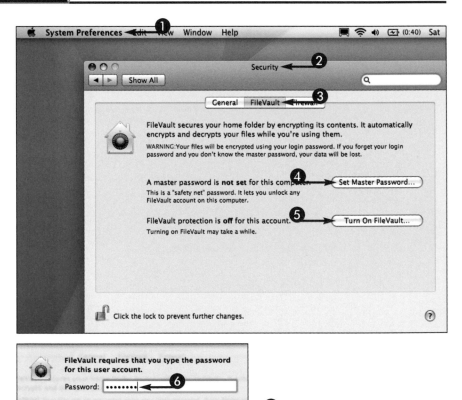

6 Enter the password needed to access the current user's data.

7 Click **OK**.

8 If you want data to be deleted securely (overwritten so it cannot be recovered from the Trash), check the **Use secure erase** check box.

9 If you want MacBook to be even more secure, check the **Use secure virtual memory** check box to encrypt data stored in virtual memory.

10 Click **Turn On FileVault**.

MacBook logs you out of the current account and encrypts all the data stored in your Home folder.

Note: When you are logged into your user account, your data is available. Make sure you log out whenever you are not using MacBook if there is any risk of it being accessed by someone you do not know or trust.

WARNING: You are ready to turn on FileVault now. After your files are encrypted, you must enter your login password or the master password to access them. If you forget these passwords, your information will be lost.

When you turn on FileVault, you will be logged out while FileVault encrypts your home folder, which might take a while. You cannot use your computer while this is occurring.

After you turn on FileVault, you cannot log in to this user account for SMB file sharing or printer sharing.

☐ Use secure erase
☐ Use secure virtual memory

Cancel | Turn On FileVault

 TIPS

When I log in and FileVault is on, I do not notice any difference. Is it working?

FileVault protects access to your data from outside your user account. For example, if someone else logs into MacBook, he or she cannot access your data without entering the FileVault password. When you are logged in under your user account and FileVault is on, you likely will not notice any difference. FileVault is designed to protect data from being accessed outside of your user account. Check the icon on your Home folder; if it is the Secure icon, FileVault is on.

What happens if I forget my password?

If you do not enter the correct password, you cannot access any data that has been encrypted (which is the point, right?). Make sure you choose a password that you can remember or that you store the password in a secure manner away from MacBook. If you forget the required password, you lose access to all the data in your Home folder. You should also create a master FileVault password in case other users forget their individual passwords. You can use this password to access all the data on MacBook.

Protect MacBook with System Security

If MacBook is used by other people, or there is some chance it will be, consider adding some extra security to prevent problems with the data stored there.

For example, you can require that a password be entered to wake MacBook up or to stop the screen saver. This is good if you sometimes leave MacBook running when it is possible for someone else to access it. Without your password, other users cannot access your information even if they get their hands on MacBook.

Protect MacBook with System Security

① Open the System Preferences application.

② Click the **Security** icon.

③ Click the **General** tab.

④ Check **Require password to wake this computer from sleep or screen saver** if you want a password to be entered to start using MacBook.

⑤ If you want to prevent automatic login, check the **Disable automatic login** check box.

⑥ If you want to require a password to change any settings through System Preferences, check the **Require password to unlock each System Preferences pane** check box.

⑦ To automatically log out, check the **Log out after** check box.

⑧ If you want to prevent remote control of MacBook to a specific device, check the **Disable remote control infrared receiver** check box.

⑨ To allow remote control with a specific device only, click **Pair.**

⑩ Hold the remote close to MacBook while pressing and holding its Menu and Next buttons at the same time.

Close System Preferences to save MacBook's new security settings.

Protect MacBook with Its Firewall

When you are using a known network to access the Internet, it should be equipped with its own firewall or NAT protection to prevent outside resources from being able to see or access MacBook. However, if you are not sure about how much protection a network provides, such as when you are connecting to a network in a public place, you should use the Mac OS X firewall to block attempts to access MacBook from the Internet.

You might have to tweak the firewall a bit to be as secure as possible while still allowing you to do what you want.

Protect MacBook with Its Firewall

① Open the System Preferences application.

② Click the **Security** icon.

③ Click the **Firewall** tab.

④ To prevent most incoming connections while allowing Mac OS X to automatically allow connections for some applications, click the **Block all incoming connections** radio button.

⑤ To allow only specific connections, click the **Set access for specific services and applications** radio button.

⑥ To add applications through which you want to allow incoming connections, click the **Add** button (+).

● Services and applications that are allowed to have incoming connections are shown on the list.

⑦ Click **Advanced**.

⑧ Check the **Enable Firewall Logging** check box to create a log of incoming connections.

⑨ To prevent MacBook from being detected on a network by services you did not request, check the **Enable Stealth Mode** checkbox.

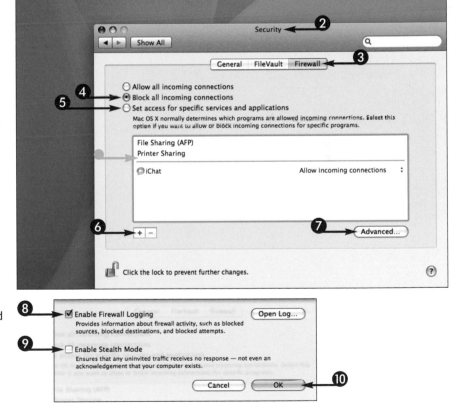

Synchronize Files with Other Computers

If you use MacBook and another computer, such as an iMac, you should keep documents you work on synchronized on each computer so that changes you make on MacBook are reflected on the iMac and vice versa.

There are several ways to make sure you have the most current version of documents in both locations. If you have .Mac, you can use your iDisk as the synchronizing mechanism; this is good because the process is mostly automatic. You can also use a smart folder to identify files that have changed recently so that you can synchronize them manually.

Synchronize Files with Other Computers

SYNCHRONIZE FILES USING AN IDISK

1. Open the System Preferences application.

2. Open the **.Mac** pane.

3. Click the **iDisk** tab.

4. Click **Start**.

   MacBook creates a copy of your iDisk on its hard drive.

5. Click the **Automatically** radio button.

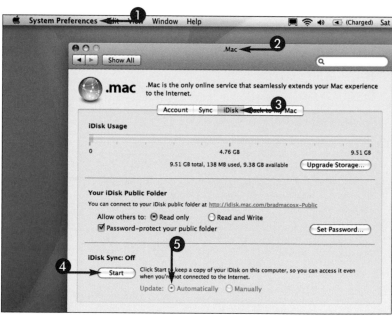

MacBook synchronizes the version of files on the local iDisk (on your hard drive) with the one stored on the Internet.

6. Save documents that you want to keep in sync on a folder on the iDisk.

7. Use steps **1** to **5** to configure your iDisk on each computer that you want to keep in synch.

   Each computer you configure accesses the same version of the files on the iDisk.

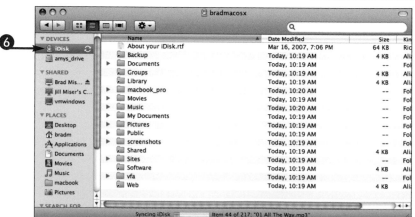

SYNCHRONIZE FILES USING A SMART FOLDER

1 Create a smart folder on MacBook that uses criteria by which you want to identify files you have changed while traveling with MacBook.

Note: See Chapter 4 for the details of creating a smart folder.

2 When you return from a trip, use the smart folder to find all the documents you have changed recently.

3 Copy the changed files from MacBook to the computer on which you want to sync them.

Note: Configure file sharing to make it easy to copy files between computers (see Chapter 7).

Name	Kind	Last Opened
224595 fg1721c.tiff	TIFF image	Today, 10:20 AM
224595 fg1721.tiff	TIFF image	Today, 10:20 AM
224595 fg1720c.tiff	TIFF image	Today, 10:18 AM
224595 fg1720.tiff	TIFF image	Today, 10:18 AM
VFAspendMa...ions_bm.doc	Microsoft Word document	Nov 13, 2007, 3:35 PM
VFAspendMa...1092007.doc	Microsoft Word document	Nov 13, 2007, 11:15 AM
spdmgr_prospect_log.xls	Microsoft Excel workbook	Nov 13, 2007, 10:55 AM
status_planning_9_8.doc	Microsoft Word document	Nov 13, 2007, 9:38 AM
status_planning_9_29.doc	Microsoft Word document	Nov 13, 2007, 9:38 AM
status_planning_9_22.doc	Microsoft Word document	Nov 13, 2007, 9:38 AM
status_planning_9_15.doc	Microsoft Word document	Nov 13, 2007, 9:38 AM
status_planning_9_1.doc	Microsoft Word document	Nov 13, 2007, 9:38 AM
status_planning_8_4.doc	Microsoft Word document	Nov 13, 2007, 9:38 AM

46 items

TIPS

What about synchronization applications?

There are third-party applications that keep files stored in multiple locations in synch. You designate a source folder and a target folder, and then you determine the direction of the sync, such as from the target to the source or in both directions. Based on your settings, the application automatically performs the required synchronization. One example is ChronoSynch, available at www.econtechnologies.com.

What do I need to do about backing up files I changed while traveling?

Chapter 19 discusses Time Machine, which enables you to back up all the information on MacBook in case you ever need to recover data that is lost from MacBook's internal hard drive. As soon as you get back to where your backup hard drive is located, connect the hard drive to MacBook; the backup process launches immediately so that any changes you made while traveling are protected in the current backup.

Connect a MacBook to Other Devices

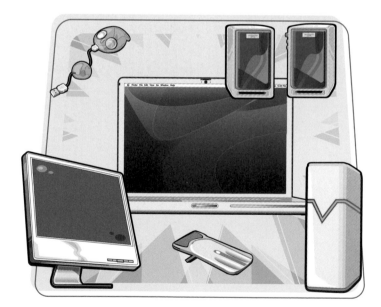

MacBook packs a lot of functionality in a small container, and you can do a lot without ever connecting MacBook to other devices; but there is no reason to limit your MacBook to its built-in capabilities. There are many great devices that you can connect to MacBook to get even more out of it. This chapter contains a sampling of some of the more useful devices to which you might want to connect MacBook.

Expand Storage Space with an External Hard Drive

All MacBooks include a hard drive on which you store the operating system, applications, and your own files and folders. Over time, you might run low on available disk space, especially if you do large video or DVD projects. You can connect MacBook to an external hard drive to expand the working storage space available to you.

Expand Storage Space with an External Hard Drive

CONNECT AND POWER AN EXTERNAL HARD DRIVE

1 Connect the hard drive to a power source and turn it on.

You should hear the drive spin up and see its power light.

2 If the hard drive supports FireWire, use a FireWire cable to connect its FireWire port to the FireWire port on MacBook.

Note: Most hard drives include the cable you need to connect to MacBook. However, some do not. Check the package information to make sure the cable is included. If it is not, you have to buy a cable separately.

3 If the hard drive supports USB2 but not FireWire, use a USB2 cable to connect its USB port to one of the USB ports on the Mac.

The hard drive is ready to format and partition.

FORMAT AND PARTITION AN EXTERNAL HARD DRIVE

1 Open the **Applications** folder, then the **Utilities** folder, and then open the **Disk Utility** application.

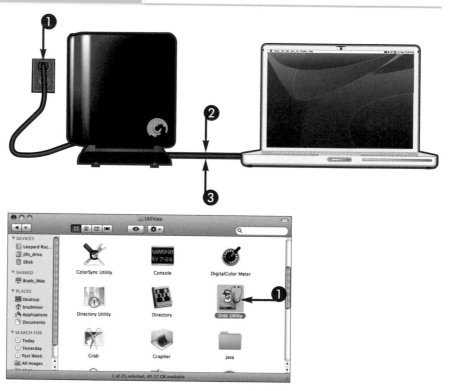

chapter 18

● When Disk Utility opens, you see all available disks in the left pane.

② Select the external hard disk.

③ Click the **Partition** tab.

● You see the number of partitions in which the disk is currently organized; a new disk has one partition.

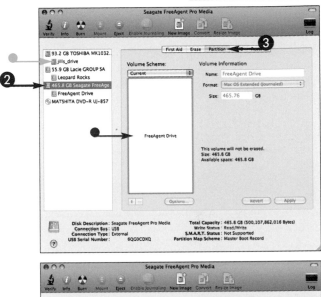

④ On the **Volume Scheme** pop-up menu, choose the number of partitions you want to create on the disk.

● The space on the disk is grouped into the number of partitions you selected. Each partition is named "Untitled X," where X is a sequential number.

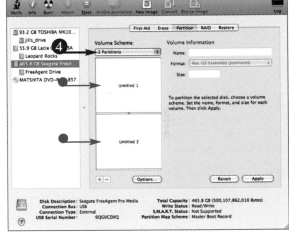

continued

Although being able to access more storage space is useful for projects and documents, it's even more important for backing up the information you have stored on MacBook. With an external hard drive, you can use Mac OS X's Time Machine feature (covered in Chapter 19) to back up your important data. Should something happen to that data on MacBook or to the MacBook itself, you can easily recover the data from the external drive.

5 Select the top partition.

● Its information is shown in the **Volume Information** section.

6 Name the partition in the **Name** box.

7 On the Format pop-up menu, choose **Mac OS Extended (Journaled)**.

8 Enter the size of the first partition in the **Size** box and press Return.

Note: *You can also change the size of partitions by dragging the resize handle located in the horizontal bar between the partitions in the box.*

The partition is named and sized.

9 Select the next partition.

10 Repeat steps **6** to **8** to name, format, and size the partition.

11 Repeat steps **9** and **10** until you have configured each partition.

The total size of the partitions equals the usable size of the hard disk.

12 Click **Apply**.

The partition warning appears; when you partition a disk, all the data it contains is erased, so make sure you do not need its data before continuing.

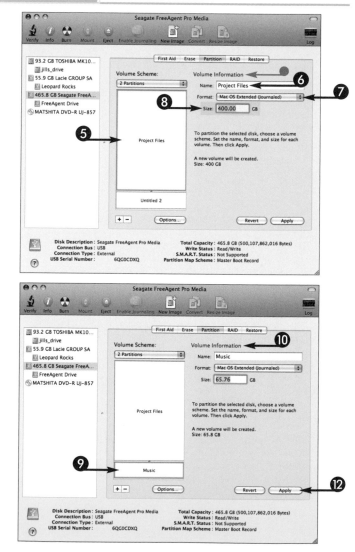

13 Click **Partition**.

Disk Utility partitions the drive according to your settings and the Time Machine dialog box appears.

14 Quit Disk Utility.

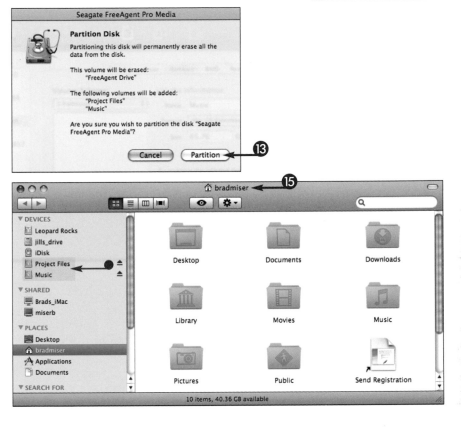

Seagate FreeAgent Pro Media

Partition Disk

Partitioning this disk will permanently erase all the data from the disk.

This volume will be erased:
"FreeAgent Drive"

The following volumes will be added:
"Project Files"
"Music"

Are you sure you wish to partition the disk "Seagate FreeAgent Pro Media"?

Cancel   Partition   **13**

15 Open a Finder window.

● You see the partitions on the external drive, and they are ready to be used just like MacBook's internal hard drive.

Note: Before disconnecting a hard drive from MacBook, click the Eject button next to its icon in the Places sidebar and wait for the disk icon to disappear from the sidebar. Disconnecting a drive without ejecting it can damage its data.

15 bradmiser

DEVICES
- Leopard Rocks
- Jills_drive
- iDisk
- Project Files
- Music

SHARED
- Brads_iMac
- miserb

PLACES
- Desktop
- bradmiser
- Applications
- Documents

SEARCH FOR

Desktop   Documents   Downloads

Library   Movies   Music

Pictures   Public   Send Registration

10 items, 40.36 GB available

TIPS

What kind of external hard drive works with MacBook?

MacBook supports any external hard drive that supports USB2 or FireWire 400. You want to get the largest drive you can afford; for backing up data, the hard disk drive should be at least twice as large as the hard disk in MacBook; for example, if your MacBook has a 100GB hard drive, the external hard drive should be at least 200GB. Finally, you can use hard drives that are Mac- or Windows-compatible. If a hard drive is formatted for Windows, you should reformat and partition it before using it (any software with it probably will not run on MacBook, but you do not need it anyway).

200GB

What is a partition and how many should I create on my external hard drive?

Partitions are logical volumes on a hard disk, which means that they behave as if each partition is its own hard disk even though they are actually on the same physical disk. You can create partitions for various purposes, such as to organize data. However, once you create a partition, you cannot change its size without reformatting it (thus erasing all its data). In most cases, you should limit the partitions on one disk to one or two so that you do not end up with lots of partitions that are too small to be usable.

Connect and Use an External Display

You can never have too much screen space to work with. In addition to making your document windows larger so you can see more of their contents, a larger amount of screen space helps you work efficiently because you can have multiple windows open at the same time.

To add screen space to MacBook, you can connect an external display.

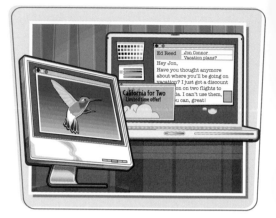

CONNECT THE REQUIRED ADAPTER TO THE EXTERNAL DISPLAY

1. Obtain an Apple Mini-DV to DVI adapter from the Apple Store or other Apple retailer.

2. Plug the small end of the adapter into the Mini-DV port on MacBook.

3. Connect the other end of the cable to the DVI port on the display.

4. Connect the display to power and power it up.

CONFIGURE THE EXTERNAL DISPLAY

1. Open the System Preferences application and click the **Displays** icon.

   A Displays pane opens on the MacBook's display and on the external display.

2. Click the **Arrangement** tab on the Displays pane on the MacBook's screen.

● You see an icon representation of each display.

3. Drag the external display's icon to match the physical location of the display compared to MacBook.

4. If you want the external display to be the main display, drag the menu bar from the MacBook display's icon onto the external display's icon.

5. If you want the displays to show the same information, check the **Mirror Displays** check box and skip the rest of these steps.

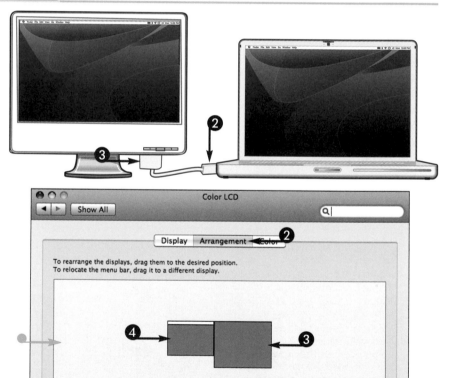

6 Select the **Displays** pane from the System Preferences on the external display.

7 Choose the resolution for the external display by selecting it on the list of available resolutions.

8 If the **Refresh Rate** menu appears, choose the highest rate available.

9 Use the other controls to configure the external display.

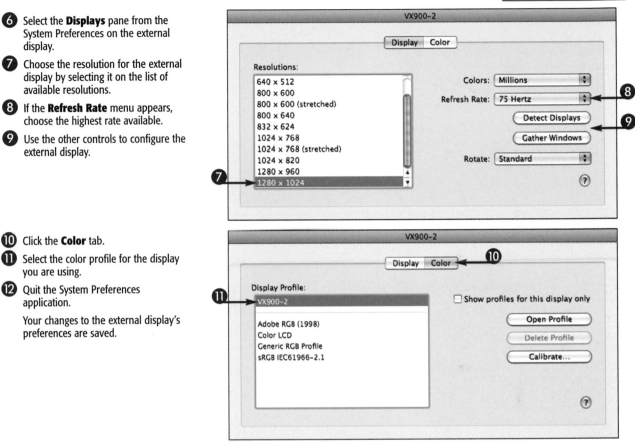

VX900-2

Display Color

Resolutions:
640 × 512
800 × 600
800 × 600 (stretched)
800 × 640
832 × 624
1024 × 768
1024 × 768 (stretched)
1024 × 820
1280 × 960
1280 × 1024

Colors: Millions
Refresh Rate: 75 Hertz
Detect Displays
Gather Windows
Rotate: Standard

10 Click the **Color** tab.

11 Select the color profile for the display you are using.

12 Quit the System Preferences application.

Your changes to the external display's preferences are saved.

VX900-2

Display Color

Display Profile:
VX900-2

Adobe RGB (1998)
Color LCD
Generic RGB Profile
sRGB IEC61966-2.1

☐ Show profiles for this display only

Open Profile
Delete Profile
Calibrate...

TIPS

What kind of external display should I get for MacBook?

MacBook supports many different displays and resolutions. The two most important considerations are size and cost. Larger displays are better because they give you more working space. Larger displays also tend to be more expensive, although that depends on the specific brands you choose. Be wary of very inexpensive displays because they tend to have poor image quality. In most cases, if you choose a display from a reputable manufacturer, such as Apple (the Apple displays are extremely high quality, but are also on the expensive end of the scale) or ViewSonic, any display you get will work well for you.

Can I use a projector with MacBook?

Yes. You connect and use a projector in the same way as an external display. When you use a projector, you typically want to turn display mirroring on so that the audience sees the same information being shown on MacBook's screen.

Connect and Use a Bluetooth Mouse

You might find that the MacBook's trackpad works really well for you and you do not want to use anything else; or, you might prefer a mouse when you are working with MacBook in one place. It is mostly a matter of personal preference.

If you do want to use a mouse, a Bluetooth mouse is a good option because it has no wires and therefore does not take up one of MacBook's precious USB ports.

① Insert batteries in the mouse and turn it on.

② Place the mouse in discovery mode; see the documentation for the specific mouse you use to see how this is done.

③ Open the System Preferences application and click the **Bluetooth** icon.

The Bluetooth pane appears.

④ Check the **Bluetooth Power** check box to turn Bluetooth on.

⑤ Check the **Discoverable** check box so that other Bluetooth devices can find MacBook.

⑥ Check the **Show Bluetooth status in the menu bar** check box to enable the Bluetooth menu so you can control Bluetooth from the desktop.

⑦ Click the **Set Up New Device** button.

The Bluetooth Setup Assistant appears.

⑧ Click **Continue**.

9 Select the **Mouse** radio button.

10 Click **Continue**.

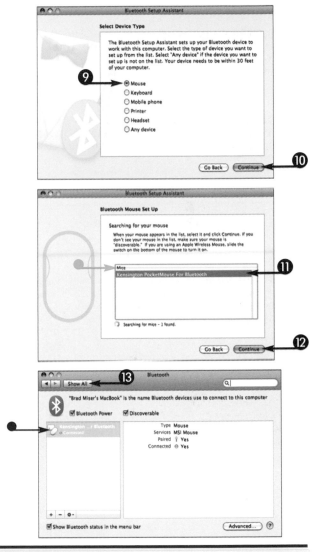

● MacBook searches for mice with which it can communicate. These appear on the list of available devices.

11 Select the mouse you are configuring.

12 Click **Continue**.

MacBook pairs itself with the mouse.

● The mouse is shown on the Bluetooth tab and you can start using it.

13 Click **Show All**.

14 Configure the mouse using the **Mouse** tab of the **Keyboard & Mouse** pane.

TIPS

Can I use other kinds of mice?

You can use any mouse with MacBook whether it is a Bluetooth mouse or not. To use a wired mouse, simply plug its USB cable into an available USB port. To use a non-Bluetooth wireless mouse, connect its receiver to a USB port. You can use the Mouse tab of the Keyboard & Mouse pane of the System Preferences application to configure any mouse.

What is the best kind of Bluetooth mouse?

The most important consideration when choosing a mouse is the comfort of the mouse in your hand. If possible, you should try moving a mouse around before buying it. Next, consider the number of controls and buttons a mouse offers. At the least, a mouse should have two buttons and a scroll wheel. Apple's Mighty Mouse enables you to click a left or right button by pressing one side or the other, scroll horizontally and vertically using its scroll ball, and program buttons on the side for specific actions.

Connect and Use External Speakers

MacBook has speakers, but their sound quality is something less than spectacular (a lot less actually). With iTunes, DVD Player, and all the other great applications for which sound is an important element, you should consider using external speakers when you have MacBook parked somewhere.

You can use a variety of speakers with MacBook as long as they are powered (also called computer) speakers. MacBook supports digital audio, which means you can connect a surround sound speaker system to MacBook, which is especially good when you use it to watch DVDs.

Connect and Use External Speakers

1 Connect the speaker input to the headphones/digital audio out port of the left side of MacBook.

2 Make the connections between the speakers, such as between the speakers and the control unit.

3 Power up the speakers.

4 Open the **System Preferences** application and click the **Sound** icon.

The Sound pane appears.

5 Click the **Output** tab.

6 Select the speakers you want to use for sound output.

7 If controls for those speakers appear, use them. The device used in this example has no output controls.

8 Play sound with an application such as iTunes (see Chapter 11).

9 Use the application's controls to set a general volume level.

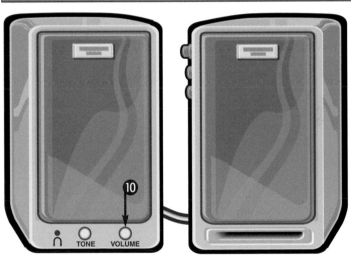

10 Adjust the volume level and other settings using the speaker system's controls.

TIPS

Why do I need a TOSLINK adapter for digital audio?
Analog audio, which is used for most headphones and two- or three-speaker systems, uses different technologies than digital audio does. MacBook has only one sound out port: the headphones/digital audio out port. Although this looks like a typical stereo mini-jack port, its appearance is deceiving. When you connect a typical stereo mini-jack plug, it behaves like a regular port, such as the headphones port on an iPod, and you get stereo sound output. To access the digital output from the port, you need a special adapter that connects to a digital audio cable and fits into the port in order to make the correct connections for digital audio. This is called a TOSLINK adapter; when you are buying a digital audio cable, look for one that includes the adapter. You can also purchase them separately.

Synchronize a MacBook with an iPhone

In addition to its amazing cell phone features, the iPhone offers iPod functionality (see Chapter 11 for synching with an iPhone for that purpose) along with calendars, contacts, e-mail, and Web browsing.

Some of the information you use on iPhone can come from MacBook. For example, if you use iCal to manage your calendar (see Chapter 15), you can synchronize your calendar on iPhone so that changes you make in iCal are reflected on the iPhone and vice versa. You can also sync your e-mail accounts, contacts from Address Book, and even your Safari bookmarks.

Synchronize a MacBook with an iPhone

① Connect iPhone to MacBook using its USB cable.

● iPhone is mounted on MacBook, iTunes opens, and you see iPhone on the iTunes Source list.

② Select **iPhone**.

③ Click the **Info** tab.

④ Check the **Sync Address Book contacts** check box.

⑤ To sync all contacts, click the **All contacts** radio button.

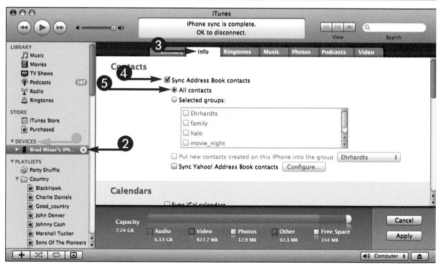

⑥ Scroll down until you see the **Calendars** section.

⑦ Check the **Sync iCal calendars** check box.

⑧ If you want to sync all of your calendars, click the **All calendars** radio button.

⑨ From the pop-up menu, choose the calendar into which created iPhone events should be placed.

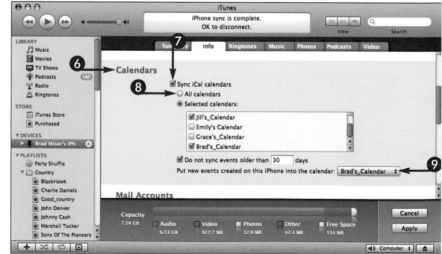

⑩ Scroll down to the **Mail Accounts** and **Web Browser** sections.

⑪ To move your e-mail accounts to iPhone, check the **Sync selected Mail accounts** check box.

Note: For information about e-mail, see Chapter 9.

⑫ Check the box for each account you want to sync.

⑬ To sync your Web bookmarks, check the **Sync Safari bookmarks** check box.

Note: For information about bookmarks, see Chapter 8.

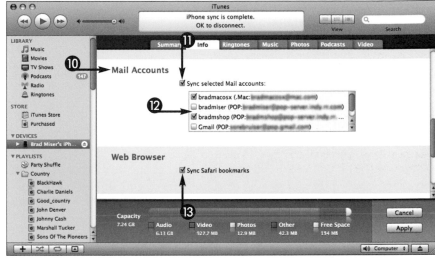

⑭ Scroll down to the **Advanced** section.

⑮ Check the box for the information you want to be replaced on iPhone when you sync

⑯ Click **Apply**.

The next time you sync, the information you configured is moved between MacBook and iPhone.

Can I sync MacBook with other kinds of cell phones?

If your cell phone supports Bluetooth, you can sync its information with MacBook too. In most cases, you can at least sync contacts. With other devices, you might be able to move calendar and other information from MacBook to the cell phone; it depends on the specific device that you use.

So, how do I do that?

To sync with a Bluetooth cell phone, you must pair it with MacBook. You do this like other Bluetooth devices using the Bluetooth Setup Assistant (see "Connect and Use a Bluetooth Mouse" earlier in this chapter). Once paired, you can choose the information that you sync between the two devices. Although not as easy and powerful as syncing with iPhone, this works almost as well.

19

Maintain and Troubleshoot MacBook

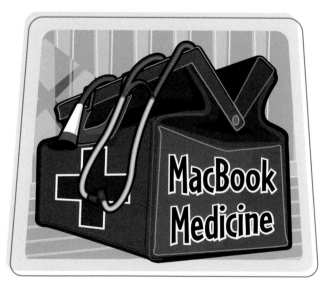

MacBooks are complicated machines. The good news is that their hardware and the Mac OS X software are so well designed that it is not likely you will experience problems. Even better news is that with a few simple maintenance tasks, you can further decrease the already small chance that you will have problems and lessen the severity of problems you do experience. It is important to know what to do when a problem happens so that you can quickly get MacBook back into action.

Keep MacBook's Apple Software Current

Apple regularly issues updates for its applications to correct these problems (hopefully before you experience them). Along with correcting problems, Apple also issues updates to improve its software by adding new features and capabilities.

Mac OS X includes built-in tools to make it simple to keep your Apple software (Mac OS X plus any Apple applications installed on MacBook) current. Keeping your software up to date is one of the most important things you can do to maintain MacBook to prevent problems.

Keep MacBook's Apple Software Current

UPDATE APPLE SOFTWARE MANUALLY

1 From the Apple menu, choose **Software Update**.

The Software Update application launches, connects to the Internet, and compares the versions of Apple software installed on MacBook to the current versions.

Note: *If the current versions of Apple software are already installed, you see a message stating that no new software was found.*

2 Select one of the available updates.

3 Read information about that update to understand what it includes.

4 To install an update, check its check box; to prevent an update from being installed, uncheck its check box.

5 Click **Install** *numberofupdates*, where *numberofupdates* is the number of updates you have selected to install.

6 Enter your administrator user name (if required).

7 Type your password.

8 Click **OK**.

MacBook downloads and installs the selected updates.

Note: *Some updates require you to restart MacBook; click* ***Restart*** *at the prompt and skip the rest of these steps.*

Software Update

New software is available for your computer.

Installing this software may take some time. If you're not ready to install now, you can choose Software Update from the Apple menu later.

Install	Name	Version	Size
☑	iMovie Update	7.1	46.1 MB
☑	iPhoto Update	7.1	61.8 MB
☑	iWeb Update	2.0.2	18.4 MB

This update addresses several areas including video and audio editing capabilities, and performance associated with opening and switching iMovie Events and Projects. This update also supports general compatibility issues, improves overall stability, and addresses a number of other minor issues.

Note: Use of this software is subject to the original Software License Agreement(s) that accompanied the software being updated. A list of Apple SLAs may be found here: http://www.apple.com/legal/sla/.

Install 3 Items

Software Update requires that you type your password.

Name: Brad Miser

Password: |

▶ Details

?   Cancel   OK

When the process is complete, Software Update window appears.

● You see a green check mark () next to each update that was installed successfully.

● Updates you did not install do not have the check mark; you can install them by checking the **Install** check box and clicking the **Install** button.

UPDATE APPLE SOFTWARE AUTOMATICALLY

1 Open the System Preferences application.

2 Click the **Software Update** icon.

The Software Update pane appears.

3 Click the **Scheduled Check** tab.

4 Check the **Check for updates** check box.

5 Choose how frequently you want MacBook to check for new software.

6 If you want important updates to be downloaded automatically, check the **Download important updates automatically** check box.

Note: If you do not check this check box, you are prompted to download the updates when they are available.

When the specified amount of time passes, Software Update checks for new software.

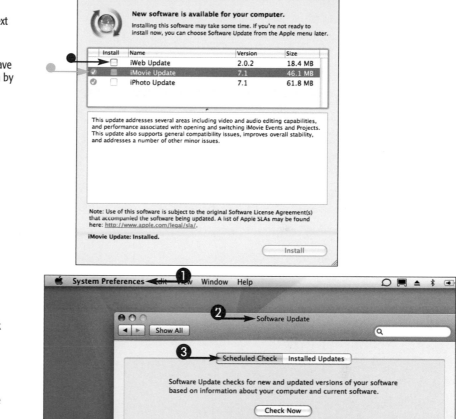

TIPS

Should I install all updates to my software?
In general, you should install all updates as they become available. Rarely, an update actually causes more problems than it solves; but that is unusual, and in such cases the problematic update is immediately followed by one that corrects its problems. Make the update process easy on yourself by configuring MacBook for automatic updates.

How do I know what updates have been installed?
Open the Software Update pane of the System Preferences application. Click the **Installed Updates** tab. A list of all the updates you have installed successfully appears.

Maintain and Update Third-Party Applications

The odds are great that you also have third-party software on MacBook, such as Microsoft Word and Excel or Intuit's Quicken. Like Apple, other software companies also issue updates to their software to fix bugs and add features.

Unfortunately, support for these updates is not built into Mac OS X. Instead, each application provides its own tools to download and install updates. Most of these also support manual and automatic updates. The details of using these tools depend on the specific application. The following sections show how to update Microsoft Office applications manually and Ambrosia Software's Snapz Pro X automatically; other third-party applications are updated similarly.

Maintain and Update Third-Party Applications

1 After launching the application, choose **Check for Updates** from the Help menu.

The application checks for updates either using built-in tools or through a separate update application.

MAINTAIN AND UPDATE THIRD-PARTY APPLICATIONS AUTOMATICALLY

1 After launching the application, open the application's Preferences tools.

2 Select the **Check for new versions at launch** check box.

Note: *This command may use different wording, but most applications provide some way to check for updates automatically.*

Each time you launch the application, it checks for newer versions. When one is found, you are prompted to download and install it.

MacBook includes lots of hardware components and many different kinds of software. Each of these has a specific version and set of capabilities. Most of the time, you do not need to worry about these details. However, there are times when these details can be very important, especially when you are trying to troubleshoot and solve problems.

Keeping a current profile of MacBook is a good idea so that you have detailed information about it when you need to solve a problem or evaluate MacBook's capabilities (such as if it meets the system requirements for hardware or software you are thinking about adding).

Profile MacBook

① From the Apple menu, choose **About This Mac**.

● The **About This Mac** window appears.

Here, you see information about the version of Mac OS X you are running, the processors in MacBook, the amount of RAM, and the current startup disk.

② Click **More Info**.

The System Profiler application appears.

● In the left pane, you see various categories of information about MacBook, such as hardware components.

③ Select an area about which you want detailed information.

● The details appear in the right pane of the window. You may want to print the information and store a hard copy.

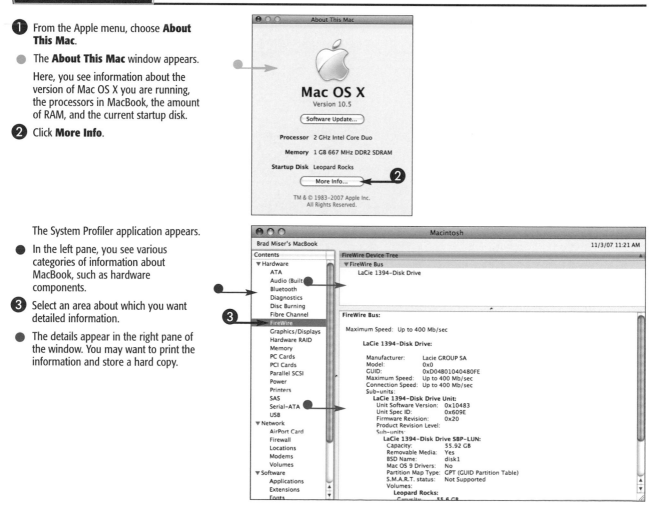

Monitor
MacBook's Activity

You cannot always tell what is happening with MacBook just by looking at its screen or observing how applications are performing. It is useful to be able to identify what is happening with MacBook in detail, especially when you are troubleshooting a problem.

With the Activity Monitor application, you can see the status of MacBook in a very detailed way. For example, you can see how much of MacBook's processing power specific applications are using, which can often tell you when an application is having a problem.

Monitor MacBook's Activity

① Open the Utilities folder within the Applications folder.

② Double-click the **Activity Monitor** icon.

The Activity Monitor application opens.

③ Click the **CPU** tab.

● In the upper part of the window, you see a list of all the processes running on MacBook.

● At the bottom of the window, you see a graphical representation of the activity of each of MacBook's processors.

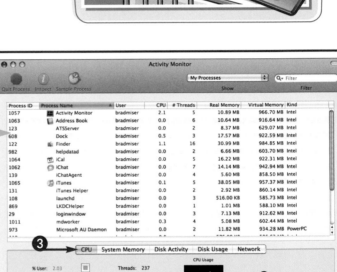

④ Click the **Disk Activity** tab.

● At the bottom of the window, you see how data is being written to the hard disk.

⑤ Click the **CPU** column heading to sort the list of processes by amount of processor activity.

You can limit the processes shown in the window to be just for applications, which can make the window's information easier to interpret.

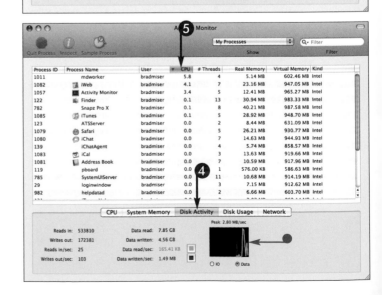

6 On the pop-up menu at the top of the window, choose **Windowed Processes**.

● The list is reduced so that it includes only processes associated with applications.

7 Click the **Disk Usage** tab.

8 Select the disk about which you want information.

● The information at the bottom of the window shows how much of the disk is being used.

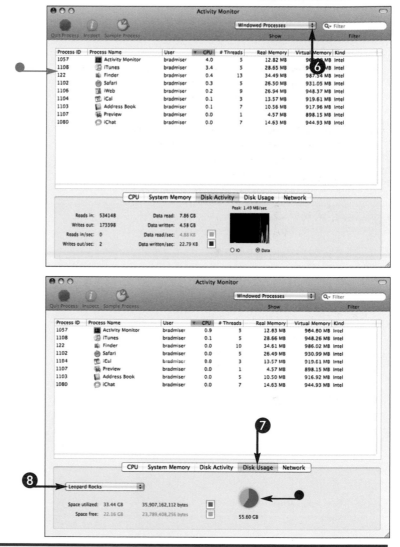

TIPS

What do I do if a process is using a lot of the CPU for a long period of time?
Switch to the application and try to quit it. If it does not quit, it is hung, meaning that its processes are locked up because it is having a problem. Go back to Activity Monitor, select the process, and click the **Quit Process** button. Click **Force Quit**. The process is stopped; forcing an application to quit loses any unsaved data in it, so make sure the application is really hung before doing this.

How can I get even more detail about a specific process?
Select a process and click the **Inspect** button. The Inspect window opens and you see several tabs providing information about various aspects of the process such as its memory use, statistics about how it is working, and the files and ports it has open. Sometimes this information is useful when doing detailed troubleshooting.

Maintain MacBook's Hard Drive

If MacBook's hard drive is not performing optimally, MacBook will not be at its best either.

You can do a lot for MacBook's hard drive by practicing good housekeeping on it to keep as much free space available as possible (see the first tip at the end of this section). If you have an external hard drive, create a second startup disk to use in case something happens to your primary startup disk. You can also use Mac OS X's Disk Utility application to maintain MacBook's hard drive and to solve some problems if they occur.

CREATE AN ALTERNATE STARTUP DISK

1. Connect and configure an external hard drive (see Chapter 18).

2. Insert the Mac OS X installation disc.

   The **Mac OS X Install DVD** window opens.

3. Double-click the **Install Mac OS X** icon.

   The Mac OS X installer application starts.

4. Follow the on-screen instructions to install Mac OS X on the external hard disk.

   The installer completes the installation and MacBook restarts using the new startup disk.

CHOOSE A STARTUP DISK

1. Open the System Preferences application.

2. Click the **Startup Disk** icon.

   The Startup Disk pane appears.

3. Select the startup disk that you want to use.

4. Click **Restart**.

   MacBook starts up from the disk you selected.

Note: You can also choose a startup disk by restarting MacBook and holding the Option key down.

MAINTAIN OR REPAIR A MACBOOK'S HARD DRIVE USING DISK UTILITY

1 Open the Disk Utility application located in the Utilities folder within the Applications folder.

2 Select the hard disk you want to maintain or repair.

Note: You cannot repair MacBook's internal hard drive with Disk Utility.

3 Click the **Verify Disk** button.

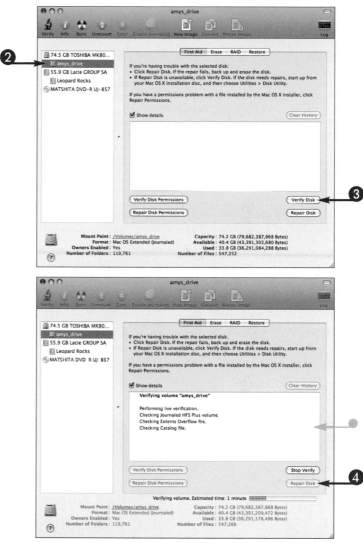

● Disk Utility checks the hard drive, and the progress appears in the window.

4 Click the **Repair Disk** button.

*Note: If you selected an external hard disk, click **Repair Disk** instead of Verify Disk because the verify function is part of the repair process.*

Disk Utility attempts to repair the problems it found. If successful, you see a success message.

TIPS

What are good housekeeping practices for a hard disk?

When you are done with folders or files, move them off the hard drive. Delete them if you are sure you will not need them again, or archive them by burning them onto a CD or DVD and then deleting them from the hard drive. You should keep your folders and files well organized so that you have a good idea of what you have stored on the disk. You should also make sure that you keep a good backup for all the important files on your hard drive.

Should I use a third-party disk maintenance application?

If Disk Utility is unable to repair a disk, you can purchase a more sophisticated disk maintenance application. These applications usually include a DVD from which you can startup in order to repair your startup disk.

Use Time Machine to Back Up MacBook

If something really bad happens to MacBook, you can lose all the files it contains. This includes music from the iTunes Store (you have to pay for it again if you want it back) along with other content such as applications you have downloaded. However, what is worse is losing data you create, such as your photos in iPhoto, movies, and documents. Much of this data simply cannot be replaced.

Use Time Machine to Back Up MacBook

1 With an external hard drive connected, open the System Preferences application.

2 Click the **Time Machine** icon.

The Time Machine pane opens.

3 Drag the slider to the ON position.

Time Machine activates and the **select drive** sheet appears.

4 Select the drive on which you want to store the backed-up information.

5 Click **Use for Backup**.

Note: When you use a hard drive for Time Machine, the hard drive's icon becomes the Time Machine icon.

amys_drive		40.4 GB
Back_Up		184.0 GB

The sheet closes and you return to the Time Machine page.

● The drive you selected is shown at the top of the pane.

6 Click **Options**.

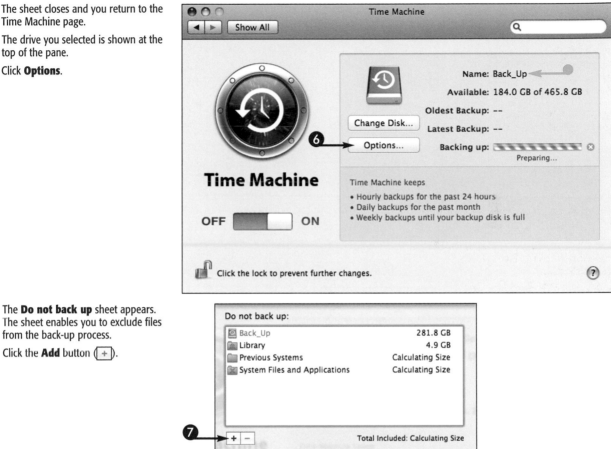

The **Do not back up** sheet appears. The sheet enables you to exclude files from the back-up process.

7 Click the **Add** button (+).

continued

Use Time Machine to Back Up MacBook *(continued)*

The way to minimize the risk of losing important data is to back it up. Mac OS X's Time Machine application is designed to make it easy for you to do this so you can recover important files easily when you need to. All you need is an external hard drive on which to store your backups.

Use Time Machine to Back Up MacBook *(continued)*

The select sheet appears.

⑧ Navigate to and select the folders or files you want to exclude from the backup.

⑨ Click **Exclude**.

⑩ If you selected system files, click **Exclude System Folder Only** to exclude only files in the System folder.

⑪ Click **Exclude All System Files** to exclude system files no matter where they are stored.

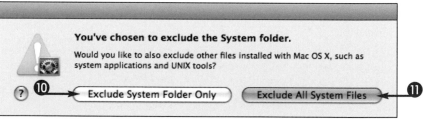

⑫ Click **Done**.

Time Machine automatically backs up your data to the selected hard drive. New backups are created every hour.

Note: *After you disconnect the external hard drive so you can move MacBook around, the next time you reconnect the external hard drive, the next backup is made.*

Do not back up:	
🖥 Back_Up	281.8 GB
🏛 Library	4.9 GB
📁 Previous Systems	Calculating Size
🗙 System Files and Applications	Calculating Size

| + − | Total Included: Calculating Size |

☑ Warn when old backups are deleted

(?) (Cancel) (Done) ⟵ ⑫

TIPS

How long is my data protected?

Time Machine backs up your data for as long as it can until the back-up hard drive is full. It stores hourly backups for the past 24 hours. It stores daily backups for the past month. It stores monthly backups until the back-up disk is full. To protect yourself as long as possible, use the largest hard drive you can afford and exclude files that you do not need to back up (such as System files if you have the Mac OS X installation disc) to save space on the back-up drive.

How else should I protect my data?

Hard disks can fail, and no matter how large your back-up drive is, it fills up at some point and you will not be able to back up all the files you might need. You should also back up important files in a second way, such as to DVD. You can do this by burning files to a disc from the Finder (see Chapter 4) and from within some applications (such as iTunes, from which you can back up your iTunes Library onto disc).

Restore Files with Time Machine

If you have used Time Machine to keep MacBook backed up, losing data from MacBook is not a big deal. (If you do not have your data backed up, it will be a very, very big deal.) You can use Time Machine to restore files that are included in your backups. You can restore files and folders from the Finder and you can recover individual items from within some applications (such as photos from within iPhoto).

Restore Files with Time Machine

RESTORE FILES IN THE FINDER

① Open a Finder window showing the location where the files you want to recover were stored.

② Launch the Time Machine application by clicking its icon (⊚) on the Dock or by double-clicking its icon in the Applications folder.

The desktop disappears and the Time Machine window fills the entire space.

● The Finder window that you opened in step **1** appears in the center of the window. Behind it, you see all the versions of that window that are stored in your backup from the current version as far back in time as the backups go.

● Along the right side of the window, you see the timeline for your backups.

● The Time Machine controls appear at the bottom.

● The time of the frontmost window appears in the center at the bottom.

③ Click the time on the timeline when the files you need were available.

④ When you reach the files or folders you want to restore, select them.

⑤ Click **Restore**.

The files and folders you selected are returned to their locations.

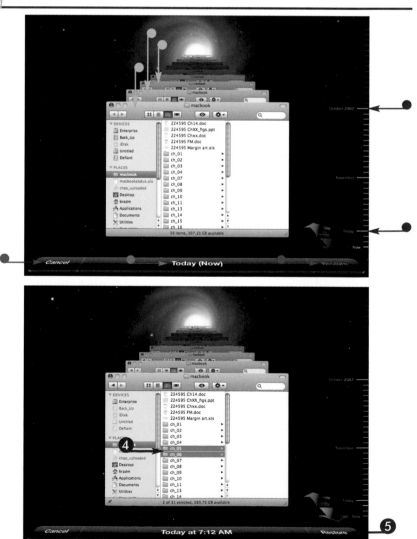

RESTORE FILES IN APPLICATIONS

① Open the application containing the files you want to recover.

② Launch the Time Machine application by clicking its icon () on the Dock or by double-clicking its icon in the Applications folder.

The desktop disappears and the Time Machine window fills the entire space.

③ Click the time on the timeline when the files you need were available.

As you go back in time, you see the versions of the application window that are saved in the backup.

④ When you get to the files you want to restore, select them.

Note: To restore all of the files in the frontmost window, click **Restore All**.

⑤ Click **Restore**.

The files are returned to the application and you can use them as if they had never been lost.

TIPS

What if an application I use does not support Time Machine? Can I still restore files for it?

Not all applications support Time Machine; currently only some Apple applications support the ability to back up and restore individual files within an application. Hopefully, more applications will support this technology over time. However, you can always use Time Machine to restore files being managed in an application by including them in the backups you create and then restoring the individual files from the Finder. This is not as slick as using a supported application such as iPhoto or iTunes, but it works well.

Troubleshoot and Solve MacBook Problems

Once in a while, MacBook is not going to cooperate with you. You might experience applications that hang (they stop doing anything while displaying the spinning color wheel icon) or quit unexpectedly; or, something odd might happen and you cannot quite put your finger on it. At the most extreme, you might not be able to get MacBook to start up at all.

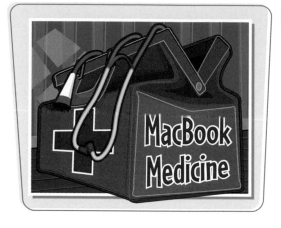

Troubleshoot and Solve MacBook Problems

Note: Restarting MacBook solves many problems you experience. Because it is easy to do, it should always be one of the first steps you try to solve a problem.

1 Restart MacBook by choosing **Restart** from the Apple menu.

Note: If MacBook does not respond to any commands or keys, press and hold the Power button until MacBook shuts off. Press the Power button again to restart it.

 2 Try to replicate the problem by doing the same things you did when it first occurred.

 3 If you cannot cause the problem to happen again, assume it was something unusual and go on about your business.

4 If you can cause the problem to happen again, use Activity Monitor to see if any applications appear to be consuming large amounts of resources.

5 Use Activity Monitor to check if the hard drive is too full.

6 To see if your problem has to do with newly installed software, generate a MacBook profile.

Note: *A MacBook profile includes such information as all the applications you have installed.*

7 Look for any applications you installed just before you started having problems.

The detailed information you collected should give you an idea of the cause of the problem.

DETERMINE IF A PROBLEM IS SYSTEMWIDE OR USER-SPECIFIC

1 Log into a brand new user account.

2 Try to replicate the problem under the new account.

Note: *If you can repeat the problem, it is systemic rather than being specific to a user account.*

3 If you cannot repeat the problem, log back into your primary user account.

The problem is likely related to something with your user account.

continued

Troubleshoot and Solve MacBook Problems (continued)

The first step in solving any problem is understanding when and how it happens, which is usually more than half the battle. Part of this is determining if the problem is general or related to a specific user account.

Troubleshoot and Solve MacBook Problems (continued)

④ Navigate to your Home folder.

⑤ Open the Library folder.

⑥ Open the Preferences folder.

⑦ Delete the preferences files for the application you are having trouble with.

Note: *The application's name is part of the preference's file name.*

⑧ Try to replicate the problem.

If you cannot replicate it, you have likely solved it.

If you can replicate the problem, continue on.

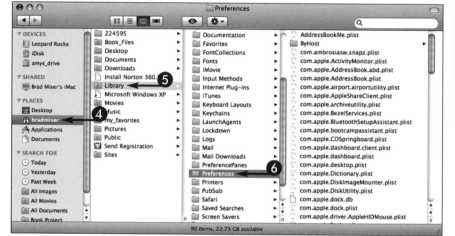

SOLVE THE "HUNG APPLICATION" PROBLEM

① Identify the application that is hung.

Note: *You can recognize a hung application by the spinning color wheel icon appearing on the screen for a long period of time.*

② Press ⌘+Option+Esc.

The Force Quit Applications window appears.

③ Select the hung application.

④ Click **Force Quit**.

Note: *If the Finder is hung, when you select it, the button becomes Relaunch, which attempts to restart the Finder.*

The application is forced to shut down.

⑤ Restart MacBook.

⑥ Update the application that hung.

Note: *See "Keep a MacBook's Apple Software Current" and "Maintain and Update Third-Party Applications" earlier in this chapter.*

If the update solves the problem, you are done. If not, seek out professional support.

SOLVE THE "MACBOOK WILL NOT START UP" PROBLEM

 1 Make sure MacBook is either connected to power or has a full battery.

2 Connect the alternate startup disk (see "Create an Alternate Startup Disk" earlier in this chapter).

3 Press the Power key.

4 Press and hold the Option key.

After a few moments, the valid startup disks are shown.

5 Click the alternate startup disk.

● MacBook starts up from the selected disk.

Note: If MacBook starts up, you know the problem is probably with the system software installed on the primary startup disk.

6 Insert the Mac OS X installation disc.

7 Launch the Install Mac OS X application.

8 Follow the on-screen steps to reinstall or repair the system software on the primary startup disk.

Note: If you do not have an alternate startup disk, you can start up from the Mac OS X installation disc by inserting it, restarting MacBook, and holding down the C key. MacBook restarts in the Mac OS X Installation application.

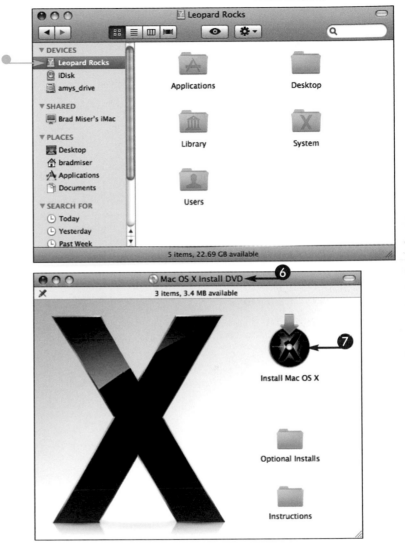

 TIPS

What are the most important things I can do to protect myself from MacBook problems?

Back up your data. You should always have current backups of your data because losing data is not just something that might happen to you; it will happen to you at some point. Second to keeping good backups of data is maintaining an alternate startup drive. If something happens to the system software on MacBook, you can restart from the alternate hard drive and get back to work, not to mention have a better chance of fixing the problem. Third, keep your Mac OS X software installation disc available. If you need to restore MacBook's system software, you need this disc.

Capture a Screenshot

When you experience a problem, being able to capture a screenshot is a great way to describe and document the problem for yourself. It is even more useful when you ask for help because you can give the screenshots to the person from whom you are asking help.

Capture a Screenshot

① Open the window that you want to capture.

② To capture the entire desktop, press ⌘+Shift+3.

An image file is created on the desktop.

③ To capture a portion of the screen, press ⌘+Shift+4.

④ Drag over the area of the screen you want to capture; release the trackpad button when the area you want to capture is highlighted.

An image file is created on the desktop.

⑤ Open the image file you created; it is named Picture Z, where Z is a sequential number.

● The file opens in Preview.

How can I capture screens with Grab?

Grab is a screenshot capture application that you can find in the Utilities folder. When G____ ____ ___ ____ enu (but no windows) opens on MacBook's screen. Choose **Capture** from the menu, the options. If you choose **Timed Screen**, for example, the **Timed Screen Grab** dialog b arranged your screen how you want it to be captured, click **Start Timer** on the dialog the screen is captured and the result is opened in a new window, where you can ch screenshot.

Get Help with MacBook Problems

One of the most important troubleshooting skills is to be able to ask for help in the right places and in the right way. Many problems you encounter have been experienced and solved by someone else already.

Get Help with MacBook Problems

1 If the problem is related to Apple hardware or software, visit www.apple.com/support.

2 Search for the issue you are having.

3 Browse the information on the Search Results page to locate the problem.

Note: If you purchased AppleCare, you can use that technical support service. See your documentation for contact information.

4 If you do not find what you need, go to www.google.com.

5 Search for the problem you are experiencing.

6 Browse the results of the search to find the information you need.

Note: If you live near an Apple retail store, call for an appointment at the Genius bar. You can often get excellent technical support for no cost if the problem can be solved in the store.

Index

Index

Index

Index

Index

Index

user accounts
administrator, 9
create, 110–113
fast user switching, 115
guest accounts, 9
log in, 8
login items, 113
passwords, forgotten, 113
pictures, 112
user name, 9

V

vCards
add contacts with, 284–285
create from Address Book cards, 285
from Microsoft Outlook, 285
video, watch video content, 223
video mode key, 5
view, windows, 25
View menu, 11
View Options dialog box, 28, 30
viruses
antivirus software, 133
protection from, 133
volume, control, 109
volume keys, 5
volumes on disk, 16

W–Z

watch movies on Web, 164
watch video content, 223
Web
AutoFill for forms, 165
download files, 154–155
introduction, 122
searches, 152–153
Web pages
Address Book, 290
e-mail contents of, 169
e-mail links to, 168–169

HomePage, 199
move through, 151
movie watching, 164
navigate to with bookmarks, 149–150
navigate to with History, 150
navigate to with links, 151
navigate to with URL, 148
opening multiple pages at once, 162–163
publish, 206–207
save, 168
widgets, create, 166–167
Web site, create, 208
Webmail (.Mac account), 204–205
Wi-Fi, 123, 127
widgets
iTunes, 53
Web, create, 166–167
window controls, Application window, 23
Window menu, 11
commands, 27
windows
applications, 81
close, 27
description, 80
expand folders, 31
Finder Preferences, 92
hide open in Exposé, 44
instead of tabs in Safari, 157
minimize, 26
move, 27
resize, 26
scrolling, 25
scrolling with keyboard, 25
title, 12
view, 25
wireless broadband card, 327
wireless networks, connect to, 324

Read Less-Learn More®

Want instruction in other topics?

Check out these
All designed for visual learners—just like you!

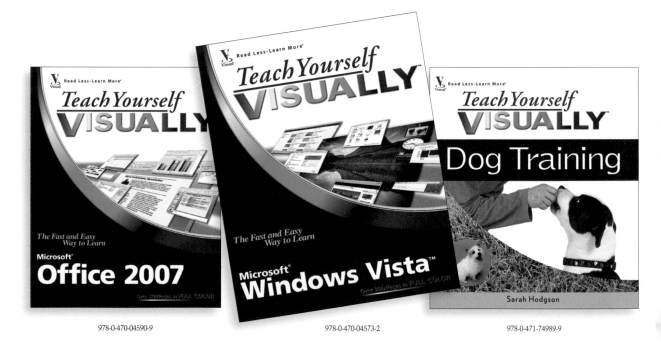

978-0-470-04590-9   978-0-470-04573-2   978-0-471-74989-9

For a complete listing of *Teach Yourself VISUALLY*™ titles and other Visual books, go to wiley.com/go/visual

Visual®
An Imprint of ⊕WILEY